"Hurtado awakens us from our cultural amnesia,' to remind us that the origin of Christianity and its remarkable success has more to do with its ability to distinguish itself from other religions in antiquity than to be one with them. Hurtado challenges readers to reconsider what have become common assumptions of religion today—that there is a single God and that religious affiliation is a voluntary choice. Without the distinctive rise of Christianity, none of these would be so."

—**April D. DeConick**, Chair of the Department of Religion, Rice University

"This is a fascinating survey of the features that made Christianity distinctive in antiquity and so—ultimately—successful. Hurtado discusses the Christian concept of an exclusive veneration of God, the trans-ethnic and trans-local religious identity, the central role of books and learning and distinctive and challenging forms of behavior within their ancient context. The glimpses into the first three centuries may even inspire contemporary Christians to find their identity and negotiate between social assimilation and difference."

—**Jörg Frey**, Chair of New Testament Studies, University of Zürich

"Comprehensive and quietly authoritative, Larry Hurtado's *Destroyer of the gods* offers its readers a three-centuries' tour of the Christianizing Mediterranean. The sweep of his panorama never sacrifices the liveliness of telling detail. For those who ask, 'What was distinctive about this new religious movement?' Hurtado offers thoughtful answers. Make room for this book, whether on bedside table or in classroom syllabus—or both."

—**Paula Fredriksen**, Distinguished Visiting Professor of Comparative Religion at The Hebrew University

"In this very accessible and readable book, Larry Hurtado shows how really distinct early Christianity was in comparison to its surrounding cultures of Greco-Roman paganism and Judaism. This was certainly true for aspects of early Christian life that are somewhat familiar to many of us, such as its stricter sexual code, but even here Hurtado shows that the early Christians took their code 'to the streets' and opposed the double standard of their day. *Destroyer of the gods* is an exciting read across a wide range of interests in early Christianity coupled with many comparisons to religious life today."

—**Jan N. Bremmer**, Professor Emeritus of Religious
Studies, University of Groningen

"In this lucid and wide-ranging book, Larry Hurtado convincingly shows how novel and distinctive early Christianity was in the religious world of the first century. He argues that early Christianity was in many respects a different kind of religion, and was revolutionary in the way that 'religion' has been understood ever since. Along the way, Hurtado sheds much light on the New Testament and on second century Christianity. He hopes to enhance 'our appreciation of the remarkable religious movement' that was early Christianity, and he admirably achieves exactly that."

—**Paul Trebilco**, Professor of New Testament,
University of Otago

"Clear and enlightening, Hurtado's coverage of the first centuries of Christianity explains why it was different, more philosophy than religion, and how its emergence as the supreme religion in the Roman world is less paradoxical than usually argued. This account is the nearest one can get to meeting an early Christian and quizzing them."

—**Robin Cormack**, Emeritus Professor, Courtauld
Institute of Art

Also by

Larry W. Hurtado

Text-Critical Methodology and the Pre-Caesarean Text:
Codex W in the Gospel of Mark

One God, One Lord:
Early Christian Devotion and Ancient Jewish Monotheism

The Gospel of Mark:
New International Biblical Commentary

At the Origins of Christian Worship:
The Context and Character of Earliest Christian Devotion

Lord Jesus Christ:
Devotion to Jesus in Earliest Christianity

How on Earth Did Jesus Become a God?
Historical Questions about Earliest Devotion to Jesus

The Earliest Christian Artifacts:
Manuscripts and Christian Origins

God in New Testament Theology

Why on Earth Did Anyone Become a Christian
in the First Three Centuries?

Destroyer
of the
gods

Early Christian Distinctiveness
in the Roman World

Larry W. Hurtado

BAYLOR UNIVERSITY PRESS

Cover Design by Will Brown
Cover Image: Protome of a Female Figure, artist unknown. Terracotta,
Tarentum (Taras), South Italy, 440–430 BC. Digital image courtesy of
the Getty's Open Content Program.

The Library of Congress had catalogued the hardback as follows:

Library of Congress Cataloging-in-Publication Dats

Names: Hurtado, Larry W., 1943– author.
Title: Destroyer of the gods : Early Christian distinctiveness in the
  Roman world / Larry W. Hurtado.
Description: Waco : Baylor University Press, 2016. | Includes biblio-
  graphical references and index.
Identifiers: LCCN 2016006230 (print) | LCCN 2016023781 (ebook)
  | ISBN 9781481304733 (hardback : alk. paper) |
  ISBN 9781481305396 (web pdf) | ISBN 9781481305389 (mobi) |
  ISBN 9781481304757 (epub)
Subjects: LCSH: Church history—Primitive and early church,
  ca. 30–600.
Classification: LCC BR165 .H77 2016 (print) | LCC BR165 (ebook)
  | DDC 270.2—dc23
LC record available at https://lccn.loc.gov/2016006230

The ISBN for the 2017 paperback edition is 978-1-4813-0474-0

Printed in the United States of America on acid-free paper.

To

Shannon
para siempre

Contents

Preface

I began this book with the simple aim of highlighting some features of earliest Christianity that made it distinctive, even odd, in the cultural environment of the first three centuries AD. As the work progressed, however, the additional observation recurred that these features that made earliest Christianity odd in that setting have subsequently shaped assumptions about religion in large parts of our world today. The focus remains historical, however. The following chapters dwell mainly on phenomena of those first three centuries, both because that is the period of my own scholarly focus over several decades and because I happen to think that, on any basis, it is the most interesting and exciting period of Christian history. But I have tried to show briefly that each of the features of earliest Christianity discussed in this book has become (especially for many people in the Western world) an unexamined commonplace notion.

Among both the scholarly guild and the wider public, there is a widespread presumption that all religions are basically the same, with insignificant variations of beliefs and practices, but essentially fitting one conceptual box. Departments of Religion in universities and colleges implicitly reflect this view, and a good many textbooks on religion(s) in various disciplines do so explicitly. At a high level of generalization, and with a careful selection of examples, it is possible to sustain this presumption. But a more wide-ranging analysis, both chronologically and across various cultures and examples, should readily put it to rest as flawed.

Some religions and religious groups do have strong resemblances to one another, and what modern scholars call "religion" has often played a similar role in various societies/cultures in various periods. Take Christianity, for example. For over fifteen hundred years of European history, institutional Christianity typically formed part of the establishment and served to promote the coherence of the various regimes with which it was allied. It was, in short, a social institution and as such affirmed, promoted, and defended the structures of society. From this specific history, there then developed the generalization, influentially among European scholars, that all religions typically play this kind of role of social conservatism.

But if we consider the first three centuries of Christianity, I submit that we have a very different picture. In those centuries that were actually so formative for what became characteristic beliefs and behavioral teachings, Christianity was certainly not part of the establishment. Indeed, as the following chapters show, in this exciting time Christianity was considered, and really seems to have been, a dangerous development that challenged what were then accepted notions of religion, piety, identity, and behavior. Indeed, in that ancient Roman setting, Christianity was perceived by many as irreligious, impious, and unacceptable, a threat to social order. From the standpoint reflected in some early Christian texts, too, Christianity was a broadscale rejection of religion as then known and practiced, and for profoundly religious reasons!

Early Christianity is not the only example of a religion or religious group that does not fit the widespread assumption that I have mentioned. But it is the example that I know best, and perhaps the single most influential one, and so I focus on it here. I think that earliest Christianity is fascinating in itself, but it is also a case study showing that the various past and present phenomena that we lump under the category of "religion" include a good many that are simply incommensurate with one another. Indeed, sometimes religion can even be frighteningly evil. I recall a conversation with a senior colleague a few decades ago in which he blithely asserted that differences among religions were comparatively insignificant, for all religions were good and should be affirmed. I replied, "I have one word for you: Jonestown." (If some readers are too young for Jonestown to mean anything, google it.) I mean no analogy to early Christianity. My point is simply that what we call "religion" comprises a considerable diversity.

But the proof is in the eating, so I invite readers to pull up to the table and take in the following chapters, in which I show that earliest Christianity was a very different kind of religious development in the Roman world. I emphasize that this is not a technical monograph. Instead, the book is intended for a wide spectrum of readers, accessible hopefully for anyone sufficiently curious about its subject to dip into it. The endnotes are intended primarily to provide some suggestions for further reading, and so the references are selective and almost entirely confined to English-language publications.

The basic ideas in chapters 1–4 were presented as the Josephine So Lectures in the China Graduate School of Theology, Hong Kong (January 2015), and I express my thanks to friends there who made my stay in Hong Kong then so comfortable. The gist of chapter 4 formed The International Centre for Biblical Interpretation Annual Lecture for 2015 in the University of Gloucestershire (May 2015) and also the Peter Craigie Memorial Lecture in the University of Calgary (January 2016), I thank hosts at both universities for their hospitality.

I also thank Jan Bremmer, whose knowledge of the ancient world and scholarly study of it is remarkable and who read earlier versions of the chapters of this book and gave me a number of helpful comments and bibliographical pointers, and my Edinburgh colleague, Philippa Townsend, who gave comments on what is now chapter 3. I also heartily thank Carey Newman and his staff at Baylor University Press for their commitment to publishing this book and their expertise in doing so. I dedicate this book to my wife, whose loving companionship over thirty-seven years now has been the dearest earthly gift I could imagine.

Edinburgh, January 2016

Introduction

Even in an age that some describe as post-Christian, the beginnings of the strange movement that was to become Christianity
in all its varieties continue to fascinate thoughtful people. . . .
Yet something more than mere curiosity about an ancient puz-
zle draws our attention to the first centuries of Christian history. Our interest in the question betrays our awareness that,
whether or not we regard ourselves as Christians or in any way
religious, we cannot altogether escape the tectonic shift of cultural values that was set in motion by those small and obscure
beginnings.[1]

This book addresses our cultural amnesia. Actually, I have two
emphases, one concerned with the past and one with the
present. I focus on several features of early Christianity that made
it unusual in the Roman period.[2] In the eyes of many of that time,

early Christianity was odd, bizarre, in some ways even dangerous. For one thing, it did not fit what "religion" was for people then. Indicative of this, Roman-era critics designated it as a perverse "superstition." Yet the very features of early Christianity that made it odd and objectionable in the ancient Roman setting have become now unquestioned assumptions about religion in much of the modern world. But we likely do not realize how unusual, even odd, these notions once were, and are still, in the larger context of human history. Nor do many of us realize that what are for us these commonplace notions originated in the rambunctious early Christian movement. So, in the following pages, we go back to that Roman era to see more clearly how early Christianity was a distinctive religious movement. We begin that journey here with a brief summary of the emergence of what became "Christianity."

The Birth of "Christianity"

About 30 AD, a new religious movement appeared, initially comprising circles of Jews in Roman Judaea, in which Jesus was central in its beliefs and practices. At some point thereafter (scholars debate exactly when), but certainly by the latter part of the first century AD, adherents of this movement began to be referred to as "Christians," initially by outsiders; and by the second century, the movement came to be known as "Christianity."[3] During his earthly life, Jesus had been the master to a group of followers, and, likely, they saw him as Messiah, or Messiah-designate. Shortly after Jesus' state execution by crucifixion, there erupted among his followers the powerful conviction that God had raised him from death and exalted him to heavenly glory, thereby designating Jesus as Messiah and Lord. This conviction produced a new and even greater fervency among the circles of Jesus' followers, and within a couple of years at most the movement had spread to other sites as well, such as Damascus and Antioch (in ancient Syria). Within a decade or two, it had spread to a number of cities in present-day Turkey and Greece, also to Rome, and likely to other places as well, such as Alexandria (Egypt). Initially made up of Jews, the movement also quickly expanded transethnically to include non-Jews, "Gentile" converts, that is, former "pagans."

From earliest days, however, there was also opposition and criticism, directed particularly against Jewish members of the movement, from some fellow Jews who seem to have found it objectionable and offensive to their religious traditions. That opposition sometimes even got mortal, as illustrated in the execution of James Zebedee (one of Jesus' close followers) ordered by Herod Agrippa (then Jewish ruler of Roman Judaea) about 42 AD, and somewhat later the execution of James "the Just," Jesus' brother and leader of the church in Jerusalem, at the behest of the Jewish high priest Ananus in 62 AD.[4] Also, and much more frequently, in the cities where non-Jews (Gentiles) were the majority population, there was often harassment, likely most often from relatives and acquaintances, and occasionally accusations and disturbances that brought the movement to the attention of some local civic authorities.[5]

All of this reflects the early translocal and numerical growth of the young movement.[6] During Nero's reign (54–68 AD), adherents in Rome were specifically targeted as the objects of a deadly pogrom and put to death by various hideous means.[7] Clearly, Christians were readily identifiable by that point there in Rome. Indeed, Tacitus refers to "vast numbers" of them arraigned under Nero's orders (*Annals* 15.44). In spite of that pogrom and other localized harassment and persecutions, however, across the following decades, the movement continued to grow. To take a set of estimates now often cited by scholars, there may have been about one thousand Christians in 40 AD, about seven to ten thousand by 100 AD, about two hundred thousand or a bit more by 200 AD, and by 300 AD perhaps five to six million.[8] One recent estimate of the number of sites where there were bodies or "communities" of Christians posits a hundred or so (many of these comprising several house-based groups) by 100 AD and two hundred to four hundred sites by 200 AD.[9] In the early third century, the Christian writer Tertullian claimed that Christians were numerous, "all but the majority in every city" (Tertullian, *To Scapula* 2). He may well have been exaggerating, but behind the rhetoric there seems to have been substance: Christianity had grown remarkably and continued to grow in that period.

As Christianity grew and became more visible, the tensions it generated both socially and with civic and imperial authorities continued and exacerbated. As we will see in the next chapter, the dominant pagan view of Christians was negative, often involving wild rumors among the general populace and more studied ridicule and critique among the elite. "A new and wicked superstition" is one such negative characterization of Christianity by the Roman writer Suetonius (early second century AD).[10]

In response, some Christian writers of the second and third centuries produced literary defenses of their faith, boldly addressing political authorities and/or the wider populace.[11] Referred to by scholars as the classic Christian "Apologists" (from the Greek word *apologia* = "defense"), these writers not only responded to accusations against Christians; they also attempted to advocate and defend vigorously Christian beliefs in the larger intellectual world of their time. These writings give us valuable insights into the situations of Christians and their impressive efforts to articulate and justify their distinctive religious stance. The stakes were high, involving not only criticism and foul rumors but sometimes the prospect of prosecution and even execution. In short, "Christian apologists had to argue for their lives," and consequently we have their rather vigorous and extended defenses of their faith.[12]

During the third century AD, there were even occasional imperially sponsored and empire-wide efforts against the movement, in spasms of violent suppression, especially under certain emperors such as Decius in 250 AD. Remarkably, however, in the early fourth century, not long after what was the most severe such persecution, which began in 303 AD under Diocletian, the movement obtained imperial approval from Emperor

Constantine, and in due course it became the official religion of the Roman Empire.

Often referred to as the "triumph" of Christianity, this story has been recounted and analyzed many times and from various standpoints.[13] But Christianity did not become successful through Constantine giving it imperial approval. Instead, Constantine adopted Christianity likely because it had already become so successful despite earlier efforts to destroy the movement. The story of early Christianity is a remarkable phenomenon, to be sure, as other analysts of it have noted. Among other great developments across a similar period of time, "this one of the period AD 100–400 might fairly be given pride of place in the whole of Western history."[14] It is simply the case that "no other cult in the Empire grew at anything like the same speed."[15] Of course, a few centuries later, Islam spread with remarkable success also. But, from its earliest moments, Islam's successes were often at the point of the sword. By contrast, the growth of Christianity in its first three centuries, the most crucial period, was largely by a combination of the power of persuasion, whether in preaching, intellectual argument, "miracles" exhibiting the power of Jesus' name, and simply the moral suasion of Christian behavior, including martyrdom. Granted, however, the adoption of Christianity as the state religion of the Roman Empire and in subsequent regimes produced thereafter a more ambiguous story in which Christian leaders sometimes used imperial authority coercively against other religious groups.

Historical and Distinctive

Frequently, the main question has been how, despite opposition, a movement of such small and obscure origins could have grown so rapidly and impressively and attained such a status.[16] It is not my purpose here, however, to address that question or even to focus on that impressive growth. Instead, I want to highlight some major features of early Christianity that made it distinctive, noteworthy, and even peculiar in the ancient Greek and Roman setting. My additional point is that these features that were so unusual in that time have become accepted as commonplaces in the modern view of what religion is, and that, I submit, is largely due to the influence of Christianity.

Granted, there have often been observations about how early Christianity resembled other religious groups of its time and how it differed from them. Certainly, Christianity did not drop from the sky but arose and developed in history, and so it can be studied as can any other historical phenomenon. There were resemblances and indebtedness to the wider cultural setting of the Roman period, especially, but by no means exclusively, with the Jewish tradition in which what came to be "Christianity" first emerged.[17] Without denying the resemblances, I want to high-light some distinctives, however, because I think that these have not been given the attention that they warrant and because they help to shape the modern world.

I will focus particularly on the first two centuries AD, with some attention also to the third century. Granted, every religious movement in history likely has had some kind or degree of dis-tinctiveness. But, as I hope to show, in the case of Christianity in these earliest centuries, both insiders and outsiders regarded it as very different, distinctive, indeed even strange and repellent. As a number of publications referred to in the notes will indicate, I am by no means alone in noting that there were things that distinguished early Christianity in the Roman world.[18] But, to my knowledge, I offer here a more focused discussion of several noteworthy features of early Christianity than is available in other current publications.

Anyone familiar with the enterprise will acknowledge that the analysis of early Christianity has been more than simply a historical exercise; ideological and theological concerns have also played a major role. One should not and cannot pretend to have a superhuman objectivity or even a lofty disinterest in the subject. Indeed, it would be difficult to find anyone really disinterested in the origins of Christianity, whatever the stance taken toward Christian faith, and I would be inclined to distrust any claim to such disinterested objectivity. But I do wish to approach the question of how early Christianity was distinctive, doing so neither in the service of Christian apologetics nor from an aggressive and skeptical stance toward Christian faith. Instead, I intend this study primarily as a historical inquiry concerned with the origins of Christianity, noting also its subsequent influence. My aim is to promote an informed appreciation of the early stages of this historically significant religious movement, especially among readers who have not previously considered the matter in any depth. Whatever you may think about Christianity as a life choice, I think this is a worthy, and even fascinating, topic for historical analysis.

Drawing upon his extensive study of new religious movements in the modern setting, Rodney Stark formulated a set of observations about why only a very few religious movements "succeed," by which he meant they continue to grow and thrive across multiple generations.[19] Of the ten features of successful religious movements that he posited, the first and third are particularly relevant here. A successful religious movement must retain a certain level of continuity with its cultural setting, and yet it must also "maintain a medium level of tension" with that setting as well.[20] That is, a movement must avoid being seen as completely alien or incomprehensible. But, on the other hand, it must also have what I mean by distinctives, distinguishing features that set it apart in its cultural setting, including the behavioral demands made upon its converts.[21] There has to be a clear difference between being an insider to the group and an outsider.

Classic liberal forms of modern Christianity have often been concerned to align themselves with the dominant culture, affirming its values, even shifting in beliefs and practices markedly to do so. But the danger in this can be that, unless there are also distinctive features (and demands) of being an adherent of a group, people cannot see the point of becoming one, or the worth of remaining one. On the other hand, as an example of a movement that probably made the bar too high for success in numbers, consider the Shakers. From a peak of about five thousand members in the nineteenth century, this communal movement has now dwindled down to one small community of three as of 2010, the latest report I have found.[22] The emphasis on celibacy was likely one factor that made it difficult for many to consider joining the movement. So, distinctiveness is important, but there is a point of diminishing return, and along with being distinctive a movement has to commend itself to its cultural setting.

We see this reflected in some early Christian writings. Among these, especially those of the "Apologists" mentioned already, consider the fascinating second-century text known as the *Epistle to Diognetus*.[23] The unknown author of this text set out to inform outsiders about the Christian movement, hoping to correct the scurrilous allegations about Christians circulating among pagans. To be sure, he boldly justifies certain Christian distinctives such as the refusal to worship the many gods of the Roman Empire (*Diognetus* 2.1-10), but he also urges that "Christians are not distinguished from the rest of humanity by country, language, or custom" and do not practice "an eccentric way of life" (*Diognetus* 5.1-2). Nevertheless, although Christians "follow local customs in dress and food and other aspects of life" in whatever city they live, they also "demonstrate the remarkable and admittedly unusual character of their own citizenship" (5.4). For example, he says, Christians do not "expose" their children (5.6), referring to the Roman-era practice of discarding unwanted babies after birth, and he also posits a nonretaliatory stance taken by Christians toward those who despise or persecute them (5.11-15). The author goes on to articulate the distinctive beliefs of Christians, including the conviction that the one true God has revealed himself decisively and redemptively in "his own Son" (9.2).

In this book, therefore, I focus on some things that were historically distinctive and identifying features of early Roman-era Christianity. Personally, I think it is perhaps particularly important to draw attention to such features in today's setting. To underscore the observation I made earlier, it seems to me that under the impetus of an understandable desire to view early Christianity in its Roman-era context, we scholars and the wider public may have emphasized similarities at the expense of, or may have neglected, early Christian distinctives. That is, there may be a tendency to highlight ways in which early Christianity undeniably shared features with its wider historical context, and not adequately note differences. To some degree, this might be an understandable reaction against, and/or a desire to avoid, simplistic or exaggerated claims of Christian uniqueness in the service of evangelistic or apologetical aims. This reaction can be traced back to the academic forebears who originated a historical approach to the study of the origins of Christianity.[24] Whatever may be the reasons for it, however, there may now be an overreaction that prevents us from seeing clearly enough how early Christianity was distinctive. I think that we presently need to do justice to features of early Christianity that marked it out in its Roman-era setting. Outsider observers of early Christianity certainly thought it was different, and so it is not out of line for us to explore what those differences were.[25]

It is perhaps especially appropriate to consider early Christian distinctives, given the growth and success of early Christianity noted already. For, in fact, of the plentiful religious traditions and movements of the Roman era, only two survive as living traditions today, those that became Judaism and Christianity.[26] Moreover, of the numerous *new* religious movements of that era, only Christianity developed into a long-term successful one that outlived the Roman era in which it first appeared. It is rare for a new religious movement to amount to much and rarer still for a new faith to sweep through a civilization in the way that Christianity did. Perhaps, only Buddhism and Islam are other examples of this.[27] In light of this, it is surely appropriate to ask whether there were things about early Christianity that helped to promote its peculiar survival and flourishing.[28] If early Christianity had been essentially unremarkable and indistinguishable in any major matter from other groups of the Roman era, then its survival and success would be all the more curious. If early Christianity essentially affirmed and reflected beliefs, values, and practices commonly shared in the Roman Empire, why would people have bothered to join? In fact, however, in several features early Christianity was unusual and noteworthy among other religious and philosophical groups of the time.

To grant that something is distinctive or even novel, however, is not necessarily to endorse it as valid. We might, for example, grant that this or that feature of early Christianity was novel but also regard it as simply bizarre, outlandish, even weird and repellent. In any case, at the risk of belaboring the point, I repeat that along with doing justice to the similarities of any phenomenon of the past and in its context, it is a proper, even necessary, part of adequate historical analysis to grasp equally clearly any features that may mark off that phenomenon and make it noteworthy.[29]

Which "Christianity"?

One further matter to address, and only briefly here, is the diversity in early Christianity. Scholars now are, or ought to be, very aware of this diversity and wary of rigid categorization of it as simply a binary alternative of "orthodox" and "heretical."[30] Perhaps especially in the second century, this Christian diversity was considerable, such that some scholars may object to talking about Christian distinctives at all, suspecting that it implies that "Christianity" comprised one cohesive religious stance in beliefs and practices, which emphatically I do not presume here. Illustrative of that early Christian diversity, in addition to those figures who are often regarded as precursors of the more familiar kind of Christianity of later centuries, sometimes referred to as "proto-orthodox" Christians, there were, for example, also "Valentinian" Christians, Marcionite Christians, and a number of other varieties, including the various so-called "gnostic" Christians.[31]

In some cases the differences were substantial. For example, Marcionites did not treat the Old Testament writings as their scriptures, and they even distinguished sharply between the Old Testament deity, whom they regarded as an inferior deity, and the previously unknown God, whom they claimed that Jesus came to reveal.[32]

In this book, however, I focus on certain features of the kinds of Christianity that came to prominence and shaped what we can think of as the emerging mainstream tradition thereafter, those circles sometimes referred to by scholars today as the "proto-orthodox" Christians. Even these Christians, however, were not uniform in their beliefs and practices. In this early period, there were no ecumenical councils or ecclesiastical or political structures to enforce uniformity. Instead, I have proposed that "proto-orthodox" Christianity itself in the first two centuries comprised a variety of Christians and Christian circles characterized broadly by a readiness to recognize one another (despite their differences), by a high regard for traditions and a suspicion of radical innovations, by a commitment to the "Old Testament" writings as scripture, and by an exclusivist "monotheistic" stance in which the deity of the Old Testament is the only valid deity worthy of worship.[33]

Indeed, the New Testament is perhaps the most significant and influential literary product of "proto-orthodox" Christian circles, and it reflects their diversity. There are four Gospels, contrasting with Marcionite Christians who accepted only one, a version of the Gospel of Luke. And these Gospels were accepted with all their differences left unharmonized, contrasting with the Christian teacher Tatian, who produced a single harmonized Gospel-book that drew on the four familiar Gospels. As well, in addition to a collection of letters of the apostle Paul, the traditional New Testament also includes writings ascribed to other apostles, again in contrast with Marcionites who accepted only Paul as a valid apostle. Readers of the New Testament know very well the differences of emphasis between the Epistle of James and

Paul's letters; and the writings ascribed to other figures, such as 1 John or the two letters ascribed to Peter, further reflect differences. Yet "proto-orthodox" Christian circles incorporated them all into their emerging "canon," thereby reflecting a certain impressive readiness to accommodate diversity.

In the social rough and tumble of religious rivalries of the first two or three centuries, these "proto-orthodox" or "catholic" Christians seem to have won out, and well before Constantine and the subsequent influence of the state in matters of religion.[34] That is, the proto-orthodox or catholic Christians were simply more successful at winning adherents in that earliest period, and their success did not depend then upon state support. We have to recognize that precisely in the crucial first three centuries the Christian tradition did begin to cohere around certain practices and beliefs, and that "proto-orthodox" Christianity emerged as the mainstream version that shaped subsequent Christian tradition.

Indeed, as we will see in the next chapter, the ancient pagan critics of early Christianity seem to have taken this "proto-orthodox" or "catholic" Christianity typically as the object of their concern and scorn, which suggests that they did not consider other versions of Christianity to be as important. So, with all due respect for the other, and less successful, versions of early Christianity, we will focus here on the kind of Christianity that came to be more influential historically.

Summary

The remarkable growth of early Christianity makes it interesting to note what identified and distinguished it in the earliest period of its development. The subsequent influence of Christianity upon world history, especially in Western countries, makes it all the more relevant to pursue this sort of question. Roman-era Christianity was certainly a historical phenomenon, and so reflected, and even sought to relate meaningfully to, that historical setting. Without denying similarities, however, I think that it is also appropriate, particularly for historical purposes, to note what distinctive features as well.

Finally, to anticipate the further discussion in the final pages of this book, I want to note that these features of early Christianity that made it odd or at least remarkable in the ancient Roman setting subsequently became familiar features of all the cultures in which Christianity was influential. So, in grasping distinctive features of early Christianity, we will also perhaps understand a bit better origins of some things that form part of our thinking as well. We take them for granted. But in the ancient Roman period, they were remarkable.

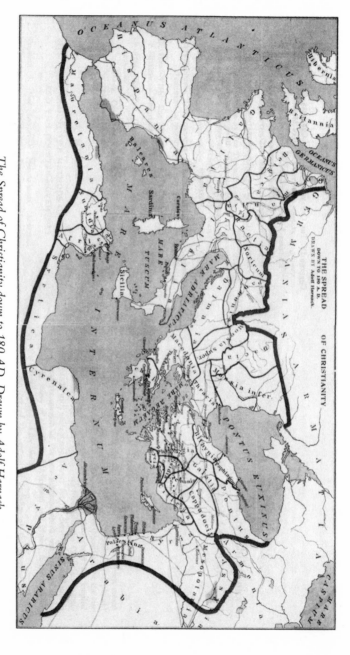

The Spread of Christianity down to 180 AD. Drawn by Adolf Harnack.
(Adolf Harnack, *The Mission and Expansion of Christianity in the First Three Centuries*. Translated and edited by James Moffatt [New York: J. P. Putnam & Sons, 1908])

I

Early Christians and Christianity in the Eyes of Non-Christians

One of the best indications that early Christianity was different in the context of the Roman world is the evidence of how outsider observers at the time saw Christians and their beliefs and practices. Even if these outsiders missed or distorted some things, I think that it is interesting to note what they thought. As we will see, invariably, these outsiders refer to Christians as different, odd, and even objectionable. This seems to be reflected both in Jewish and in pagan responses.

Jewish Responses

Since what became Christianity emerged initially as a new religious movement in Roman-era Jewish tradition, let us first consider responses from other Jews of the time. In an essay initially

published in 1999, I surveyed evidence of earliest Jewish opposition to Jesus-devotion directed against Jewish believers in Jesus.[1]
It is clear that from the earliest days the young Jesus-movement,
which then was made up of Jews almost entirely, was regarded
with hostility by at least some other devout Jews, who probably
saw it as a danger to the religious integrity of the Jewish people.
Granted, because the extant evidence is limited, it is difficult to
say with full confidence what it was specifically about the early
Jesus-movement that generated this opposition. Indeed, the only
firsthand evidence comes from the man who is perhaps the most
well-known early opponent, the zealous young Pharisee, Saul of
Tarsus.[2] Of course, we know this man as the apostle Paul, and,
ironically, he is perhaps also the most well-known proponent of
the Jesus-movement![3]

Saul/Paul

In several of his letters sent to churches that he established as
"Apostle to the Gentiles," Paul refers to his earlier stance as opponent of the faith that he subsequently came to embrace. In one
passage, he says, in his own words, that he had sought to "destroy"
this movement (Galatians 1:13). The verb Paul uses in this passage (Greek: *porthein*) connotes harsh, even violent, actions.[4] Saul/
Paul's other references to these actions suggest that they were such
as to cause him much regret later. In one of these passages, he
refers to himself as "the least of the apostles, unfit to be called an
apostle, because I persecuted the church of God" (1 Corinthians
15:9). Even if you choose to see this statement as involving a bit
of rhetorical posturing, it seems to me likely that it reflects some
level of genuine remorse.

In another letter where Paul rehearses certain specifics of
his Jewish identity, which he continued to affirm, he refers to
his previous commitment to strict observance of Jewish law as
a Pharisee. Again, indicative of the nature of his religious zeal
at that time, he points to his former actions as "a persecutor of
the church" (Philippians 3:6). Paul's language, especially his

reference to "zeal," suggests a possible connection to an ancient Jewish tradition that allowed for, and even called for, the justifiable use of violence by Jews against fellow Jews seen guilty of some major and public violation of God's law. This tradition is associated with the biblical figure Phinehas.[5]

According to the biblical story in Numbers 25:1-15, the Midianites seduced the people of Israel into idolatry, which brought the threat of divine punishment. To avert this, Phinehas took violent action against a fellow Israelite, killing both the man and the Midianite woman who is presented as having enticed the man to commit public idolatry. The result is that Phinehas is praised specifically for his "zeal" (Numbers 25:10, 13), and in ancient Jewish tradition thereafter his zeal is remembered as exemplary.[6]

For example, in the account of the Jewish revolt against the Syrian king Antiochus Epiphanes, which began with Mattathias' killing of a fellow Jew for committing public idolatry, 1 Maccabees lauds Mattathias "who burned with zeal for the law, just as Phinehas did" (1 Maccabees 2:26). In another instance, in the text known as "the Wisdom of Jesus, son of Sirach" and "Ecclesiasticus" (written ca. 200 BC), there is a section where a series of "famous men" receives praise. Phinehas is cited there for being "zealous in the fear of the Lord" (Sirach 44:23-25), his action having made "atonement for Israel" (v. 23). The learned Jewish writer Philo of Alexandria (ca. 50 BC–50 AD) likewise refers to Phinehas approvingly several times. In the most explicit reference, after urging that Jews with "a zeal for virtue" should feel obliged to act against fellow Jews seen guilty of idolatry in particular, Philo then cites Phinehas as the example to be emulated.[7]

So, in light of this ancient Jewish connection of "zeal" with the Phinehas tradition, we can surmise two things. First, Paul's references to his persecuting "zeal" suggest that at the point when he had engaged in this activity he saw himself as acting, not as some ruffian or bully, but justly in the spirit of Phinehas. Second, that means that Paul's zealous actions were likely motivated by a similar concern to punish what he saw as some serious problem about the early Jesus-movement that could not be ignored. Perhaps he saw the Jesus-movement as some kind of threat to the collective religious commitment that was expected of all fellow Jews. In any case, we likely should think of him as taking determined actions against some troubling offense(s) or danger that he perceived in the circles of early Jewish Jesus-followers.

Saul/Paul does not say, however, explicitly what their offense(s) was/were and why he initially persecuted "the church of God," and so scholars have made various proposals.[8] Was the problem that the early Jesus-followers (or some of them) were supposedly critical of the Jerusalem temple? But there is scant evidence for this proposal.[9] Or was Saul/Paul enraged over Jesus-followers supposedly being lax in observance of Jewish law, for which also it is hard to make a case? Personally, I think that Paul's zealous ire was probably provoked at least in part by what he regarded as inappropriate reverence for Jesus. Perhaps this involved both the claims made about Jesus by Jewish believers and also their devotional practices in which the risen Jesus figured prominently.[10]

We know that early Jewish believers hailed Jesus as the Messiah ("Christ"), whose ignominious death was part of God's redemptive plan, and they also proclaimed him as the divinely approved "Son" who had been exalted to a heavenly status "at God's right hand" (e.g., Romans 1:3-4; 1 Corinthians 15:1-11; Acts 2:32-36).[11] But, before the experience that Paul refers to as a divine revelation, and that turned him from opponent to advocate of the early Christian gospel (Galatians 1:15-16), what did he think of Jesus? With some other scholars, I think that Paul probably saw Jesus as a false teacher whose crucifixion was the just punishment for his actions and who, indeed, stood under a divine curse as well. In his letter to Galatian churches, Paul refers to Jesus as having become "a curse for us," and then, alluding to Jesus' crucifixion, Paul invokes this biblical text: "Cursed is everyone who hangs on a tree" (Deuteronomy 21:23). I suggest that this Galatians passage likely reflects Paul's rethinking of his earlier view of Jesus' death as one accursed by God. So, I propose that prior to his revelatory experience, Paul thought of Jesus as accursed. But then, as reflected in the Galatians passage, he came to see Jesus' accursed death in radically different terms, as redemptive for believers, and so part of the divine plan.[12]

It is important to recall that in addition to suffering a state execution by the authority of the Roman governor, Jesus had probably also been condemned by the Jewish temple authorities. That would help account for Paul's earlier view of Jesus as accursed. Although we have no direct evidence from the temple authorities themselves as to specifics, it is reasonable to judge that they accused Jesus to the Roman governor as a seditious threat, likely as a messiah-claimant, and as such a king, which would have amounted to a challenge to Rome's rule. After all, the high priest held office at the pleasure of Rome, and the priestly authorities knew that their responsibilities included alerting the Roman governor of any perceived threat. Their accusation of Jesus as a royal messiah-claimant, thus, would have served to alert the governor to such a threat, and it appears to be the charge on which Jesus was crucified.

But I think that the priestly authorities also likely condemned Jesus as a false teacher or false prophet.[13] This would have allowed them to see their denunciation of Jesus to the Roman governor as also an action in defense of the Jewish religious tradition. That is, they could have presented Jesus as standing under God's condemnation as well as Pilate's. So, at the least, the early Jewish-Christian claim that Jesus had been vindicated by God in resurrection-power and was now installed as the true Messiah would likely have seemed objectionable, even outrageous, to conscientious Jews such as Saul the Pharisee. Zealous for his ancestral traditions, as he claims, he was willing, therefore, to take direct action against fellow Jews because they seemed to threaten in some significant manner the religious integrity of the Jewish people.

In a subsequent chapter, I shall have more to say about some specifics of how the early Jesus movement represented a significant "mutation" in ancient Jewish religious tradition. For now, it is sufficient to note that from a very early point there are ample references to serious tensions between Jewish adherents of the Jesus-movement and fellow Jews, and that these are portrayed in early Christian texts typically as focused on Jesus. Granted, the earliest evidence of this is in early Christian texts. I have already noted that in Paul's letters we have the firsthand references to his own actions against the Jesus movement. In other early Christian texts as well, we have indications that his actions were by no means unique. There are, for example, a number of references in Acts of the Apostles to Jewish opposition to the young Jesus-movement, in Jerusalem (4:1-22; 5:17-42; 7:54-60; 8:1-3) and in other cities as well (e.g., 13:44-47; 14:1-7; 19–20). Recall also the Acts 12:2 reference to the execution of James Zebedee by Herod Agrippa, the Jewish ruler of Roman Judaea, about 42 AD. In addition, we have the outsider report by the Jewish historian Josephus, who recounts the execution of another leading figure in the Jerusalem church, James, Jesus' brother, by the Jewish High Priest Ananus.[14]

There may well have been other factors as well, but I submit that Jewish-Christian claims about, and reverence for, Jesus were deemed highly objectionable and likely comprised at least a contributing basis for opposition from at least some in the larger Jewish population of the day. But, whatever the cause(s), it is clear that the early Jewish believers in Jesus were regarded as comprising a distinctive development in Roman-era Jewish tradition.

Pagan Criticism

We also have references to Christians and early Christianity by pagan writers, and these, too, reflect a view of early Christianity as different, and objectionably so. These pagan critics were members of the cultural elite of the time, such as philosophers, rhetoricians, and literary figures, people from the Roman-era intelligentsia. So their views likely reflect, and were intended also to influence, the views of people of their own social levels. It is

interesting that these pagan writers typically refer to Christians as
dissonant and out of step, and as in tension with the larger culture
of the time in some matters.[15] In the early second century (ca.
112 AD), the Roman writer Tacitus described how Nero sought
to deflect accusations that he himself was responsible for the fire
that destroyed much of Rome in 64 AD. Tacitus says that Nero
blamed Christians for the fire (*Annals* 15.44.2–5) and launched
a vicious pogrom against them.[16] In this account Tacitus himself refers to Christians as "hated for their abominations" and as
promoting "a deadly/dangerous superstition." Tacitus claims that
under Nero's orders "an immense multitude" of Christians were
arrested, who were convicted of "hatred of the human race," and
then were subjected to various hideous forms of death. In addition to suffering "mockery of every sort," they were torn apart by
dogs, or nailed to crosses, or set afire to serve as human torches
for Nero's nighttime spectacle.

Historians of all stripes tend to treat Tacitus' report as basically accurate.[17] So, already by the reign of Nero in the 60s of the
first century AD, it was possible to identify and distinguish adherents of the Jesus-movement in the general populace, at least in
Rome. Indeed, it is interesting that Tacitus seems to indicate that
"Christians" (Latin: *Christiani*) was a term known and used by
the general populace to refer to adherents of the Jesus-movement,
apparently already by the time of Nero's pogrom against them.[18]
Moreover, it appears that "Christians" were already then the
subject of accusations of unspecified "abominations."[19] Indeed,
from early Christian texts, we get the sense that at local levels
there were often hostile rumors, public harassment, and occasionally even local judicial proceedings against Christians well
before Nero's infamous action.[20] These rumors were likely the
sort of wild accusations that we know from other sources, that,
for example, Christians engaged in orgiastic sex, incest, and cannibalism. I will return to these accusations later in this chapter.

In another account of Nero's rule, Suetonius, writing
roughly contemporaneously with Tacitus, very briefly refers to

punishments that were meted out to Christians as "a class of people given to a new and wicked superstition" (*Nero* 16.2). The term used both by Tacitus and by Suetonius to characterize Christianity, "superstition" (Latin: *superstitio*), connoted then religious beliefs and rituals they deemed excessive, repellent, or even monstrous.[21] The basic point to underscore here, however, is that both writers refer to Christians and their religion as different, and objectionably so, and not as simply one type of Roman-era religious option among and like others.

Pliny

In still another pagan writer of the early second century, we get a similar impression. Pliny "the younger" (ca. 61–112 AD), a friend of Tacitus, was sent as imperial legate to Bithynia-Pontus (in modern-day Turkey) about 110 AD. During his time in that office, he wrote to Emperor Trajan about his investigation of people denounced to him as Christians (Pliny, *Epistles* 10.96).[22] We cannot linger over all the several fascinating features of this letter, which include our earliest outsider description of early Christian worship gatherings.[23] I confine myself here to indications of how he regarded and treated Christians.

He claimed to have no previous personal experience in the investigation of Christians (which, of course, is indirect indication that such official actions were already taking place elsewhere as well), and so he was unsure of the nature of the crime(s) usually alleged against them.[24] But, nevertheless, he reports his rather decisive actions against those accused as Christians. He says that he first gave them three opportunities to renounce their faith, and, if they steadfastly refused despite his threats, he either ordered their execution or, if they were Roman citizens, had them sent to Rome for further trial. So, Pliny clearly thought that being a Christian was in itself sufficient grounds for his punitive actions, even execution, although the obstinacy of some Christians in the face of Pliny's demands and threats gave him a further justification.[25]

Some of those denounced to him either denied that they ever were Christians or claimed that they had ceased to be Christians some time earlier. Pliny says that he released any of these who would confirm these claims by reciting a prayer to the gods, making supplication to the image of the emperor with incense and wine, and cursing Christ, "things which (so it is said) those who truly are Christians cannot be made to do" (*Epistles* 10.96.5–6).[26] Moreover, Pliny reports that he also tortured a couple of Christian women about what Christians did in their gatherings, learning from them only that the Christians met early "on a fixed day" to chant "a hymn to Christ as to a god" and also took an oath committing themselves to upright behavior. Then, later in the day, they met again to share "ordinary and harmless food." Even though he found no indication of criminal actions, Pliny nevertheless judged Christians as holding "a perverse and extravagant superstition." He also predicted that his firm actions would stem its spread and restore the revenues of the pagan temples that were "almost deserted," along with celebrations of the traditional rites of the gods.

Clearly, Pliny regarded Christians as comprising a problem significant enough for him to take such strong actions: torturing Christians for information, demanding that those accused apostasize, and handing over for execution or further trials those who refused to comply with his demands. It is also important to note that the response of Emperor Trajan to Pliny's letter was essentially an affirmation of Pliny's actions. He agreed that those accused and convicted of being Christians were to be punished, unless they recanted and demonstrated this by "worshipping our gods."[27]

Furthermore, it is interesting to note Pliny's claims that there were numerous Christians in Pontus at that point in various towns and villages, and that the growth of Christianity was having a markedly negative effect on the institutions devoted to the traditional deities and the economic activities associated with them.[28] Of course, Pliny may have been exaggerating a bit. But it seems to me quite plausible that the social and economic effects of Christian withdrawal from the worship of the gods, or simply the fear of such effects, may have been at least one cause for the denunciation of Christians to Pliny and likely to other local officials. I will explain why I say this.

Those Christians who withdrew from worshipping the gods obviously ceased sacrificing to them and ceased frequenting their temples, and that had economic consequences for various people. In addition to gifts made to the temples, for example, as thanks for a god granting a petition, there were local craftsmen who sold various items to those who frequented the temples, such as miniature images of the gods and *ex voto* objects, which were items purchased and then given to the temple to express thanks for favors from the gods.[29] Then there also were others who raised and sold sacrificial animals on license from temple authorities, and still others who produced food for these animals. In short, the ancient temples represented a significant sphere of economic activity, and so any denunciation of the gods, any withdrawal from their worship, or even the threat or prospect of this would have been seen as threatening to the many with vested interests in the various components of the operation of temples.[30] Indeed, we have an early representation of this concern in a scene in Acts of the Apostles (19:21-40), where artisans engaged in making miniature shrines of the goddess Artemis start a major disturbance in reaction to the preaching of Paul, fearing that their livelihood will be endangered.[31]

This economic factor may well be an important distinguishing feature in the basis and nature of the antipathy of many pagans toward early Christianity. In ancient Rome there were occasional repressions of other religious groups deemed foreign and/or guilty of some particular offence, but these tended to be "sporadic and of short duration."[32] For example, the Isis cult suffered repression in Rome itself several times, but in each case it was allowed back into the city at some point thereafter. There were also cases where Jews were expelled from Rome. But in each case, after a while, they too were allowed back.[33] There was not anything like the repeated and increasingly hostile stance taken by the Roman authorities against early Christians. Moreover, whatever the particular offences that prompted the actions against various foreign cults in Rome, none of them constituted a threat to the worship of the traditional deities. New cults were typically seen as additions to the cafeteria of deities and religious groups of the Roman world. Not even Jews were such a threat. For, although there were Jewish texts of the time that expressed disdain for the pagan gods, there is no indication that Roman-era Jews actually attempted seriously to persuade the non-Jewish population to abandon their deities. That Jews themselves typically abstained from worshipping the gods was viewed by pagans as an ethnic peculiarity. But early Christianity—because it was programmatically transethnic in its appeal, and more aggressive in attacking what it called "idolatry"—was a new and more serious danger.

There is another striking development reflected in the letters between Pliny and Trajan about Christians. As we have noted earlier, Pliny readily admits that he found no evidence of any actual crime or confirmation of the various wild accusations about Christians that circulated in that time. Nevertheless, he confidently proceeded to execute those who maintained their Christian faith, simply for their refusing to recant it. This means that already in his day Roman jurisprudential practice, though not yet formal legislation, was being shaped somewhat in response to Christians. In particular, note Pliny's reference to requiring those denounced as Christians to prove their innocence by reverencing the gods and the emperor's image and by cursing Christ. These seem to be specific judicial innovations not to my knowledge attested previously in the handling of any other type of crimes or people brought before Roman justice.[34]

In this, as in some other matters, early Christianity seems to have been seen as something different that required new or modified measures to deal with it.[35] In short, the letters exchanged between Pliny and Trajan over the judicial treatment of Christians show that, already at that point, "Christianity is placed in a

totally different category from all other crimes." As far as mag-
istrates such as Pliny were concerned, "[w]hat is illegal is being a
Christian: the crime is erased by a change of heart," which was to
be registered by the ritual actions that Pliny demanded.[36]

We may have another indication of this de facto criminal-
ization of Christianity in the exhortations in the New Testament
writing, 1 Peter (4:12-19), to bear up under "the fiery ordeal that
is taking place," in which believers are "reviled for the name of
Christ." In this passage, the author, some early Christian writing
in the name of Peter, goes on to distinguish between suffering on
account of criminal actions such as murder or theft and suffering
"as a Christian." The latter likely reflects the sort of judicial situation described by Pliny, in which believers were condemned simply for firmly maintaining Christian faith. As a named illustration
of this, at about the same time, Ignatius, a leader in the church of
Antioch (Syria), was arrested and transported to Rome for execution, a process similar to what Pliny says he ordered for Christians
who were Roman citizens.[37] In the case of Ignatius, however, it
appears that the Roman authority in Antioch was content to seize
a church leader, and did not go after Christians as a group.

To be sure, Roman authorities such as Pliny likely felt that
they were simply punishing what they saw as the unreasonable
and even antisocial stance of Christians. Nevertheless, to underscore the point, both in making the profession of Christian faith
punishable and in the peculiar judicial process by which people
could absolve themselves of the accusation of being Christians,
we seem to have new Roman judicial developments in response
specifically and distinctively to early Christianity.

Galen

There are still other second-century pagan writers who refer to
Christians, giving us further indication of how they were viewed.
In the case of one well-known pagan of the day, the famous
physician Galen (129–199? AD), we have a comparatively more
positive view.[38] Galen refers to Christians and Jews, sometimes

likening them to each other, and treating both groups as followers of a type of teaching that he criticizes as insufficiently reliant
upon philosophical reasoning and as too much based on claims
about divine revelation that have to be taken on faith. Indeed,
it may well be that Galen was the first pagan author to draw
comparisons between Greek philosophy and the early Christian
movement.[39]

Even though Galen was critical of Christians, his was more
of an intellectual critique, and he does not echo the sort of wild
charges about Christians that we see reflected in some other
texts of the time—for example, that Christians indulged in cannibalism and orgiastic rites.[40] Also, although Galen regarded
Christianity as a defective philosophy, he expressed a certain
admiration for Christians, particularly mentioning their courage
in the face of death, their self-restraint in matters of sex, food,
and drink, and "their keen pursuit of justice."[41] It is not entirely
clear what this last phrase refers to, but I wonder if it may be
the writings of second-century apologists such as Justin Martyr,
who boldly appealed to Roman authorities to treat Christians
fairly and prosecute them for any actual crimes, but not for being
Christians.

It bears noting that the virtues that Galen commended in
Christians were among those highly regarded particularly in
second-century philosophical circles: "valour, temperance, and
justice."[42] What especially impressed Galen was that Christians,
who were dominantly people of subelite social levels and not
philosophically trained, demonstrated these virtues with a dedication that matched "that of genuine philosophers."[43] That is,
Galen admired Christians for exhibiting qualities that he associated more with the philosophical elite of the time and that he
regarded as requiring training in philosophy.

Marcus Aurelius

Galen's commendation of Christians may have been a bit conde-
scending, but at least he did not display the outright hostility of

some others of the day. This contrasts, for example, with the more disdainful attitude of Emperor Marcus Aurelius (121–180 AD), who referred to the readiness of Christians to die for their faith as "mere obstinacy" (i.e., in British slang, "bloody mindedness"; *Meditations* 11.3). Moreover, Marcus Aurelius' scorn for Christians should probably be read in light of the executions of Roman Christians, such as Justin and others that took place under his rule. That is, he not only disdained Christians but was ready to have at least some of them executed under his own orders. Note that this is the same Marcus Aurelius who was a gifted student of philosophy and whose "Meditations" reflect a keen interest in ethics and various matters of learning.[44] Clearly, his own cultural sophistication did not prevent him from taking rather strong actions against Christians. He must have felt that they were sufficiently at odds with Roman culture, especially its religious foundations, that firm action was justified.

Lucian

There is an even stronger expression of disdain for Christians, however, in the satirical account "The Death of Peregrinus," written by Lucian of Samosata sometime in the late second century.[45] Lucian describes the lead character, Peregrinus, as essentially a charlatan who feigns a conversion to Christianity, using his skills at deceit to rise to some prominence among Christian circles in Palestine, people Lucian treats as credulous and easily duped. Then, because of Peregrinus' prominence, someone denounced him as a Christian to the Roman authorities, whereupon he was arrested and sent to jail. The Christians of the town sought his release, however, and when that failed they took pains to make his prison stay as pleasant as they could. They brought food to him and even bribed the guards to be allowed to stay with Peregrinus overnight. They looked upon him as a martyr-to-be and showed him all the reverence customary among them that was given to one of their number who was ready to die for the faith. But the Roman governor released Peregrinus, not wishing to make him a martyr. So he departed, travelling about and taking advantage of Christian hospitality in other various cities. At some point, however, he was observed eating forbidden food, probably partaking of food offered as sacrifice to pagan gods, and was excommunicated.

Scholars debate whether Peregrinus is a fictional or real figure and, if the latter, how much Lucian's account is a caricature of him. But one thing that comes through clearly is Lucian's own mockery of Christians. To cite Lucian's characterization of them,

> The poor wretches have convinced themselves, first and foremost, that they are going to be immortal and live for all time, in consequence of which they despise death and even willingly give themselves into custody, most of them. Furthermore, their first lawgiver [Jesus] persuaded them that they are all brothers of one another after they have transgressed once for all by denying the Greek gods and by worshipping that crucified sophist himself and living under his laws. Therefore they despise all things indiscriminately and consider them common property, receiving such doctrines traditionally without any definite evidence. So, if any charlatan and trickster able to profit from this comes among them, he quickly acquires sudden wealth by imposing himself upon such simple folk.[46]

Note in particular that Lucian saw the great transgression of Christians as their refusal to honor the traditional deities, worshipping instead Jesus. This seems to have been sufficient to prompt Lucian's other sneering comments and general disdain.

Celsus

In yet another second-century pagan writer, Celsus, we have this disdain expressed in a full-scale critique of Christianity, entitled "The True Word," written circa 175–180 AD.[47] The "true word" of his title refers to what Celsus posits has always been a line of true teaching, which was essentially pagan religion informed somewhat by Greek philosophical notions, and Celsus lays out a running contrast between this and the teachings of the upstart Christianity of his time. About three-quarters of Celsus' critique of Christianity survives because several decades later the early Christian writer Origen wrote a refutation of it in which he quoted large portions.[48] We know nothing else about Celsus other than his authorship of this literary work. He is otherwise "an unknown eclectic philosopher with strong Platonic leanings whose major focus was practical ethics rather than abstract metaphysical concepts."[49] Ironically, therefore, Celsus would have been lost to history had he not produced this literary attack against Christianity and had not Origen agreed to refute it decades later. In short, what made Celsus a noted figure in history subsequently is the very religious movement that he sought to discredit!

Possibly Celsus hoped to convert Christians back to paganism "by shaming them out of their religion."[50] Granted, the text appears to address Christians. But Origen says that he had never heard of Celsus' work at the point when he was asked to refute it. So, although Celsus may have hoped to dissuade Christians from their faith, I think that he wrote mainly for others of the pagan cultural elite of the time. He likely hoped that they would be interested in his critique of what they may have regarded as a growing threat to the dominant religiocultural outlook. In support of my suspicion, it appears that Celsus was read by, and influential for, subsequent pagan critics of Christianity.[51] Moreover, as a general observation, apologists for or against any cause may formally address their opponents, but they are typically and mainly read by those already aligned with their position.

In any case, to his credit, Celsus seems to have made an effort to acquaint himself with the Old Testament and also with early Christian writings treated as scriptures, especially the Gospels. Although Celsus occasionally commended Christians for their ethics, he generally portrayed Christianity as an inadequate philosophical-theological option and Christians as a bunch of intellectually inferior people.[52] He ridiculed the Old Testament writings and the Gospels' narratives as well, with special harshness for Jesus' life and teachings. Celsus gives perhaps our earliest reference to the claims that Jesus was an illegitimate child, that he learned magic in Egypt, and that, upon returning to Palestine, Jesus claimed to be a god.[53] As to reports of Jesus' miracles, in Celsus' view these simply showed that Jesus was a wicked sorcerer.

Celsus also ridiculed Christian teachings about Jesus' incarnation and about his resurrection. The latter idea was especially repellent to Celsus, as to many other pagans of that time. Although he granted that the soul may have, or may be given, everlasting life after death, it was unthinkable that it should ever be reunited with a body.

With other pagan critics, Celsus portrayed Christians as simpletons, and he characterized their teachers as like quack physicians, charlatans passing off simplistic teachings but unable to take part in a real philosophical debate. He alleged that Christians welcomed the worst kinds of people into their fellowship, in an unfavorable contrast with other religious movements of the time that, he posited, rightly invited only those who had purified themselves through extended training and testing. He also accused Christians of destroying families by promoting tensions between children and their parents, and he alleged that Christians were antisocial and comprised a threat to the civil and political order.

Moreover, along with other pagan critics, he complained about Christians' refusal to honor the traditional gods. Indeed, despite all the alleged stupidities of Christians, Celsus expressed a willingness to tolerate them, if only they would honor the gods and follow the polytheistic customs that everyone else, excepting, of course, Jews, affirmed. By their refusal to do so, Celsus contended, Christians questioned the validity of the gods upon which the social and political order rested and so were guilty of impiety and, at least implicitly, of promoting sedition. If masses of people followed the Christians in their madness, Celsus declared, this would provoke the wrath of the gods and the social and political order would fall into anarchy and chaos. So, Celsus posited, there were high stakes in the religious choice on which he weighed in against Christians and in favor of "the true word."

In considering the specifics of Celsus' critique of Christianity, we should not overlook the larger observation that he was willing to devote himself to the task of researching and writing such a major refutation. It seems to me a likely inference, therefore, that Celsus perceived Christianity as a sufficient threat that such an effort to refute it was justified and, perhaps, even required. Celsus characterized Christians as lower-class simpletons easily deluded, their faith more to be pitied than admired. But I suggest that there is more than meets the eye in Celsus' refutation.

For if Christianity was really confined to the dregs of Roman society, it would hardly have been seen by a cultural sophisticate such as Celsus as much of a threat. I think that he would hardly have thought it worth his time to prepare such an extended critique of it. So I suspect that, in fact, by Celsus' time Christianity had begun to make converts in circles and levels of Roman society that mattered in his eyes. In other words, from his standpoint, Christianity was beginning to make converts from the wrong social classes. It was becoming a real and present danger! Several decades later, the Neoplatonist Porphyry produced a work against Christians comprising fifteen books in length, indicating that earlier critiques from figures such as Celsus apparently did not have their desired effect in halting the growth of the Christian movement, including growth in upper social levels.[54]

Remember that by Celsus' time Christians such as Justin Martyr were producing major defenses of Christianity in which they attempted to address philosophical objections to Christian faith. As well, the sheer numerical growth of Christianity in this period likely posed a problem for its opponents. To reiterate the figures on early Christian growth cited earlier, there may have been about seven to ten thousand Christians by 100 AD, about two hundred thousand Christians by about 200 AD, and perhaps as many as five to six million by 300 AD, though unevenly distributed across the empire.[55] So, various factors, including the numerical growth of Christianity and its upward creep through societal levels, along with those formal literary defenses of Christian faith could well have combined to make Celsus think that a full-scale critique was needed.

Similarly, Lucian's extended parody of Christians in *Peregrinus*, also written in the late second century AD, suggests to me that by that time Christians had become sufficiently numerous and visible in Roman society that he could expect the cultured readers for whom he wrote to recognize and enjoy his caricature. "Literati" such as Lucian would not waste their time writing extended parodies of religious movements that were little known or were considered insignificant. That is, both Celsus and Lucian may inadvertently give us further indications of the success and social salience of Christianity in their time.

Whatever the case, there were also other pagan critics of Christianity in the second century, among them Cornelius Fronto (ca. 95–166 AD), the orator appointed by Emperor Antoninus Pius as personal tutor to his sons, Marcus Aurelius and Lucius Verus. Unfortunately, Fronto's critique does not survive. But in the work entitled *Octavius*, the Christian writer Minucius Felix, active in the early third century AD, puts in the mouth of one character an extended speech ascribing various evil things to Christians, including incest and murder, and in which he refers to a speech by Fronto as having made similar claims.[56] In the eyes of this character and, likely, in Fronto's eyes as well, Christians are monstrous and utterly repugnant, "the very dregs of the nations."[57]

As noted earlier, these sorts of outlandish accusations against Christians are also reflected in other early sources, including Christian texts that were written to refute these claims. These wild charges of incest, cannibalism, and human sacrifice, however, were not newly fashioned for Christians. They had been invented originally as slander by Greek-speaking cultured pagans, the individual component accusations previously made against groups and societies outside or at the margins of ancient Greece. But the innovation involved in applying the charges against Christians was that they were lodged against an identified group *inside* the ancient Roman-era society. "This was a completely new development," and these accusations show that a number of Roman-era pagans saw the Christians as both different from themselves and also as not observing accepted religious behavior, particularly by not worshipping the gods.[58]

Summary

The second century in particular was a time of serious clashes between defenders of the established religious culture and early Christianity, a time when "pagan suspicions about Christians surfaced and found expression in savage attacks and sarcastic remarks."[59] But we should note that this was also a time when figures such as Justin Martyr made serious efforts to articulate and defend Christians and Christian faith in writings addressed to the imperial authorities and the wider public.[60] In their energetic efforts to engage their cultural setting, second-century Christian apologists exhibited what has been termed "an intellectual acceleration." Although Christianity did not count for much at the beginning of the second century, Eric Osborn judged that by the end of the century "Christianity was on the way to dominance in the Roman empire."[61]

Osborn's statement is perhaps a bit of an exaggeration, shaped a good bit by subsequent developments, particularly the "triumph" of Christianity under Constantine, developments that were likely not anticipated by anyone, pagan or Christian, in 200 AD.[62] Certainly, however, the second century was the time when pagans in the upper levels of Roman society began to take much greater notice of Christianity, whether hostile or benign in nature.[63] As we have noted, the general pagan reaction to early Christianity seems to have been negative: popular and sophisticated complaints, allegations, ridicule, critique, harassment, and even some state-approved efforts, at least by local authorities such as Pliny, to stamp it out. There were certainly other groups as well that sometimes came in for criticism and, occasionally, for official actions against them such as temporary banning. But these were more ad hoc and temporary. By contrast, the social, and then political, opposition to Christianity amounted to something distinctive. For pagan critics such as Celsus, other new religious movements of the time were "mildly contemptible," but Christianity was "a social phenomenon fraught with danger."[64] Granted, the treatment of Christians varied from place to place and from one emperor to another. But the combination of popular abuse, cultured critique, and official repression across the better part of three centuries, locally at first and then empire-wide toward the end, has no parallel.[65]

Indeed, in light of the social and, increasingly, the political consequences of being a Christian in these early centuries, one might well wonder that the movement grew and why people became Christians.[66] But, obviously, those who did so under those circumstances had strong reasons. There must have been things about early Christianity that made it worthwhile to become an adherent in spite of social harassment and potential prosecution. So, not only was early Christianity different in some key respects, but also participation in Christian faith must have offered things that attracted converts and compensated for the considerable social costs incurred in becoming an adherent.[67] But we cannot go further into that topic here. I would simply observe that one of the curious gaps in recent scholarship on the origins of Christianity is an adequate treatment of what made early converts think it worth those costs.[68]

The evidence surveyed in this chapter, along with other data that we will note in the following chapters, indicate that in the early Roman period people saw early Christianity as distinguishable from the many other groups and movements of the time. Actually, it appears that a good many outsiders, who were the overwhelming majority of the populace, regarded Christians and

Christianity as objectionably different and certainly not simply one group among an undifferentiated lot. In the following chapters, I discuss some of the specific features that generated this attitude and that made early Christianity distinctive.

2

A New Kind of Faith

If you were to go out into the streets of almost any city today, at least in most Western nations, and ask people, "Do you believe in God?" you would probably get one of three replies: "Yes," "No," or "I'm not sure." Likely, no one would ask what you mean by "God" or which deity you have in mind. Even modern atheists presume that there is only one God to doubt! But in the longer and wider context of human history, this is a curious assumption. Its prevalence in large parts of the world today is largely due to the cultural impact of Christianity.[1]

In the rich and diverse religious environment of the Roman world, early Christianity was different in the pattern of its beliefs and its religious practices. Among the particular features that distinguished Christianity from traditional "pagan" religious practice and from the many other new religious movements of the time was the firm insistence that there is only one "true and living God," and the demand that its adherents had to drop all worship of any other deity. Arguably, early Christianity represented not simply belief in one particular deity among many but, actually, in some respects a different kind of religion. As we will see in this chapter, early Christianity was so different that many Roman-era people recoiled from Christian beliefs and practices, accusing Christians of rank impiety and even atheism.[2]

"Religion"

Before we consider the religious environment of early Christianity, however, we have to engage a terminological issue over the word "religion." It is not simply a pedantic matter but helps us to see more clearly some differences between our time and the Roman era.

The modern use of the term "religion" can actually cause some problems for us in understanding that Roman setting. In the modern sense, at least in many "Western" countries, "religion" and equivalents in other Western languages can be regarded as a kind of activity distinguishable from other areas of life, such as politics, economics, or science. Also, at least in most Western countries, affirmation of religious beliefs and participation in religious practices and groups are now typically seen as voluntary, personal, and optional. You choose whether to be "religious" or not, and, if you choose to be religious, you also choose what this will involve and which religion to take up and follow. Indeed, you can even construct your own religion "a la carte," selectively combining features from one or more religious traditions.[3]

So, we refer to various "religions"—such as Judaism, Christianity, and Islam—that we typically regard as essentially distinguishable versions of a common thing called "religion." When used this way, "religion" appears to designate a particular genus or species of human activity, perhaps like warfare or music. We assumed that religion assumes various particular expressions or forms but in essence is supposedly similar and readily recognizable across time and various cultures. So, for example, in this generic sense "religion" is often defined as comprising a set of beliefs and rituals directed toward and/or concerned with deities and as serving to connect people and the material world with transcendence and to give ultimate meaning to life.[4]

But this generic concept of "religion" as a basically similar feature of human cultures across time actually emerged in European thinking only in the last few centuries and in connection with European exploration and colonial expansion. In this historical development, "religion" seems to have functioned, at least in part, as a category by which to capture and classify features of the peoples and cultures encountered in this colonizing expansion.[5] Also, the specifics of the concept of "religion" in this sense were heavily shaped by Christianity, and Europeans often sought to understand and portray ritual practices of other cultures through the lens of Christian categories. What European colonizers and subsequent cultural heirs imagined incorrectly was that they could use European Christianity as a kind of template or master model of what "religion" was and could then characterize and categorize the various beliefs and ritual practices of colonized peoples on that basis.

In at least some cases, however, this involved more distortion than accurate perception. For example, in some forms of classical Theravada Buddhism, there is no particular deity, and "worship" as understood typically in Christian tradition, the adoration of God, is hardly a feature. To cite another example, in the case of what came to be called "Hinduism," we are really dealing with an array of traditional forms of beliefs and practices in India with various historical origins, not a single "religion" with a particular historical beginning and a set of fixed doctrines.[6] Likewise, ritual practices of at least some forms of "traditional religions" of various peoples seem as much or more to do with keeping potential spirit-dangers at bay and avoiding offending them, rather than "worship" and adoration of, and a positive relationship with, a deity as conceived, for example, by Christians. That is, in many cases, "religious" ritual practices can be intended to placate deities or even to avoid their attention altogether. Also, the ritual practices of various traditional peoples were obviously meaningful for them, but it would be a bit misleading, even cultural imperialism perhaps, to say that those who performed these ritual practices typically aimed to express or obtain some sort of "ultimate meaning." My point is not that one or another kind of religion is self-evidently superior; it is only that the variety of religious practices and beliefs is considerable and extends well beyond what we may presume.

Certainly, in the ancient Roman era also, things were very different from what "religion" has come to mean for most Westerners.[7] Indeed, it is not even clear that ancient Greek or Latin or other ancient languages had a term that corresponded directly to the modern concept and uses of the term "religion." The Greek term *eusebeia*, for example, tended to designate "reverence" or "respect," which, to be sure, could be shown toward gods and so could connote what we might call "piety." But you could also show *eusebeia* toward parents or other legitimate recipients.[8] That is, *eusebeia* was more what we might call an attitude or a "virtue," involving reverence for appropriate figures, and certainly did not designate specifically what the modern term "religion" typically connotes. The term *theosebeia* is more specific and comes a bit closer to "religion," meaning basically service to or reverence of a god, "religiousness" in that sense. An early Christian writing addressed to a "most excellent Diognetus" purports to respond to his interest in learning about "the religion [*theosebeian*] of the Christians," and the text goes on to explain and defend key Christian beliefs, worship practices, and other behavior.[9] Likewise, another Greek term, *thrēskeia*, typically designated the particular ritual actions involved in giving reverence to a deity, such as offering sacrificial gifts.

But the key thing to underscore that is different between "religion" in the ancient world and in the modern Western world is this: We tend to think of "religion" as a distinguishable area of life. We also imagine that "religion" in some common, generic sense (drawn heavily from the particular features of Christianity) is an essential and ubiquitous feature of humans of all times and places. But this is a dubious assumption, "a surprisingly thin veneer that dissipates under close historical scrutiny."[10]

To take a specific example of a form of religious life in the ancient Roman world, consider the Greek term *ioudaïsmos,* which is often translated into English as "Judaism." This translation can work mischief, however. For to moderns, "Judaism" tends to designate a particular "religion," a defined system or tradition of beliefs and religious practices that can be distinguished from other "religions" such as Christianity. So, for example, when we read translations of the apostle Paul's statement in the New Testament letter to the Galatians (1:13) about his "earlier life in Judaism," we can easily misunderstand what he wrote. It is all too easy to presume that Paul meant that formerly he was an adherent of one particular "religion" called "Judaism" but then changed to another. So, readers may infer that the Paul who wrote Galatians thought of himself at that point no longer as a Jew but as a "Christian."[11]

In Paul's own time, however, the Greek word *ioudaïsmos* seems to have designated more the activity of promoting *a Jewish way of life* exhibited particularly in the observance of the commandments of Jewish law.[12] The cognate verb *ioudaïzō* ("judaize") was used then to mean to take up Jewish religious practices—that is, *ioudaïsmos*—and/or to promote their observance by others. Consequently, in referring to his former "manner of life in *ioudaïsmos*" in Galatians 1:13, Paul actually meant his former earnest activity as a Pharisee in promoting among fellow Jews a rigorous commitment to what we might call "Jewishness," the observance of defining Jewish practices. He contrasts this former activity with his subsequent divine calling to preach the gospel to the nations ("Gentiles"). But he does not indicate that he has left one "religion" for another. He has not left what we mean by "Judaism" for what we may refer to as "Christianity." Neither category, as we

use the terms, was even available to him then. I repeat for emphasis: Paul simply means that, in contrast with his former efforts
promoting among fellow Jews a more scrupulous observance of
Jewish practices, he now acts as divinely deputized emissary of
the God of Israel and his Son, specifically called to win obedience
to his gospel among all nations.

The modern English word "religion" derives etymologically
from the Latin word *religio*, but, as is clearly the case here, etymol-
ogy is not always helpful for establishing the subsequent meaning
and usage of words. For, at least in the time of early Christianity,
the Latin term *religio* had a certain variety of connotations, often
designating sacred rites and sacrificial practices—that is, actions
that can comprise reverence or worship given to this or that deity.
But, similarly to the Greek word *eusebeia*, the Latin word *religio* did
not always designate such actions concerned with gods. At least in
some early instances, it could simply connote conscientiousness or
being scrupulous about various duties or responsibilities.

It is neither possible nor necessary to belabor further the point
that "religion" as the term is used today, and the modern concept of "religion" as well, comprise developments that actually
separate us from the ancient setting and so can make it difficult
to engage that setting accurately. Granted, modern scholars often
use the term "religion" in describing the beliefs and practices
associated with various deities of the Roman era, but that reflects
our use of the term and our way of organizing things.[13] That is
not necessarily a problem, so long as we understand that we are
using a modern term that derives from our view of things to label,
and help us to discuss, phenomena of another time and setting.

A recent study of the modern notion of "religion" refers to
the "redescriptive" task of scholarship concerned with the ancient
past—that is, the analysis and characterization of phenomena of
the ancient world in terms that make them more meaningful to
us.[14] So long as we are self-critical about this task, I agree that this
can be legitimate. So, in what follows, I will refer to "religious"
beliefs and practices, meaning by that adjective simply beliefs and

practices that typically were connected to the various sorts of gods and divine beings of the Roman period.

We also need to recognize that for Roman-era people generally, what we call "religious" *practices*—that is, primarily sacred/traditional rituals—were more central and more characteristic, more obvious and explicit, than "religious" beliefs.[15] Nevertheless, beliefs about the gods were integral to these practices, even if the beliefs were typically implicit and not the focus of much attention.[16] For example, people of the Roman period obviously presumed that a given deity existed, this notion serving as a necessary premise for offering sacrifice to the deity. They also presumed that, under some favorable circumstances, a given deity would respond to petitions, this notion serving as a logical premise for making a petition to the deity for some kind of assistance. People of the ancient world did not tend to use our categories of "religious beliefs" and "religious practices"; but, as I have just indicated, it is probably helpful and legitimate for us to do so, in order to understand for ourselves the relevant phenomena.

So, in the following pages, we will first take some measure of the religious environment in which early Christianity appeared, and then note how it represented a different kind of religion, both in beliefs and in practices. In referring to early Christianity as a distinctive or different kind of religion, I reluctantly make a terminological choice that is at odds with the bold stance taken by my friend, the respected ancient historian Edwin Judge. He has urged that "it is hard to see how anyone could seriously have related the phenomenon of Christianity to the practice of religion in its first-century sense."[17]

He has a point. Granted, in a number of ways early Christianity lacked things that typically, and for most ancient contemporaries essentially, comprised "religion": no altar, no cult-image, no priesthood, no sacrifices, and no shrines. On the other hand, the key neuralgic issue between Christians and their critics and opponents in those early centuries was worship, and that sounds "religious" to me. Pagan opponents of Christians certainly noted their rituals, as reflected in Tacitus' reference to Christianity as a *superstitio*, and in Pliny's reference to the Christian practice of singing "a hymn to Christ, as to a god."[18] Also, pagans demanded specifically that Christians should worship the traditional gods. Recall that pagans such as Celsus were willing to tolerate Christians and their other various objectionable features, if only they would worship the traditional gods. But Christians were noted as typically refusing to do so, declaring that they worshiped only the one biblical deity and, still more offensively, that everyone else ought to do likewise. Granted, Christians deployed various arguments, including philosophical ones, to justify their stance and to mitigate thereby the negative reactions that it generated. Also, to be sure, the pagan demand to worship the traditional gods was intended to secure and promote social and political unity as well as what we would call "religious" conformity.

But I insist that at least as we use the term, it was for non-Christians fundamentally a *religious* issue. Christian religious practices and beliefs, about which I will have more to say later, were set over against the practices and beliefs of the ancient "pagan" world at large. Furthermore, in the eyes of early Christians as well, it was what we would call a "religious" issue, their key concern of fidelity to the one true God set over against what they saw as the many false and unworthy deities of the day. Granted, neither pagans nor Christians called it a "religious" matter, for the terminological reasons that I have stated, but I repeat that I think it is reasonable for us to do so.

"A World Full of Gods"

To turn now to a brief survey of the religious character of the early Roman Empire as a context in which to view early Christianity, the first thing to note is the sheer plurality of divine beings to which people directed various kinds of reverence.[19] It was "A World Full of Gods."[20] Indeed, there were deities of various kinds and various spheres. There was, for example, the traditional

Roman pantheon of deities presided over by Jupiter, who was often identified as and with Zeus, the chief deity in the Greek traditional pantheon. But, in addition to these gods, by the time of earliest Christianity the Romans had adopted or allowed other deities as well that originated from various parts of the empire. There was a virtual cafeteria of Roman-era deities from the many nations. And, as in a cafeteria, you did not have to restrict yourself to any one or any number of the gods. Indeed, any such exclusivity was deemed utterly bizarre.

As an illustration, consider the little town Val di Non, located in the Alpine foothills of northern Italy, where archaeologists found inscriptions dedicated to Jupiter, Minerva, Apollo, Saturn, Mercury, Mars, Venus, Diana, Luna, Hercules, Mithras, Isis, and (the only deity truly native to that area) Ducavavius. This was not a major metropolis but a small provincial town, and yet note the diversity of deities. We also have inscriptions from Philippi (in Macedonia) that reflect a Greco-Roman mixture of deities including linked ones, Jupiter/Zeus, Juno/Hera, Minerva/Athena, as well as Vertumnus (an Italian deity), and others amounting to some two dozen or more. Likewise, in evidence from other sites farther to the East such as Nicomedia (in present-day Turkey), there are over forty deities mentioned.[21]

The most well-known deities were associated with particular peoples, particular geographical areas, particular areas of life, particular forces of nature, and particular cities. Each of the many peoples of the Roman Empire had their own traditional, and multiple, deities, and in that period the tendency was to recognize and welcome them all. In general, the attitude toward this rich diversity of gods was "completely tolerant, in heaven as on earth."[22] As illustrated in the evidence from Philippi just cited, people were often entirely willing, even eager, to link particular deities from various places who bore similar characteristics, seeing them essentially as alter egos of the same deity known by different names among different peoples. This has been referred to in a recent study of the ancient world as the "translating" of gods from one people to another.[23]

Moreover, in other cases, deities that had originated in one or another location were simply adopted by people in other places and reverenced under their traditional names, these deities thereby acquiring a much wider following than in their native habitat. This could involve a major transformation or refashioning of the deity. Perhaps the most famous and successful ones were Mithras and Isis, each of which derived from a more localized deity and was transformed to receive a wider popularity.[24] The Mithras cult, for example, seems to have been developed and populated by soldiers of the Roman army, and so most of the shrines are found where the army was stationed, including Britain. In the case of Isis, likewise, we have a goddess originally of somewhat modest significance in her native Egypt that came to be heralded even more widely by many in the general population as the goddess of the whole empire (*oikoumenē*) and that was often portrayed as reverenced by various peoples under various names.[25]

In addition to such "high" deities, there were also lesser and other divine beings that, nevertheless, figured regularly in religious practices. In Rome, for example, these included beings called *Lares* that functioned as guardians over various settings. The most common were domestic *Lares* of each household (Latin: *Lares domestici*), which represented spirits of family dead who had been elevated to a special kind of spiritual existence on account of their goodness and/or importance. These spirits protected the family, and all members of the household were expected to reverence them daily in offerings and prayers at the *Lararium*, a small altar typically placed in the Roman house. But there were also protective *Lares* of bridges, crossroads, and other sites, and even *Lares Augusti*, seen as guardians of the Roman state. In comparison with the more well-known gods, the *Lares* typically had more restricted spheres of power, but they likely figured much more frequently in the day-to-day ritual life of people.

As well as the diversity of divine beings in the Roman period, we must also note the ubiquitous place of the reverence given to them in the lives of people of that time. Here is a particular instance where the modern notion of "religion" as a separate sphere distinguishable from politics or social life simply does not fit. We may think of "religion" as something you do, for example, on Sundays, or, if you are Jewish, on Sabbath. But in the Roman Empire what moderns call "religion" was virtually everywhere, a regular and integral part of the fabric of life. As we have noted, members of Roman households, the family and their slaves too, gathered daily to reverence the household *Lares*. Residents of a given city might be expected to take part in periodic expressions of reverence such as processions and sacrificial offerings to the guardian god or goddess of the city. Even in ordinary activities such as giving birth, or eating, or travelling, in the meetings of guilds and other social groups, or in the formal meetings of a city council, people typically offered appropriate expressions of reverence to the relevant divinities. For example, at many such occasions a "libation" of wine might be made, that is, a bit of wine spilled out in honor of the tutelary deity of the occasion. At the highest and widest level, there were also deities identified as guardians and the ultimate bases of the empire itself. In short, from the lowest to the highest spheres of society, all aspects of life were presumed to have connections with divinities of various kinds. There was really nothing like the modern notion of a separate, "secular" space of life free from deities and relevant ritual.

It is also important to underscore the point that all deities were deemed worthy of reverence. To deny a deity worship, and that typically meant sacrifice, was, effectively, to deny the god's reality. Individual pagans of that time did not feel it obligatory to reverence each and every deity, but, in principle, all gods were entitled to be reverenced. So, the people of the Roman period generally found no problem in participating in the worship of various and multiple deities.

People did not select this or that deity as their personal god to the exclusion of others. But they did typically approach or invoke or appeal to various deities, as was appropriate to the occasion. To repeat, there were various divinities linked with various sites, occasions, venues, and spheres of life. The gods typically had individual portfolios. So, for example, if you set out on a sea voyage, you might well appeal for a safe journey to a sea deity, such as Poseidon. Or, if you or a member of your family needed healing from some injury or illness, you would appeal to an appropriate deity, such as Asclepius. If, however, you needed a bit of help in matters of love, you might appeal to Aphrodite, or to some powerful *daimon* (a class of spirit-beings) by using magical invocations. If you were a member of a given guild, such as bakers, you would join with other members in rituals reverencing the patron divinity of your guild. There were also deities linked to the various army legions. Meetings of city authorities would typically include the acknowledgment of an appropriate deity associated with the city.

There was no worry that any one deity would be offended if you offered worship to other deities as well. Of course, it was especially important to reverence the gods of one's own people, land, or city, a matter to which I return for further discussion in the next chapter. But there was no need to avoid reverencing other deities also. Indeed, for people in the Roman era generally, "piety" meant a readiness to show appropriate reverence for the gods, any and all the gods. That meant, as the occasion called for it, reverencing any of those recognized as gods by any of the peoples that made up the empire. So, for example, on a visit to some other city or land, you might be invited to take part in rites associated with the deities of that place, and you would typically accept the invitation without hesitation. Outright refusal to worship deities was deemed bizarre, even antisocial, and, worse still, impious and irreligious.

The massive place of "religious" activity in the Roman era is reflected in the many temples and shrines. Temples were often built right in the city center, and multiple temples could take up a major portion of central city space.[26] There were altars for sacrifice, and other opportunities to donate to a deity and its temple. As we noted earlier, there were people engaged to raise animals for sacrificial rites in the temples. There were craft workers who made small images of the deities for personal usage and as souvenirs of a visit to a temple. There were *ex voto* objects that you could purchase and leave in a temple as thanks for a deity's answer to a prayer-request, such as a small carved foot signifying the healing of your foot. People wanted things from their deities, and the deities liked gifts. So, it was a mutually convenient relationship, and reverencing the gods involved a significant part of life.

Gods and "Idols"

This is particularly where the religious beliefs and stance of early Christianity stand out as different. Christians were expected to avoid taking part in the worship of any deity other than the one God of the biblical tradition. I discuss the inclusion of Jesus as effectively corecipient of early Christian reverence later in this chapter. Given the ubiquitous place of the gods and their rituals in Roman-era life, however, it would have been difficult for Christians simply to *avoid* all such rituals without being noticed. Christians likely often also had to *refuse* to join in the worship of the various divinities and so had to negotiate their relationships carefully, especially, no doubt, those involving family and close acquaintances.

This refusal to reverence the many gods that was demanded of early Christians would have included refusing to offer worship to household divinities, to the tutelary deities of cities, to the traditional gods of the various cities and peoples of the Roman world, and even to the deities that represented the empire itself, such as the goddess Roma, and that conferred legitimacy to Roman rule. Indeed, Christians were expected to treat all the many deities of the Roman world as "idols," from the Greek term *eidōlon*, meaning "image" or "phantom." That is, Christians were to treat all the various traditional gods as beings unworthy of worship, as false and deceptive entities, or, even worse, as demonic beings masquerading as deities. In short, precisely that which was generally considered piety (*religio* or *eusebeia*), reverencing the many gods, was, for early Christians, idolatry, impiety of the gravest sort.

We get a glimpse of this demanding and exclusivist attitude in what may be the earliest extant Christian writing, the apostle Paul's letter in the New Testament known as 1 Thessalonians (written ca. 50 AD). Sometime earlier in his missionizing visit to the city, Paul had established a church (Greek: *ekklēsia*) in Thessalonica comprised of former pagans whom he converted. In this letter he writes to them to offer encouragement, to give some teaching on matters that were reported to him as issues in the church there, and to explain why he had not been back in person for some time. Early in this letter, Paul commends the Thessalonian believers for their enthusiastic reception of the gospel, declaring that they had become an example for believers in all of Macedonia and Achaia. Indeed, he claims that everywhere he went among other circles of Christian believers he found that the enthusiastic conversion and firm commitment of the Thessalonian church were known and applauded (1 Thessalonians 1:2-7).

Then, in a passage much more directly relevant to our focus here, Paul characterizes the Thessalonian believers' response to the gospel specifically as turning away from idols, "to serve a true and living God, and to await his Son from heaven, whom he raised from the dead, Jesus, who delivers us from the coming wrath" (1:9-10). Note the sharp and unhesitating polarization in the language here between the one rightful deity and the "idols," the latter term Paul's obviously derisive characterization of the entire panoply of deities of the Roman world! As noted, our word "idol" comes from the Greek term *eidōlon*, a term that in ordinary Greek usage could connote something that is a mere phantom. Obviously, this was not a term used to refer to the gods by those who worshipped them! Instead, Paul's use of "idols" here, as in early Christian texts generally, reflects the distinctive ancient

Jewish usage of the term to designate the many deities of the other peoples of the ancient world, these deities thus referred to as only and falsely *seeming* as beings worthy of worship. I emphasize that this pejorative use of the Greek word *eidōlon* ("idol") to designate deities is not found in ancient pagan usage but is common in Jewish and Christian texts.[27] It rather clearly reflects a blatant disdain and even derision for all the pagan gods.

Actually, in ancient Jewish and Christian texts, there is a whole distinctive vocabulary expressing this disdain for the gods. To confine ourselves to Pauline texts for a few illustrative examples, in addition to references to "idols," there are references to the temple of a pagan deity as an "idol temple" (Greek: *eidōleion*; 1 Corinthians 8–10), to "idol meat" (Greek: *eidōlothuton* [sacrificial meat offered to a pagan deity]; e.g., 1 Corinthians 8:1, 4, 7, 10; 10:19), to "idolatry" (Greek: *eidōlolatreia* [the worship of the gods]; e.g., 1 Corinthians 10:14; Galatians 5:20), and to the "idolater" (*eidōlolatrēs* [a person who worships the gods]; e.g., 1 Corinthians 5:10, 11; 6:9; 10:7). Just as *eidōlon* is not used in classical/pagan texts to refer to the gods, so these other words are not used *at all* outside of Jewish and Christian texts.[28]

Sampling a few additional texts will give us a deeper sense of how the pagan gods and their worship were treated in early Christian discourse. In 1 Corinthians 8–10, Paul engages at length some questions about how his pagan converts were now to conduct themselves in relation to the pagan deities. This was an unavoidable topic particularly for converted pagans living in pagan cities. These believers remained members of their families, and so, even if their own particular household had converted to Christian faith, they still likely had pagan relatives in their extended families who would expect them to join in reverencing relevant divinities. Likewise, Paul's converts still had to function socially and in their respective occupations or businesses, and so had to judge what social activities they could take part in without being false to their new faith commitment. And recall again that pretty much all social life involved some gestures of reverence made to various divine beings.

Paul begins his teaching in 1 Corinthians 8–10 by referring to sacrifices to the various gods as "offerings made to idols" (*eidōlo-thuta*; 1 Corinthians 8:1) and then to "eating offerings to idols" (v. 4). On the one hand, he affirms that "an idol is nothing in the world," for there is only one God (v. 4). Indeed, rather consistently across his discussion here, Paul refers derisively to "idols," "idolatry," and "idol offerings."[29] On the other hand, in a still more negative statement (10:20), Paul declares that pagan sacrifices are offered "to demons and not to God [or to a god]," and he urges, "I do not want you to be partners with demons." Clearly, this sort of language marks out a rather firm and distinct stance in the religious environment of the time!

Of course, however, as I have already noted, this vocabulary and the exclusivist stance it reflects were not invented by Paul or early Christians but first developed in ancient Jewish circles to express disdain for the various gods of other peoples. This was indicative of the ancient Jewish concern to distinguish the one biblical deity from all others, and to do so especially in worship. Given the Jewish religious matrix in which the young Christian movement emerged, it is obviously not surprising that this concern was affirmed also in the early churches of Jesus-followers and thereafter, at least in the forms of early Christianity that later came to be regarded as normative.[30] But, you might well ask, if this negative attitude toward the gods was already expressed by Jews, how remarkable and noteworthy could it have been for early Christians to echo it as well?

The Particular Christian Offence

The difference and distinguishing feature of the early Christian stance against "idolatry" is this: In the eyes of ancient pagans, the Jews' refusal to worship any deity but their own, though often deemed bizarre and objectionable, was basically regarded as one, rather distinctive, example of national peculiarities. Whether resident in Roman Judaea or in their many diaspora locations, Jews were commonly thought of, and thought of themselves, as a distinct people, an *ethnos*, a "nation" in that sense. The wider Roman-era public was well aware of, and generally accommodated, the ethnic diversity that made up the empire. Non-Jews, "pagans," seem to have found the Jewish refusal to honor their gods offensive, however, or at least annoying, and this must have contributed to the anti-Jewish sentiments expressed in a number of contemporary texts.[31] But, in general, however strange they seemed, the national peculiarities of various peoples were taken in stride, Jewish peculiarities included. Every people had its peculiarities, and, on the matter of the worship of the gods, so did the Jews, only more so!

But, to underscore the point, the early Christian circles such as those addressed by Paul and reflected in subsequent Christian texts were often or even dominantly what Jews called "Gentiles"— that is, non-Jews, former pagans. These people could not claim any traditional ethnic privilege to justify their refusal to worship the gods.[32] For, prior to their Christian conversion, these individuals, no doubt, had taken part in the worship of the traditional gods, likely as readily as other pagans of the time among their families, friends, and wider circles of their acquaintances. One month or even one week earlier, perhaps, they could have been joining family and friends in sacrificial rites to various deities. But then, after embracing the sort of message that Paul preached, after being baptized as adherents of the local Christian church, they were to desist from this activity . . . totally.

Having adopted the new stance demanded by their conversion to Christian faith, they were to withdraw particularly from making sacrificial offerings to the gods of their household, their city, and the empire, and now were to practice the exclusivity in matters of worship that was expected of members of the *ekklēsia*. These newly converted Gentile Christians would have seemed to fellow pagans, however, to be making an abrupt, arbitrary, bizarre, and unjustified shift in religious behavior. This total withdrawal from the worship of the many deities was a move without precedent, and it would have seemed inexplicable and deeply worrying to many of the general populace. In their eyes, people other than Jews simply had no right to do this, and, no doubt, it would have drawn a lot of objection and even harassment, perhaps especially from the families and closest acquaintances of Christian converts. It would have seemed to the general public a kind of religious and social apostasy, an antisocial stance. Moreover, withdrawing from the worship of the gods could also lead to being arraigned before local authorities, although this initially seems to have been sporadic. I have discussed the social and political consequences for pagan converts to Christianity a bit more fully in earlier publications, and so here I will be brief.[33]

Recall, for example, that participation in the reverencing of household gods (the *Lares domestici*) was expected of all members of the Roman household. It was considered an important expression of solidarity with the others of the household in securing its continuing safety and welfare. Likewise, participation in the honoring of the tutelary deities of one's city in sacrifice, processions, and other rituals was an important expression of solidarity at that level. For at least many in the general populace, these city gods were guardians against such risks as plague, fire, or other disasters. So, refusal to participate in the reverence due these deities could be taken as a disloyalty to your city and as a disregard for the welfare of its inhabitants. Further, there were gods believed to uphold and legitimate the larger Roman imperial order; indeed, in the case of the goddess Roma, there was a deity that embodied the Roman order. So, to refuse to worship these deities could be taken as a deeply subversive action or at least a disregard for the political order.[34] To repeat the point for emphasis, when pagan converts withdrew from the worship of the gods that they had formerly worshipped, this was a particularly acute matter, much more objectionable than Jews' refusal to worship any deity but their own. The latter was an ethnic peculiarity, but that gave no justification for non-Jews to shirk their inherited responsibilities to their own gods.

Of course, a pagan might choose to convert fully to Judaism as a proselyte, which meant becoming a Jew and ceasing to be a member of his or her own ancestral people. By such a drastic act, proselytes effectively changed their ethnic status and so could thereafter try to justify a refusal to participate in worshipping the pagan gods as expressive of their new ethnic membership and religious identity.[35] But this was not the move that Paul's pagan converts made.

Those former pagans who joined Paul's churches, for example, did *not* thereby become Jews. Indeed, Paul was at pains to emphasize that his pagan converts must *not* become Jewish proselytes. For Paul saw his mission to "Gentiles" as bringing to fulfillment biblical prophecies that the nations of the world would forsake idols and, *as Gentiles*, would renounce their idolatry and embrace the one true God.[36] That is, unlike Jewish proselytes, Paul's pagan converts did not change their ethnic identity. They did not cease being what they were in terms of family, civic, and ethnic identity and responsibilities, except with regard to their religious responsibilities. But, again, this meant that in the eyes of fellow Gentiles/pagans, these converts to the Jesus-movement had no right to excuse themselves from reverencing the gods.

Paul wrote, "There is no longer Jew or Greek, there is no longer slave or free, there is no longer male or female; for all of you are one in Christ Jesus" (Galatians 3:28), but any careful reader of his letters should readily see that in fact there continued to be all these types of believers, identified and often addressed by Paul as such. Apparently, therefore, what Paul meant more precisely was that these various ethnic, social, and biological categories were no longer to function in a negative manner, as status indicators, for example, or as a basis for invidious discrimination among members of the churches that he established. That is, whether you were Jew or Greek, slave or free, male or female, this was now to be secondary to your status "in Christ," as a member of the new social and religious entity, the *ekklēsia* (church). Irrespective of their particular ethnic, social, or biological categories, therefore, all believers were now to take on a new and supervening identity in Christ and so were to treat one another as fellow members in a body newly defined by faith in Christ. I will return to this theme of "religious identity" in the next chapter. For now, it is sufficient to note that this new sense of themselves as being "in Christ" did not involve any official or outward change in the ethnic, social, or sexual status of Paul's converts.[37]

Consequently, to return to the focus here, Gentile converts to the gospel remained Gentiles; they did not become Jews either physically or ethnically, or in some "spiritual" sense either. To be sure, their initiation into the church made them adherents of Christ, and members of the multinational family of Abraham, to use one of Paul's theological tropes. But they remained what they were ethnically, and biologically: Gentiles or Jews, free or slaves, and either males or females.[38]

I repeat again that converted pagans had no precedent or established justification for withdrawing from the worship of the gods of their families, cities, and peoples. Furthermore, when we add in the sort of rhetoric that is reflected in texts such as Paul's letters, in which the various gods are all collectively referred to as "idols" (that is, illusory and deceptive beings) and their worship is designated "idolatry" (that is, pointless and even sinful), we can readily imagine the tensions, offense, and outrage that seems often to have resulted.[39]

Indeed, the exclusivist stance of early Christianity was so odd, unjustified, and even impious in the eyes of ancient pagan observers and critics that they often accused Christians of being atheists, just as Jews had been labeled previously![40] For example, in the account of the martyrdom of Polycarp, an elderly second-century Christian leader, the hostile crowd demanding his execution are pictured as shouting, "Away with the atheists!"[41] The charge of "atheism" reflects the view of many of the Roman era that Christians were seriously impious and irreverent, failing to exhibit the proper religious stance toward the gods. Recall the general pagan view that all deities deserved to be reverenced, which made the Christian stance of refusing to worship any deity other than the God of biblical tradition an utterly bizarre and unjustifiable position. In short, the radical selectivity and exclusivity of early Christian worship was neither acceptable nor even readily comprehensible to the wider Roman-era public.

Given the social pressures against their stance, we may, therefore, wonder how consistently and fully Gentile Christians carried through in the abandonment of "idols" called for by teachers such as Paul.[42] It may be that some Gentile believers did not make a full break from reverencing the panoply of gods, under the pressures from family and wider social circles. That would be a perfectly natural reaction to the social pressures involved. But I find scant basis for any notion that Paul or others in early Christian writings accepted that pagan converts would continue to take part in events that included the worship of pagan deities— that is, sacrifices to them and sacrificial meals in their honor. Whatever the consistency of actual practice among Gentile converts to Christian faith, there is, for example, little ambiguity in Paul's teaching in 1 Corinthians 8–10 about what they were *supposed* to do. They were to devote themselves exclusively to the one God of the Jewish scriptures, "the God and Father of our Lord Jesus Christ." I simply cannot see any other way of taking what Paul says in texts such as 1 Corinthians 8:4-6:

> Indeed, even though there may be so-called gods in heaven or on earth—as in fact there are many gods and many lords—yet for us there is one God, the Father, from whom are all things and for whom we exist, and one Lord, Jesus Christ, through whom are all things and through whom we exist.

In a recent survey of religions of the Roman world, however, the authors opine that early Christian exhortations to religious exclusivity likely reflect many or even most Christians of the time taking a more relaxed attitude toward sacrifices to the pagan gods.[43] Maybe. But, again, I find this sort of confident assertion puzzling. For I think that there is scant evidence for the assertion that the *majority* of Christians were quite so indifferent to the demands of their faith. Otherwise, how would we explain that it was the "orthodox" vision of Christian exclusivity that proved successful numerically against other versions of Christianity that may have tolerated a less exclusive stance?

Granted, the stern words of the author of Revelation against those who ate "food sacrificed to idols and practiced fornication" (Revelation 2:14, 20) suggest that there were some Christians who did not observe the religious exclusivity advocated more typically in early Christian texts. But it seems to me dubious to ascribe such an accommodationist stance to *most* Christians in the earliest centuries. The more exclusivist stance certainly was the more familiar one affirmed in Christian texts and also the one typically noted and objected to by outsiders. In the Roman-era setting, it was the demand for, and the practice of, an exclusivism in worship that set Christianity off from most other religious groups.[44]

We have noted that there were several important components of what we would call "religion" in the ancient world that were missing in early Christian groups, which also made early Christianity a very different kind of religion. There were no images of their deity, no Christian altars or sacrifices, these ubiquitously essential in religious life throughout the Roman world. There was no Christian priesthood either, at least for the first couple of centuries or so, and no temples or shrines.[45] The absence of these things definitely made early Christianity odd as a religious movement in that time.

An odd religious movement, certainly, but a "religious" movement, nonetheless. For, although earliest Christians did not have such things as images or altars or shrines, they did have rituals that expressed their beliefs and that functioned as actions/events in which special divine transactions with their God took place.[46] Prominent among these rituals was an initiation rite, "baptism," which seems to have been common to various Christian circles.[47]

In earliest references to the rite, the name of Jesus was invoked over the person being baptized. It is also plausible that the person being baptized invoked Jesus by name. This use of Jesus' name seems to be what is referred to as being baptized "in/into the name of Jesus" (e.g., Acts 2:38; 19:5).[48] Analysis of similar Greek formulas that appear in documents recording acquisition or disposition of goods or property suggests that the phrase "in/into the name of Jesus" expressed the notion that the person baptized became thereby specially connected to Jesus, perhaps signifying that the person came under the ownership of Jesus.[49] In any case, early Christian baptism clearly functioned as a religious rite.

Further, this baptismal rite functioned differently from the many ritual washings that formed a part of other religious groups of the time. These washings were typically to cleanse a person in preparation for entrance to a temple and participation in sacrifice or other "cultic" activities. But early Christian baptism functioned as the rite by which one became a member of the *ekklēsia*, the distinctive circle of people comprising the Christian group. The other water/washing rites functioned to prepare one to enter a ritually unclean space, and so were practiced repeatedly, for example, as preparation for each visit to a temple or other sacred space. But Christian baptism was a one-time rite that functioned to mark the separation of the initiate from his/her pre-Christian past and to signify transition into membership in the new faith community, the *ekklēsia* (church).[50]

There also seems to have been a common ritual of invoking or acclaiming Jesus that was a crucial part of the corporate worship gathering. Paul appears to allude to this practice in Romans 10:9-13. In this text, Paul says that "if you confess with your mouth the Lord Jesus and believe in your heart that God raised him from the dead, you will be saved" (v. 9). It is striking that he then directly appropriates an Old Testament statement to summarize his point: "Whoever calls upon the name of the Lord will be saved" (v. 13). What makes this striking is that the biblical expression Paul uses here, "to call upon the name of the Lord," regularly refers to worshipping God in Old Testament texts such as Joel 2:32.[51] But Paul clearly uses the expression here to refer to the practice of a reverential invocation of "the Lord Jesus." Indeed, in another text Paul designates members of the early Jesus-movement simply as "all those who in every place call upon our Lord Jesus Christ" (1 Corinthians 1:2), this ritual act serving as a sufficient expression of their faith stance.

A shared meal with deep religious significance also seems to have been a widely observed early Christian practice.[52] Of course, shared meals were a typical feature of various groups and occasions in the Roman world.[53] In particular, group meals often followed animal sacrifice to a god, part of the animal given to the god by burning, part given to the temple/priests, and the remainder shared as a meal by those who made the offering. Furthermore, there were these meals and others as well—sometimes held in private homes and sometimes in a dining room that formed part of a temple complex—that were in honor of a god. The invitations to these meals were sometimes written as coming from the god.[54] These meals in honor of pagan deities may be especially relevant for comparison with those that were also a regular part of earliest Christian gatherings.

Indeed, in his exhortations to the Corinthian church to avoid idolatry, Paul makes a direct contrast between taking part in a meal in honor of a pagan deity and partaking of the church meal: "You cannot drink the cup of the Lord and the cup of demons. You cannot partake of the table of the Lord and the table of demons" (1 Corinthians 10:21). But, of course, the contrast also involves an implicit comparison. At least in Paul's churches, the meal that he also calls "the Lord's supper/banquet" (1 Corinthians 11:20) is clearly much more than simply an occasion for Christians to share food and have a good time. For Paul links the meal with the redemptive death of Jesus, and Paul warns that partaking with a wrongful attitude, particularly showing disdain for other believers, can even make you liable to divine judgment (1 Corinthians 11:23-32).[55] In effect, Paul portrays the Christian shared meal as one where the *Kyrios* Jesus is spiritually present and presiding in power.

We also know that—from at least sometime in the second century AD, and quite plausibly earlier still—Christians were developing their own patterns and practices of prayer.[56] It appears, for example, that recitation of "the Lord's Prayer," with some variations in wording, was an early practice reflected and encouraged in several texts of various provenances.[57] As well, we have reference to prayers to Jesus (e.g., 2 Corinthians 12:8), and to God and Jesus jointly (e.g., 1 Thessalonians 3:11-13), and also references to Jesus as heavenly intercessor to God on behalf of believers (for example, Romans 8:34; 1 John 2:1). These prayer practices, Jesus integral to all of them, comprised another feature that identified and distinguished the religious ethos of early Christianity. By sometime in the second century AD or so, Christian prayer practices often also included a preferred posture: standing, with outspread hands and facing the East.[58]

Even the practice of assembling weekly for corporate worship, which seems to go back into early first-century circles, was unusual among other religious groups of the time. For example, the more typical pagan practice was for individuals to approach this or that deity for favors when they were needed. Group worship was associated more with special days of the year or month that were connected with particular deities. The only real analogy and precedent for the weekly meetings of Christian circles was Jewish synagogue practice, which, of course, again reflects the Jewish matrix in which the Jesus-movement that became Christianity first emerged. I emphasize, however, that in comparison with the wider Roman-era pagan religious context, the early Christian emphasis on *corporate* worship by members of a given *ekklēsia*, and on *gathering regularly*, comprised a distinctive pattern of religious practice.

In short, unquestionably, the pagan converts in early Christian circles who followed the demands of their newly embraced faith to abstain completely from worshipping the many gods of the Roman world held a distinctive, even novel, religious stance in beliefs and practices. In the preceding chapter, we noted the critical attitudes of pagan sophisticates such as Celsus, and the firm judicial stance taken against Christians by Pliny. Also, the religious stance of early Christians often ignited harassment and, sometimes, social conflict, for example, as in the accounts in Acts of the Apostles. Clearly, ancient pagans thought that early Christianity was different, and objectionably so.

The Christian God

But the differences between early Christianity and its larger religious environment went beyond simply refusing to worship the gods and the distinguishing Christian ritual practices noted. For everyone in the Roman era, worship practice was crucial, perhaps the most obvious expression of one's religiousness. But early Christian *beliefs* about their God are also worth notice. From the earliest Christian texts onward, we see fascinating expressions of these beliefs.[59] I hope to highlight a few things sufficiently to make the point.

First, the lack of images of their deity reflected the Christian belief that their God was, in our terms, radically transcendent, not capable of being represented adequately in any image, not capable of being perceived in the ways that we perceive, capture, and comprehend the things of our world. Perhaps the most explicit early expression of this is in 1 Timothy 6:15-16, where the author describes God in such august terms:

> He who is the blessed and only Sovereign, the King of kings and Lord of Lords. It is he alone who has immortality and dwells in unapproachable light, whom no one has ever seen or can see; to him be honor and eternal dominion.

Of course, once again, this draws on and reflects a developed Jewish view of the biblical deity, which has roots far back into

prohibitions against making any image, in texts such as Deuteronomy 4:15-20, and in the dramatic account in Exodus 33:12-23
where God refuses Moses' request to see God's glory: "you cannot see my face; for no one shall see me and live" (v. 20). Also, in
early Roman-era Jewish writers such as Philo of Alexandria, we
certainly have an emphasis on God's utter transcendence and inef-
fable nature.[60] Likewise, in Greek philosophical tradition, there
were voices that posited an ultimate deity transcending all things,
including the named deities to which sacrifice was offered. But
there are also some interesting differences that distinguish early
Christian beliefs about their God, especially in comparison with
the larger pagan traditions of the time.

In the philosophical traditions, an ultimate and radically transcendent deity was often postulated, but you did not typically
engage that transcendent deity directly. For example, you did not
usually sacrifice to this deity or implore it directly. Instead, the
same philosophers who posited the lofty views of a transcendent
deity were content for the worship of the traditional, lesser deities
to continue and, indeed, typically took part in this themselves.[61]
But the early Christian stance was that the one, true, and radically transcendent God was, nevertheless, also available to a direct
relationship with people. Christians believed that you could pray
directly to this God and hope to be heard. You could worship this
God directly and know that it was welcome. Indeed, prayer and
worship directly to this one God was typically urged as the only
proper and legitimate worship in Christian circles. In contrast to
the practice and views of the pagan world, including specifically
philosophical traditions, Christians were to treat the many other
deities of the time as unworthy beings, and the worship of them
as idolatry.

But there was a still more unusual and, in the eyes of pagan
sophisticates, outlandish Christian notion: the one, true, august
God who transcended all things and had no need of anything,
nevertheless, had deigned to create this world and, a still more
remarkable notion, also now actively sought the redemption and

reconciliation of individuals. And what was the proffered reason for this remarkable redemptive purpose? God loves the world
and humanity! Of course, in early Christian teaching, God's love
was particularly demonstrated in God's provision of Jesus, God's
"Son," for the redemption of the world. Among the earliest and
most lyrical expressions of this belief are Paul's statements in
Romans 5:1-11 and his soaring lines in Romans 8:31-39. The
latter text concludes in these bold lines:[62]

> For I am convinced that neither death, nor life, nor angels, nor
> rulers, nor things present, nor things to come, nor powers, nor
> height, nor depth, nor anything else in all creation, will be able
> to separate us from the love of God in Christ Jesus our Lord.

The notion that there is one true and transcendent God, and
that this God loves the world/humanity, may have become subsequently so much a familiar notion, whether or not it is actively
affirmed, that we cannot easily realize how utterly strange, even
ridiculous, it was in the Roman era. When ancient pagan thinkers
spoke of human "love" for a god or gods, they typically referred
to an *eros*, not an erotic love in our sense, but a desire for association with the divine or the sublimely beautiful qualities represented by the deity. When they referred to the attitude of the gods
toward humans, they sometimes posited deities of particular cities
or peoples as kindly disposed toward them, in these cases using
the Greek term *philia*, depicting a kindness and friendly quality.[63]
The Greek term early Christians preferred, however, to depict
their God's love, and the love that they were to show as well for
God and others, even their enemies, was *agapē* and its cognate
verb *agapaō*. These words appear very infrequently in pagan texts
of the time but copiously in early Christian texts. For example, in
the New Testament, *agapē* appears some 143 times, and the verb
agapaō 116 times. These words also appear prominently in some
Jewish Greek texts. So the early Christian preference for *agapē* and
the cognate verb *agapaō* may be another instance of the influence
of the Jewish matrix of the early Christian movement. It may be

that Jews and then early Christians preferred these words because they seemed to connote a more sober love, emphasizing a moral commitment to the one loved. These terms also had the effect of marking off early Christian discourse about their God from pagan discourse about the other deities of the time.[64]

We should certainly recognize that ancient people could have a genuine sense of religious awe, gratitude, and devotion to their various gods, and individuals could feel a particular affection for their favored deities. We do have references to this or that pagan deity as merciful or generous. But the notion that the gods love humanity with anything approaching relational intensity ascribed to God rather ubiquitously in early Christian texts is, to put it mildly, hard to find in pagan texts of the Greek or Roman period.[65]

Again, the greater similarity is with the Jewish tradition, for there too we have a transcendent deity that can be approached directly, and also even the notion that the one God chose the people of Israel and maintains a profound covenant-love/faithfulness with them.[66] Nevertheless, although Roman-era Jews thought that their deity was really the creator and rightful ruler of all peoples, the particular theme of God's love for the world and humanity at large is not really emphasized with anything like the prominence that we find in early Christian texts. Indeed, the emphasis on God's love and the appeal for an answering "love-ethic" characterizing Christian conduct comprise something distinctive. We simply do not know of any other Roman-era religious group in which love played this important role in discourse or behavioral teaching.[67]

So, the differences between early Christianity and the larger religious environment went beyond simply preferring one particular deity among the others, and beyond an exclusivist worship practice. There were also different notions about what the term "god" (Greek: *theos*) meant, or at least for Christians there was a distinction between "gods" and the one God (*ho theos* = literally, "the god"). The early Christian notion posited one utterly transcendent deity who could not be compared with the many traditional gods at all and could not even be comprehended fully, so great was this God. And yet, and with equal emphasis, Christians maintained that this one deity, not some subordinate being, was the sole creator of all things and also sought to relate to the world and humanity in redemptive love, such that even the humblest of individuals could be recipients of this love and could be adopted into a filial relationship with this God.

For many pagan critics, all this was, quite simply, preposterous, as reflected, for example, in Celsus' critique of Christianity. But, to judge from the continued growth of early Christianity amidst social hostilities and periodic prosecutions, this body of beliefs, though preposterous in the eyes of some pagan critics, seems to have been winsome to many others. Indeed, these beliefs may have been among the factors in that growth, comprising part of "the social and religious capital" that early Christianity offered.[68]

One God . . . and One Lord (Jesus)

Early Christian beliefs and practices were not only distinctive, and in some ways novel, in the ancient "pagan" context. They were also distinctive in the context of Roman-era Jewish religious tradition, although for a different reason. In comparison with the devotional pattern that was typical of ancient Jewish tradition, the early Christian movement was identifiable and distinguishable particularly by the extraordinary reverence typically given also to Jesus along with God.

To avoid anachronistic notions, I must first emphasize here again that what we may call the very earliest "Christian" circles were comprised, at least mainly, by Jewish believers. Indeed, across the first few decades, even as numerous circles made up mainly by Gentiles (pagan converts) arose, such as those formed through Paul's mission to the Gentiles, Jewish believers—such as Paul, Barnabas, Peter, and others—continued to be prominent.

Furthermore, well into the second century AD and beyond, there continued to be circles of early Christianity that were made up of Jews. What is sometimes referred to as "Jewish Christianity" in that sense was for a long while a noteworthy part of the larger Jesus-movement.[69]

Especially in the earliest years of the young movement that became "Christianity," therefore, I repeat that we should not imagine two fully distinguishable religions called "Judaism" and "Christianity." Instead, in this very early period, we are dealing with a new religious movement that emerged initially *within* the ancient Jewish tradition and as a distinctive form of that tradition. Ancient Jewish tradition took in a variety of other movements as well, including religious parties such as the Pharisees, and still more radical groups such as the Qumran community. I note once more that we should not, therefore, imagine a singular and developed "Christian" stance over against some monolithic "Judaism," especially in the first century AD. The Jesus-movement was initially one among a number of Jewish religious options of the Roman era.

Rather quickly, however, the Jesus-movement became translocal and transethnic. Indeed, Paul was convinced that he had been given a divine calling to proclaim the gospel especially to non-Jews, and so he carried out an aggressive and programmatic project of doing this. Probably by the end of the first century AD, the Jesus-movement was dominantly made up of non-Jews, who sometimes distinguished their religious stance quite starkly from that affirmed by most Jews of the time. In Ignatius of Antioch, a church leader in the early second century AD, for example, we see early references to "Christianity" and "Judaism" as more fully distinguishable and contrasting entities that he refers to with these terms.[70] But, to underscore the point again, in the earlier decades of the first century the emergent "Christian" religious stance was a development within the variegated Jewish tradition of the time.

So, let us consider further the early Jesus-movement in relation to that larger Jewish tradition, and in particular how the
Jesus-movement was distinctive within that variegated tradition.
We have noted already that, from the outset, early Christians,
whether Jewish or Gentile, typically shared the ancient Jewish
exclusivist stance regarding the gods.[71] They refused to worship
any deity but the one biblical God. Moreover, at least most early
Christian circles, whether comprised of Jewish or Gentile Jesus-
followers, treated as scriptures those writings that were regarded
similarly in larger Jewish tradition of the time.[72] In these and
other ways, most early "Christians," including particularly Gentile believers, could seem to be following essentially a peculiar version of Jewish "religion." Indeed, it appears that at least
some pagans of the time saw similarities too. Recall some of
Galen's comments cited in chapter 1, in which he refers to Jews
and Christians as following or comprising a shared or a similar
philosophy.

But in a number of publications over a few decades now,
using a term from biology as a metaphor, I have referred to the
Jesus-movement as a novel "mutation" in ancient Jewish tradition.
In positing a "mutation," I have focused especially on the ways
that Jesus featured in the beliefs and practices that comprised the
devotional pattern that characterized early Christian circles. For,
although the early Jesus-movement echoed the Jewish rhetoric
and the practice of reverencing only "one God," Jesus-followers,
or "Christians," whether Jewish or Gentile, also typically accorded
to Jesus a place in their beliefs and worship practices that was
without precedent or parallel in the wider Jewish tradition of the
time. I have referred to this as comprising a distinctively "dyadic"
devotional pattern, in which Jesus was linked uniquely with God,
referred to as "the Father" in some early Christian discourse. As
I have discussed this more fully in those previous publications, I
will only summarize a few key matters here.[73]

From the beginning—that is, from the earliest known days
after Jesus' execution—he was central in early proclamation and

belief in the circles that comprised the Jesus-movement. The gospel message focused very much on Jesus' significance as Messiah (Greek: *Christos*; e.g., Acts 2:36), as the vindicated and unique "Son" of God (e.g., Romans 1:3-4), and as the divinely appointed "Lord" (Greek: *Kyrios*) who had been raised by God from death and installed at God's "right hand" (e.g., Philippians 2:9-11). Especially in the earliest days, the startling conviction that God had raised Jesus from death was obviously crucial and was the ignition point for the new level of enthusiasm among Jesus-followers and for the emphasis on these high claims about him. The proper response to the claims that Jesus' followers urged was to accept them and to live in full trust in Jesus' status and efficacy as, for example, savior and unique intercessor before God, Jesus' death proclaimed as made redemptive by God "for our sins" (e.g., Romans 4:24-25). In New Testament texts, both Jews and Gentiles are summoned to accept these claims about Jesus, treating him now as the unique agent of God's redemptive purposes (e.g., Acts 4:12), and Jews as well as Gentiles underwent a baptism in Jesus' name as their typical initiation rite into membership in the Jesus-movement.

Let us consider again Romans 10:9-13, a text we looked at briefly earlier. Paul declares in this passage that "if you confess with your lips that Jesus is Lord and believe in your hearts that God raised him from the dead, you will be saved" (v. 9). In the preceding verses of Romans 10 and several times in Romans 9–11, Paul expresses deep concern over the fate of his ancestral (Jewish) people on account of the rejection of the gospel by the great majority of them. In Romans 9:1-5, Paul registers his sorrow and anguish over Jewish unbelief in the gospel, indicating his willingness to suffer God's curse himself if it would bring about a recovery from their unbelief. In Romans 10:1-2, Paul records his prayer that fellow Jews will be "saved," and he laments again their unenlightened response to the gospel message about Jesus. Then, in Romans 11, Paul refers to his people as having "stumbled" in their unbelief in the gospel, but he insists that this does not mean their ultimate downfall and permanent estrangement from God's purposes. Instead, Paul declares boldly his confidence that in God's ultimate purpose Jewish unbelief will be overcome: "And so all Israel will be saved" (11:26).[74]

All this obviously means, therefore, that in Paul's view the necessity of confessing Jesus lay upon Jews as well as upon Gentiles.[75] Toward the end of Romans 10:9-13, Paul makes this entirely clear in his statement that "there is no distinction between Jew and Greek; the same Lord [in the context, obviously the Lord Jesus] is Lord of all and is generous to all who call upon him" (v. 12). Indeed, in Philippians 2:9-11, Paul writes that not simply all people but also all spheres of creation are to acknowledge Jesus' supremacy as "Lord" in response to God's appointment of Jesus as the one to whom all are now to give this obeisance. So, for Paul, and for other early Jewish Jesus-followers as well, recognition of Jesus' status as Messiah and Lord was incumbent upon fellow Jews as well as non-Jews. To refuse to recognize Jesus' status was, in their eyes, blind disobedience to God. And that meant that what became "early Christianity" was not simply some new Jewish religious party, such as the Pharisees seem to have been. It was something more radical. The early Jesus-movement was, to use modern terminology, more "sectarian," making an exclusivist claim to which all others should give assent.

The Pharisees were essentially Jewish rigorists as to observance of Jewish law, including a body of their traditional interpretations of it. Granted, they also seem to have urged a similar dedication to observance by fellow Jews.[76] One scholar recently characterized their aim as the "sanctification" of the whole nation of Jewish people through a collective observance of the Pharisaic understanding of Jewish law.[77] The point I underscore here, however, is that the Pharisees were a distinguishable religious "party" but were not a closed and exclusivist "sect."[78] That is, although they may have wished that other Jews should observe God's law more diligently and according to their understanding of it, we have no indication that they claimed to be the only true elect or that they regarded non-Pharisees as under God's judgment for not living as Pharisees. This contrasts, for example, with the attitude reflected in texts found at Qumran, in which there are strict rules for membership among the elect, and other Jews are included along with non-Jews (pagans) among the "sons of the pit" who would suffer divine wrath in the coming judgment.[79]

The Pharisees also form a contrast with what appears to have been the stance of the early Jesus-movement. As we have noted, Jewish believers in Jesus such as Paul clearly seem to have felt that the gospel announced a decisive new act of God in which Jesus was now made the one whom all, Jews and non-Jews, were to "call upon" and recognize as Lord.[80] That is, Jews wishing to be faithful to their ancestral God must now acknowledge Jesus; otherwise, they are actually being disobedient to their own God.

This amounts to a distinctive, exclusivist stance in the context of ancient Jewish tradition as well as in the context of the ancient pagan environment. That is, although membership in the Jesus-movement was voluntary, so far as members were concerned it was also obligatory, both for Jews and for non-Jews, if they wished to obey God. The early Jesus-movement was not the only exclusivist Jewish sect, but it certainly did not present itself as simply one optional form of Jewishness among others. It had distinctive beliefs, claims, and practices, and these focused particularly on the figure of Jesus.

The peculiarly "dyadic" nature of earliest Christian belief, in which Jesus is highlighted uniquely along with God, is also readily apparent in 1 Corinthians 8:4-6, a text that we considered earlier in connection with the larger Roman-era religious environment. Over against the many deities of the time, Paul declares that there is really only "one God, the Father, from whom are all things and for whom we exist, and one Lord, Jesus Christ, through whom are all things and through whom we exist." The point I want to focus on here, however, is how this statement combines the exclusivity of Paul's Jewish tradition with the duality that distinguished earliest Christian faith: both God ("the

Father") and Jesus are given an exclusivity in the repetition of an emphatic "one" with each of them. And, likewise, there is a universality ascribed to each, along with a distinction between them: *all* things are *from* and *for* God; and *all* things are *through* Jesus. God is the author, source, and ultimate purpose of all things, and Jesus is the unique agent of creation and redemption of all things.

In short, we have here a splendid and concise example of how the ancient Jewish confession of the uniqueness of the one God appears to have been adapted and widened, so to speak, to accommodate Jesus as a second distinguishable figure who, nevertheless, is uniquely linked with the one God and with a corresponding universal role. That classic Jewish confession, known as the *Shema* (framed in the words of Deuteronomy 6:4), can be translated, "Hear, O Israel: The Lord our God is one Lord."[81] We may think of 1 Corinthians 8:4-6 as a modification of the *Shema*, or perhaps as merely alluding to it, or as shaped by it. In any case, the important point to note is that Jesus is linked with God uniquely and that this distinguishes the early Jesus-movement (early "Christianity") from other forms of ancient Jewish religion as well as from the larger religious environment of the early Roman period.

In addition to the centrality of Jesus in early Christian belief and confession, he also was accorded a distinctive and unique place in the devotional practices of earliest circles of believers. Over the years, I have emphasized this as particularly important, especially in light of ancient Jewish concerns to protect God's uniqueness most crucially in matters of worship practice. I want to emphasize here two key points.

First, as I have repeatedly shown in previous publications, we have a whole constellation of practices that make up a noteworthy devotional pattern in which Jesus is central. For example, recall that the entrance rite to early Christian fellowship, baptism, involved the invocation of Jesus' name ("calling upon" him). Moreover, it appears that in Aramaic-speaking (Jewish) circles, as well as in Greek-speaking ones, the corporate worship gathering included the act of invoking Jesus as "Lord," as reflected in the

Maranatha appeal in 1 Corinthians 16:22.[82] That is, this veneration of Jesus in the context of gathered worship seems to have commenced in circles of *Jewish* Jesus-followers and then quickly became standard practice in Pauline churches and subsequently in early Christian tradition.

Chanted hymns or odes celebrating Jesus, and perhaps also directed to him, are referred to in New Testament writings and also seem to have formed a regular part of early Christian worship as well as biblical Psalms seen as prophetical of Jesus.[83] Recall Pliny's report discussed in chapter 1 that in their gatherings Christians sang "a hymn to Christ as to a god."[84] Furthermore, as we noted earlier, Paul refers to the common, sacred meal of churches as "the Lord's supper" (1 Corinthians 11:20), the meal in honor of Jesus "the Lord," who was deemed present and presiding, as the pagan cult deities were at the meals in their honor. Indeed, to cite again a crucial text, so central was Jesus in earliest devotional practices that Paul designates believers simply as "all those who call upon the name of the Lord Jesus Christ" (1 Corinthians 1:2), referring to the ritual practice of acclaiming and invoking him.

In summary, the various devotional practices characteristic of earliest circles of the Jesus-movement effectively incorporated Jesus along with God as rightful recipient. Along with the high claims made about Jesus, this constellation of devotional practices is quite simply remarkable, even astonishing. For it amounts to treating Jesus in ways that liken him to God, yet without displacing God in any way. Instead, in their devotional practices as in their beliefs, earliest Christians associated Jesus with God uniquely, both linking them and distinguishing them in a distinctive "dyadic" pattern.

My second point is that this seems to have been a genuine novelty. In a book originally published in 1988, I surveyed ancient Jewish tradition for any parallels or precedents for this sort of phenomena and could find none.[85] To be sure, as I showed in that book, ancient Jewish tradition often portrayed this or that figure, sometimes a high angel, sometimes a biblical hero, and sometimes one of God's attributes portrayed in personified mode, acting as God's unique agent, sometimes in creation, sometimes in redemption, and/or in other tasks. I referred to this as comprising a "chief agent" concept in ancient Jewish tradition, and I proposed that it may have given earliest Jewish Jesus-believers a kind of conceptual category in which to begin to situate the resurrected/exalted Jesus next to God. But none of these other "chief agent" figures held the sort of huge place in the faith professions and religious practices of ancient Jews that Jesus held in circles of the Jesus-movement from the earliest years. That is, none of the "chief agent" figures gives us a proper precedent or full parallel, especially for the place of Jesus in earliest Christian devotional practice.

So, I contend that this dyadic pattern of belief and practices, involving God and Jesus, marks out the Jesus-movement among the variegated Jewish tradition of the Roman period. The Jesus-movement comprises a distinctive "mutation" in ancient Jewish tradition. It is not simply that the early Jesus-movement spoke of Jesus instead of any other "chief agent" or messiah. That in itself would have given the Jesus-movement a particularity. But there is much more. From our earliest evidence, the risen/exalted Jesus held a central place in the religious confession and beliefs, and also in religious practices including corporate worship, of circles of Jewish and non-Jewish believers that is categorically without precedent or parallel and that comprises a novel "dyadic" pattern. Not simply the particulars but also the *pattern* of belief and practice was different and distinctive in comparison to any other kind of Jewish group of the time.

I will cite what is sometimes offered as an exception, but I do not think it is one. In an ancient Jewish writing known as *1 Enoch*, a composite writing comprising several distinguishable portions put together across a couple of centuries or more, there is a portion that is called "the Parables (or Similitudes)," *1 Enoch* 37–71.[86] In this material there appears a figure referred to variously as "the Chosen/Elect One," "the Messiah," and "the

Righteous One," and also in several Ethiopic expressions often translated indiscriminately as "son of man." This figure is posited as "named" and chosen before creation (48.2, 6), and he will also be the agent of God's final supremacy on behalf of the righteous and against the wicked (e.g., 48.4-10; 52.4-9). He will then sit upon a glorious throne (51.3; 61.8) and receive obeisance from all the rulers of the earth. But note that, along with a variety of other heavenly beings, this figure is pictured as joining in the worship of the one God (61.10-11). As glorious as he is, the "Chosen One" is not the recipient of this worship or even the corecipient of this worship with God. The conquered kings of the earth will "fall on their faces" before him and "supplicate and petition for mercy from him" (62.9), but he is not pictured as receiving the corporate worship of God's own people. Moreover, this figure appears in dreams and visions of the future and is not the recipient of the actual devotional practices of any known ancient Jewish circle. That is, whatever these passages envision at some future point when the figure appears, there is no evidence that circles of Jews, even those who wrote the "Similitudes" of 1 Enoch, met to reverence this figure in the ways that Jesus was reverenced in early circles of the Jesus-movement. So, I stand by my contention that the intensity and types of reverence given to Jesus in earliest Christian circles comprise a historic innovation that sets them off within the ancient Jewish tradition in which they first emerged.

Summary

I hope that the preceding discussion has been clear enough to require little by way of further elaboration here. Over against the wider Roman-era piety of reverencing all the gods, the early Jesus-movement of Jewish and non-Jewish believers shared a traditional Jewish exclusivity in refusing what they regarded as "idolatry" and insisting that only the one God of the biblical tradition should receive worship. Also, in comparison with the dominant expressions of the Jewish tradition, the early Jesus-movement was distinctive, particularly in the programmatic inclusion of Jesus as central in their religious beliefs and practices. In the initial years, of course, what became early "Christianity" was a novel movement within the Jewish tradition and was characterized by this distinctive "dyadic" pattern in which the one God and Jesus were central. But it is also clear that this unique place of Jesus in this movement was a source of profound tension, at least for some other Jews, who likely viewed it as an unacceptable mutation.[87] My main point, however, is that early Christianity was characterized by a distinctive pattern of religious beliefs and practices that made it distinguishable in the larger Roman world. Indeed, for reasons discussed in this and the subsequent chapters, I think we have to say that early Christianity represented a new kind of what we would call "religion," something that had not quite been seen before, and something that proved revolutionary in what "religion" came to mean thereafter.[88]

3

A Different Identity

Periodically, in societies such as Britain, a census is taken, in which various questions are posed to help the government and other agencies know better the nature of the population. In such a census, one of the many questions will likely be your national background or race, and in another question you will likely be asked to indicate your religious affiliation or identity. That the two questions are posed separately in such a census reflects the modern notion of a "religious identity" as something distinguishable, in particular distinguishable from one's nationality. So, in response to such questions, you can mark yourself as "White British," for example, and yet your religious affiliation or identity may be any of a number of choices, such as Christian, Buddhist, Muslim, or even no religion. (Indeed, on one such British census, a surprising number of people identified their religion as "Jedi"!)

But in the Roman era, as typical throughout antiquity and in many societies to this day, what we would call religious identity was conferred at birth and was not really a distinguishable conceptual category. Practically everyone was presumed to honor the gods, and your own gods were supplied as part of your birthright. As we noted in the preceding chapter, there were household divinities that you acknowledged simply by being a member of a given household, whether family member or slave. In addition, there were deities of your city, your people, and your nation; and so your religious duties of reverence were shaped very much by who you were, where or to whom you were born, and where you lived.

Granted, ethnic identity is, and has typically been, to some degree "constructed," at least as to the specifics of what it involves, and so it is subject to development or even change. But, for at least most people of the Roman era, their ethnic identity was basically given at birth, and gods linked to that ethnic group came as part of the package. Consequently, ancient historians and ethnographers such as Herodotus typically relate as integral the laws, customs, gods, and traditional religious observances of the various cultures and nations that they describe (Herodotus, *Histories* 3.38).

So, for example, if you were a Roman, in addition to your own particular family/household divinities (*lares*), there was the traditional Roman pantheon: Jupiter, Juno, Mars, Venus, and the rest. If you were Greek, there was a corresponding pantheon: Zeus, Hera, Athena, and others. If you were Egyptian, there were the gods of Egypt. And the same went for Syrians, Phrygians, Gauls, and all the other various peoples of the Roman world.

The Jewish people, wherever Jews lived in the Roman world, were likewise a defined "nation," and most Jews seem to have retained a sense of being Jewish and so part of their own "nation" or people, even if they were also inhabitants of Greece or other lands. But in their case, as noted earlier, in place of a pantheon of deities to be worshiped there was only the one deity, and they typically did not engage in sacrifice to the gods of the various lands where they may have been born and may have lived. In short, for Jews as for other peoples/nations, what we call "religious identity" was simply a component of ethnic identity. To be sure, Jews perceived themselves, and were perceived by others, as following a pattern of religious behavior different from other peoples. But their peculiar religious behavior—specifically, their refusal to take part in the worship of other gods—was understood as simply a peculiar feature of the Jewish people.

Indeed, in the ancient Roman setting, being part of a given people/nation and the nature of one's normal religious responsibilities were so closely connected that it might well be anachronistic to try to separate what we moderns call "religion" from what we call "ethnicity" or "culture." In chapter 1, we note that "religion" as a separate sphere of life is very much a modern notion, foreign to the ancient world.

We see illustrations of how one's gods and one's ethnic identity were linked in the way that Roman deities were reverenced and Roman forms of religion were practiced in the colonies of Roman citizens in various parts of the empire.[1] That is, as a Roman citizen, wherever you lived, you felt linked, or obliged, to Roman deities. So, if you moved to some place other than Rome, you took your deities with you. They remained your deities because of who you were. Something similar was the case with other peoples as well. For example, the various peoples who migrated to Rome, or were taken there, from other places often sought to continue the worship of their respective nations. Egyptians brought with them deities such as Isis, and other peoples did the same. Sometimes, traditional Romans were not terribly happy at the influx of foreign deities, but it went with Rome being the imperial magnet city that it was.[2]

To be sure, there was also a kind of translocal and transethnic religious identity that was expressive of the wish of various people to associate positively with the Roman Empire. For example, there are instances of Greek/eastern cities that adopted various Roman rituals and religious institutions. In some cases, this was

a rather clear and direct transplant of Roman deities and practices, and in other cases it involved adaptation as well as adoption of Roman religious influences.[3] There are also instances of
dedications/offerings by various eastern towns sent to Rome and
her deities, expressing gratitude for Roman help and/or Roman
benefaction. In short, the expansion of Roman imperial power
brought also the spread of the cults and deities of Rome.[4] So,
Roman deities could be included among the deities reverenced by
people other than Romans. But this was a result of Roman political and cultural influence; the reverencing of Roman deities was
simply what ancients judged to be a natural way to acknowledge
and respond positively to that influence. If that seems to us not
quite a "pure" religious motive, however, that is, again, because
our notions of "religion" do not map directly onto the concepts
and practices of the ancient world.[5]

A particularly novel expression of a religious response to
Roman power was the establishment of a cult of *Dea Roma*
("Goddess Rome") as a new deity in various eastern sites such
as Smyrna, Delos, and Miletus, dating from as far back as the
early second century BC. "Roma" seems to have been the per-
sonification of the deified Rome, and temples to her and statues
of her proliferated quickly.[6] This was not a case of eastern peoples adopting a prior Roman religious practice, however, for no
cult of Roma is attested in Rome itself earlier than the reign of
Hadrian in the second century AD, some three centuries or more
later. Instead, the rise of *Dea Roma* in the eastern provinces was
a creative and voluntary development. Nevertheless, it certainly
was indicative of Roman power, and a desire of people in eastern
provinces of the empire to be identified with that Roman power
was reflected in religious practices such as this divine personifi-
cation of Rome itself.

In addition, we must take note of the development of cults
of emperors, which was another kind of transethnic and translocal religious activity.[7] Contrary to the rhetoric of some publications, however, there was no one organized "imperial cult."[8]

Instead, there were various initiatives taken that were expressive of a desire to honor Rome and the emperors. In some cases, the initiative was taken at local level, influential people in a given city promoting reverence for the emperor. In other cases, there were provincial cults established by provincial assemblies, which carried more of an official status. There was also a distinction between the worship of the living emperor, which developed earlier in eastern areas of the empire, and the worship of deceased emperors, which was the form of cult more acceptable in Rome itself. There, the traditional preference was for official offerings to be made on behalf of the living emperor to the traditional Roman gods.[9]

All of these various forms of "imperial cult" are expressions of what we can call a "religious identity," in these cases the devotees seeking to identify themselves with reference to Rome, her power, and her rulers. But there were distinctions between the forms of reverence given to emperors, based on whether the devotees were citizens or subjects of Rome. Roman citizens living in the provinces had their own religious associations distinct from those of the subject peoples of those provinces, and this was expressive of the notion that Roman citizens had a special relation to the emperor.[10]

For my purpose here, however, whatever the form of devotion to the Roman emperor, it expressed a facet of what we can call one's religious identity. To be sure, that religious identity also involved what we would regard as a political stance. Whether you offered sacrifice to the emperor or on his behalf, either way you were defining yourself, in part at least, in relation to him. But, to restate the point, we should not write off emperor cults as simply political and not genuinely religious. To do so would be to impose distinctions that simply were not appropriate for that ancient setting. For at least some of those who took part in emperor cults, there probably was a genuinely religious sentiment, at least in a sense that they would recognize, even if it was not distinguishable from their admiration of Roman power. Granted, however, it was also not at all bad for your career prospects or social status to be seen to be participating in and, even more so, to be involved in promoting emperor cult.

In summary, emperor cults were translocal and transethnic expressions of religious identity. Despite the differences noted, they all served to link people in various parts of the empire through the various kinds of reverence offered to or for the emperor. In this sense, the imperial cults and the emergence of the cult of *Dea Roma* are examples of religious identity beyond what was entailed in someone's native locale or ethnic membership. Obviously, however, this religious identity was tied to a translocal political regime, the Roman Empire, and, through their participation in the religious expressions of Roman power, devotees expressed their wish to be associated and identified with that regime and its claims.

But it is also very important to emphasize that the cults of the emperor were not in competition with, nor did they displace, the traditional gods and their worship in the various lands of the empire. Throughout the Roman period, even in the eastern areas, for example, where emperor cults emerged with particular enthusiasm, people in the various cities of the East also continued their traditional rites focused on their ancestral deities.[11] That is, both in Rome and in other areas of strong Roman influence as well, traditional gods and their worship continued to be prominent. So, participation in emperor cults was simply one facet or layer of what we might regard the religious identity of devotees. It certainly did not replace the ethnic/religious identify of people, and also it did not become typically the primary religious identity of most people who took part in emperor cults.

Voluntary Religion

There were, however, also other religious groups in the Roman world to which you could become an adherent by choice, taking on thereby the worship of a deity that was not part of your birthright. These various gods and groups were not particularly associated with Roman rule or rulers; and so becoming an adherent was not expressive of some political stance. So, to us, these groups may seem closer to a purely "religious" phenomenon.

We can designate them as even more clearly examples of what we could term "voluntary religion," in which individuals made a choice to become a devotee of a given deity and to take up the practices involved. The so-called "mystery cults" of the Roman period noted in an earlier chapter are the obvious examples.[12] They were given this designation as "mystery" cults by earlier scholars on account of the sometimes secretive rituals involved in joining some of them, but their secrecy should not be exaggerated.[13]

For my purpose here, however, the main point is that some of these "mystery cults" show that one's religious adherence, practices, and affiliations could extend beyond those connected to one's family or native people. So, thereby, participation in these cults exhibited an expression of religiousness distinguishable from, or at least additional to, the more traditional forms that were conferred by birth. Consequently, in this voluntary feature, these "mystery cults" may give us something of a *partial* analogy for the way that early Christianity, whether in its earliest "Jesus-movement" form or later, likewise made an appeal to individuals transethnically and translocally. Among these "mystery cults," two in particular will serve here as examples: the cults of Mithras and Isis.[14] Each of these deities mutated significantly from a native version to one appropriated more widely by people of other and various locales. Each cult, however, is quite distinguishable from the other.

Mithras was originally an eastern deity, but, in the form that we find in the Roman world, he had devotees in various sites across the empire.[15] In fact it now appears that the Mithraism that we know in the Roman period was actually a cult designed in the Roman West, with very tenuous connections to the Persian origins of the deity. The Mithraic cult seems to have had a special appeal for non-commissioned ranks of the Roman army, as reflected in the Mithraeums, the dedicated places for adherents to conduct their rituals that are found in a number of sites where there were Roman garrisons. Although unattested before the first century AD, Mithraism went on to great success and visibility, especially during the second and third centuries. Although Mithraism had no ethnic base, its success across a large geographical area is remarkable.[16] The key to its success was likely the social network provided in the Roman army.

But, contrary to notions of some earlier scholars that Mithraism might have succeeded to a status like that enjoyed by Christianity under Constantine, this was never in the cards.[17] For one thing, the exclusion of women certainly made that unlikely. Also, in some features, Mithraic associations seem to have been more like a kind of freemasonry or men's club, functioning perhaps essentially as a male-bonding association, and only males were admitted. Meetings were occasions in which adherents enjoyed good food and wine, and certain rituals were performed involving officials adorned with various fantastic masks and in subterranean settings. Also, one could progress through various grades of membership, much like ranks in the military. By contrast, there is no indication that grander themes featured, such as the promise of immortality, for example.[18] Nevertheless, given the more flexible notions of what "religion" included in the Roman world, Mithraism can be cited as an example of voluntary religiousness. The relevant point here is that you became a participant in Mithraism by choice, not by birth.

Isis seems to have been still more broadly successful.[19] Although originally a deity of modest significance in her native Egypt, Isis in the Roman period became an object of international reverence in various sites from Egypt to Britain. There were elaborate sanctuaries built to serve her worshippers, priests to officiate in them, and images of Isis in these sanctuaries and also adorning various objects of the time, such as lamps for usage by devotees. Indeed, it is a fair conclusion that the many depictions of Isis with the infant

Horus provided the model for the later images of the Madonna and the infant Jesus.[20]

The most well-known literary references to Isis are the treatise by Plutarch (*Isis and Osiris*) and, still more popularly read to this day, Apuleius' *Metamorphoses*. The latter text includes accounts of priests of Isis conducting the morning ceremony of opening one of the sanctuaries in her honor, and it depicts the central male character of the text having a glorious vision of Isis, whereupon he becomes an enthusiastic devotee.

From these accounts, we learn of elaborate public festivals in her honor and learn also that Isis was identified with or as goddess figures of various places, another instance of the "translation" of a deity across various nations noted earlier. In addition to these public events, devotees also observed Isis rites in their homes. Indicative of the apparently genuine feelings generated in devotees of Isis, there is the lengthy list of over fifty attributes claimed by the goddess in the Isis "aretalogy" from Kyme (in modern-day Turkey), which collectively portray her as practically the source of everything good in human culture.[21]

Unquestionably, the various voluntary cults of the Roman period such as these appealed to individuals across the empire for various reasons. To underscore the point, they also clearly show that in that period one's religious identity and practices could involve more than the deities of one's family, city, or nation. Indeed, devotees of this or that voluntary religious circle sometimes identified themselves specifically as such. Initiates of the Isis cult, for example, called themselves *Isiaci*. There were priests of Isis and some Isis devotees as well whose shaved heads marked them openly as the property of Isis.[22] We also know of an association of "Poseidoniasts," a group of traders in Berytus (Beirut), who apparently took their name from the god Poseidon and thought of themselves as under his protection.[23] Indeed, for some pagans, participation in this or that "mystery cult" may have served as their main religious practice and identity.[24] We do not know this, but it seems to me a reasonable possibility to keep in mind.

But I think that it is not likely to have been very common. Indicative of the rather nonexclusive nature of the voluntary religious groups of the time, the "Poseidoniasts" that I mentioned appear on an inscription that records them dedicating a statue of Isis in thanks for her "good will," the devotees of one deity thereby also readily giving devotion to another! As a further illustration, Apuleius, who wrote so enthusiastically of initiation into the Isis cult, also claimed to have undergone initiation into various mystery cults and to have "learned mysteries of many a kind, rites in great number, and diverse ceremonies" (*Apology* 55).[25] Even the explicit self-identification of some Isis adherents on their tombstones does not imply that their religious life was confined to Isis worship, and we have some explicit evidence that it was not.[26]

There is certainly no indication that any of these various cults demanded an *exclusive* devotion, to the neglect of reverencing other deities connected with one's family, city, or nation. It is highly likely, therefore, that at least most devotees saw their participation in these groups as an augmentation of their other religious practices and associations, not as a replacement for them. To be sure, participation in Isis worship, for example, comprised a noteworthy exercise of voluntary religiousness. So, to reiterate the point, in that feature it was *partially* analogous to the sort of voluntary religiousness involved in becoming a participant in Christian circles. But the analogy breaks down precisely in the demand placed upon all Christians that they must make their Christian commitment the *exclusive* basis of their religious identity. In short, early Christianity was the only new religious movement of the Roman era that demanded this exclusive loyalty to one deity, thereby defining all other cults of the time as rivals.[27]

We might also consider Roman-era philosophical schools as other examples of voluntary associations based on shared commitments. These, too, were translocal and transethnic in scope, and they may have fostered a certain sense of fraternal relations with like-minded individuals wherever they were. Adherence to a given philosophical tradition lent to you a certain group identity distinguishable from that derived from your family, city, or ethnicity. But, as the case with the various "mystery cults," once again, adherence to this or that philosophical school did not involve, and certainly did not require, any renunciation of other religious associations and practices. As was the case in joining a mystery cult, your adherence to a philosophical tradition was essentially an augmentation to your other social and religious associations. In no way did it comprise a fundamental change in how you understood your religious identity.[28]

Early Christian Religious Identity

By contrast, as we have repeatedly noted, Christians were expected to absent themselves from the worship of all of the many gods. Granted, from the various exhortations in early Christian texts to abstain from "idolatry," we may surmise that for some pagan converts it was difficult to resist the pressures from family and friends, and the attractions to continue in some of their previous religious activities, which could include enjoyable features such as feasting and drinking with family and friends. Given the ubiquitous linkage of the gods to so many social activities, it is understandable that Christian converts may have found it difficult to know how to negotiate their new commitment and their continuing social life.

There is an early indication of this in Paul's extended treatment of various matters about "food offered to idols" in 1 Corinthians 8–10, a text noted earlier. His discussion in this passage was certainly prompted by questions about what his pagan converts could and could not do in regard to such things as taking part in a dinner in a pagan temple (8:10-13), eating meat sold in the market that may have come from sacrifices to the various gods (10:23-26), and responding to an invitation from a pagan to a meal that might involve acknowledging these gods (10:27-30).[29] As noted already, that Paul felt it necessary to warn the Corinthian converts sternly against what he called "idolatry" suggests that there were some in the church there who either were uncertain about some matters of participation in the larger society, or may have been inclined to make choices that Paul regarded as unacceptable compromises.

We have additional evidence of similar issues in another text cited earlier, the statements to the seven churches in Revelation. In the oracles to the churches in Pergamum and Thyatira (2:12-29) particularly, there are stern words against what appear to be certain figures whom the author accuses of advocating that believers may "eat food sacrificed to idols and practice fornication" (2:14-16, 20-21).[30] The figures condemned in these passages in Revelation are referred to derisively as "Jezebel" and "Balaam," the names of two notorious Old Testament figures traditionally associated with idolatry. We do not know their actual names, but they apparently claimed to be Christian prophets and on that basis encouraged behavior that the author of Revelation considered unacceptable for believers.

Specifically, they may have claimed prophetic authority for teaching that it was acceptable for Christians to take part in meals that involved the recognition of pagan deities. These meals could have included those actually held in honor of pagan deities, often in rooms that formed part of a temple complex of a god. But also there were meals of trade guilds that involved gestures that honored their patron deities, as well as meals that formed part of a variety of other pagan festivals.[31] If at one time you had participated in these activities, but then renounced them, you could be in for a good deal of harassment and ostracism.[32]

The figures condemned in Revelation may have urged that believers should feel free to take part in such meals, regarding them simply as social occasions that did not really conflict with Christian faith. We do not know their rationale for this policy, but they likely had one in advocating a stance that involved greater freedom for participating in various social activities that were tinged with religious connotations.[33] Of course, the figures referred to as "Jezebel" and "Balaam" did not see themselves as heretics or engaged in deceiving the churches. They likely thought that their teaching was acceptable, even divinely authorized.

In any case, from these stern messages to these churches in Revelation we get a sense of the different views taken among early Christians about how far they could go in fulfilling their commitment to the one God while also attempting to maintain some level of wider social acceptance.[34] It cannot have been easy for them to live out conscientiously a commitment to avoid anything that smacked of "idolatry" and yet remain also a member of their own families and circles of friends, many or most of whom did not share their Christian faith.

But I repeat that the consistent line taken in the various texts that make up the New Testament and that came to be affirmed with growing force as representative of emergent "proto-orthodox" Christianity was a rather exclusive one: believers were to abstain from the worship of any of the deities of the Roman world except the one God of biblical tradition and God's Son, Jesus. To judge from the frequent complaints about the matter by pagan observers and critics noted in an earlier chapter, it does seem that at least most Christian believers did so. In the dominant sort of early Christian teaching, believers were to base their religious life entirely on their relationship with this one deity and their participation in Christian conventicles. Matching their exclusive worship practice was what we can term an exclusive religious identity. In this, I submit, we have a new kind of religious identity that is very different from what was typical of the Roman period.

Of course, I note again that early Christian exclusivism in matters of worship was not totally unique. It echoed the stance of the Jewish religious matrix in which the Jesus-movement initially emerged. But, nevertheless, I think that we can distinguish the nature of the religious identity of early Christianity from that of the ancient Jewish tradition in which the Jesus-movement emerged. The basic difference is this: "Jewishness" in religion, and so Jewish religious identity, was always connected in some way or other with the Jewish people, who were thought of in the ancient setting as a "nation" (Greek: *ethnos*). But, to repeat for emphasis, from well within the very first couple of decades, the Jesus-movement became transethnic in composition. That is, from this early point onward, early Christian religious identity was not tied to one's ethnicity and did not involve a connection to any particular ethnic group.

Granted, there were pagans who admired ancient Jewish tradition and associated themselves with synagogues, individuals such as Cornelius, the Roman centurion portrayed in Acts 10. According to the account, he "feared God," gave alms to "the [Jewish] people," and prayed to the God of the Jews (10:1-2). The author may have meant that Cornelius refrained from worshipping pagan gods, but it is difficult to see how a Roman army officer could have done so entirely. Certainly, so far as I know, there was no *requirement* for non-Jews who showed an interest in Jewish religion to abstain totally from reverencing the pagan gods. In any case, however much Jews were ready to welcome the interest of such individuals, Jews never really considered them full members of the Jewish people/nation. Gentiles who expressed some level of interest in Jewish religion were not thereby identified religiously as "Jewish." So, these admirers of Jewish religion do not constitute an exception to the point that a genuinely Jewish religious identity required membership in the Jewish people, whether by birth or by full proselyte conversion.[35]

Of course, there were Jews settled all across the empire, and beyond, and they took up life in these various settings, working to fit in however they could and seeking to contribute to the life of the various locales in which they dwelt. But, typically, they also continued to think of themselves as part of the Jewish people, with a certain distinctiveness in their various diaspora settings, especially in matters of worship.[36] Early Christians likewise reflected a sense of being part of a larger translocal association, but their association *cut across ethnic lines*, taking in people of various nations, their only connection to believers in other places and of other nations being a shared religious commitment.

Another important point—this commitment involved both beliefs and practices. It has been a mistake in some earlier scholarship to distinguish early Christianity simply as a religion of beliefs, in contrast with ancient Judaism and the larger pagan religious environment characterized equally simply as focusing on practices and rituals. Pagans did not codify their beliefs in the way that Christians came to do, but there were clearly beliefs, even if more implicit than explicit, basic to pagan religion. As I noted in the previous chapter, people presumed that the gods existed and were responsive to prayers and offerings, for example, as the premise on which to approach them for favors.[37]

Likewise, as also noted previously, along with the profession of certain beliefs, early Christians were expected to take part in certain ritual actions that marked them as such. To cite one text as illustrative, consider again Paul's concise summary of the religious stance that he advocates in Romans 10:9-13. He urges confessing "with your lips that Jesus is Lord" as well as believing "in your heart that God raised him from the dead" (v. 9). The act of "confessing" here and elsewhere is obviously an oral ritual action, perhaps one done corporately in the early Christian assemblies. So, in addition to belief, it was necessary also to "confess" or declare that belief in bodily/ritual action. Belief and ritual actions went hand in hand.

As a further illustration of this, recall also that initiation into early Christian fellowship was typically by the rite of baptism, which involved both water and the invocation of Jesus over and/or by the initiate. The place of a common meal ("Lord's supper/banquet," "thanksgiving meal"/eucharistia) as part of gatherings of early Christians is another indication that particular religious practices were as central as beliefs in defining them and expressing their religious identity.

Early Christian prayer practice is yet another instance of the combination of beliefs and ritual. We have noted that Jesus

functioned in early Christian belief and prayer practice as authoritative teacher and model of prayer, as unique intercessor for
believers, and as corecipient or recipient of prayer himself. In the
earliest evidence, Christians sometimes prayed to Jesus, and in
other cases they directed their prayers to God "in Jesus' name."
As I have shown in an earlier publication, this particular "dyadic"
shape made early Christian prayer practice distinctive in the
Roman period, thereby further contributing to a particular early
Christian religious identity.[38]

I return now to the emphasis on the translocal and transethnic
nature of early Christian identity, particularly connecting circles
of Jewish and Gentile believers. Consider first an early illustrative passage in 1 Thessalonians where Paul portrays the Gentile
Thessalonian believers as imitating Jewish believers in Roman
Judea in undergoing harassment and opposition (2:13-16). That
is, he links his pagan/Gentile converts and Judean/Jewish believers as participants in a shared religious endeavor and identity. This
transethnic link of circles of Jewish and Gentile believers is even
more tangibly shown in Paul's extended effort to enlist his Gentile churches to take part in a financial collection for the Jewish
church in Jerusalem.[39] In Romans 15:22-33, Paul reports that the
collection has been gathered successfully and that he will soon be
en route to Jerusalem to deliver it to the Jewish believers there.
Clearly, he had been able to generate a strong sense of solidarity
between at least some of his Gentile churches and the Jewish Jerusalem church.

But in Paul's view, Jewish believers, among whom he
counted himself, remained Jews, and his pagan converts likewise
retained their various ethnic identities. Granted, having turned
from "idols" to the service of "a true and living God" (1 Thessalonians 1:9), the Thessalonian believers are now distinguished
by Paul from "the Gentiles who do not know God" (4:5). But
reflecting his Jewish outlook, here and elsewhere in his letters
Paul generally uses the term "Gentiles" (Greek: *ethnē*, literally
"nations") to refer to non-Jews collectively.[40] He states that his

own personal mission was to win "the obedience of faith among all the Gentiles" (Romans 1:5). As Paul describes the converted "Gentiles" (former pagans) in Thessalonica and elsewhere in his missionizing, they have now become "sons of light and of the day" (1 Thessalonians 5:5). As such, they have a new behavioral pattern and the assurance of their salvation from the divine wrath that will fall upon those who continue in the works of darkness (1 Thessalonians 5:6-11). That is, he portrays his pagan converts as having acquired a radically new religious identity.

But I repeat that they have not become Jews. Their baptism did not make them members of the Jewish people/nation. They remained Gentiles. In the case of the Thessalonian converts, they remain Greeks. But, in their religious life, they have become a different kind of Gentiles. They have now become obedient to the true God, the biblical/Jewish God and his Son, to whom now they are to give exclusive religious devotion and from whom they are now to derive exclusively their new religious identity. To repeat a point made in chapter 2, this was new territory and an unprecedented status for his pagan converts.[41] To put it in more prosaic terms, early Christians took up a new kind of religious identity that, uniquely, was both exclusive and not related to their ethnicity.

The specifically transethnic dimensions of the early Christian movement, and the particular religious identity associated with participation in it, are further illustrated in various texts, ranging from Paul's letters onward. In Galatians 3:28, Paul famously declares that by their baptism "into Christ," their ethnic, social, and gender distinctions ("Jew or Greek," "slave or free," "male or female") are to be regarded as relativized radically, all believers of whatever ethnic, sexual, or social class now "one in Christ Jesus." But I repeat my observation from chapter 2: Paul did not treat these distinctions as actually effaced. So, for example, he insisted that married men and women continue to have conjugal obligations to each other (1 Corinthians 7:1-7), and he persisted in referring to himself proudly as a member of his ancestral people, a "Hebrew" and an "Israelite," as well as being a "servant of Christ" (e.g., 2 Corinthians 11:22-23). But he also insisted that "in Christ"—that is, in the fellowship of Christian faith—these distinctions were no longer to be regarded as defining believers in the ways that they had functioned before. In particular, these distinctions were no longer to function as ways of justifying discrimination in the treatment of one another. Instead, their new identity conferred through their participation in the *ekklesia* ("in Christ") was to shape both how they saw themselves and how they saw fellow believers. In other passages in the New Testament, we find a similar sentiment (e.g., 1 Corinthians 12:13; Colossians 3:11).

Labels

Let us consider now some terms used among early believers to refer to themselves. By the second century AD, "Christian(s)" had become probably the one most widely used, both by insiders and by outsiders.[42] According to Acts (11:26), the term was first used to refer to members of the young Jesus-movement in Antioch (Syria), and it appears to have been applied to believers initially by outsiders. The ending of the plural form of the Greek word (*christianoi*; singular form: *christianos*) resembles the ending on the names of groups identified and aligned with this or that figure, often politically aligned groups. Note, for example, the *Herodianoi* ("Herodians") mentioned in Mark 12:13, who were likely partisans/supporters of the Herodian royal house. "Christian" appears in the New Testament only two other times after the initial instance in Acts 11:26. In Acts 26:28, "King Agrippa" responds (mockingly?) to Paul's enthusiastic advocacy of the gospel, exclaiming, "Are you so quickly persuading me to become a Christian?" In 1 Peter 4:16, the author comforts readers over the possibility of suffering "as a Christian," as distinguished from suffering for criminal behavior.

It is now commonly accepted that *christianos* and *christianoi* show the influence of Latin upon Koine Greek, the endings *-ianos/-ianoi* reflecting the Latin noun endings *-ianus/-iani*, as in the words *Brutianus*, *Augustianus*, and *Caesarianus*, and other such epithets known from the Roman period. It is also commonly accepted that such terms identify a person as belonging to the figure and/or group designated, connoting variously dependence on (with reference to slaves or those retained in service to someone), allegiance to, or political or military support of a named figure.[43] So, *christianoi* or the Latin equivalent term, *christiani*, designated people linked with "Christ" (Greek: *Christos*; Latin: *Christus*), obviously reflecting the prominence of the use of this term for Jesus in early Christian proclamation and faith.

The early Christian use of the term *Christos* originally asserted the claim that Jesus is "Messiah," the promised savior figure sent from God.[44] *Christos* used in this way was a direct translation of the Hebrew word *Maschiach* (literally "anointed one"). But this was a distinctively Jewish, and then Christian, use of the term *Christos*. In ordinary Greek usage, the word was simply an adjective meaning something like "rubbed/oiled," as with a salve. So, as that would have made little sense to them, it appears that pagans who heard early believers proclaiming Jesus as *Christos* may have taken it as some new name. Consequently, referring to believers as "Christians" may simply have designated them as people who made a figure called "Christ" such a prominent feature of their talk and their behavior. That is, it essentially designated them as partisans of this "Christ."

As with some other examples in the history of religion, thus, "Christian" seems to have begun as a term used by outsiders, probably with a certain derisive connotation, and then at some point thereafter was adopted among believers as a self-designation.[45] Illustrative of this, in comparison with the few uses of the term "Christian" in the largely first-century texts that make up the New Testament, instances subsequently multiply, both in Christian and in non-Christian texts.[46] But scholars have made various proposals about the specific time and circumstance in which followers of Jesus were first called "Christians." Because the term reflects Latin linguistic influence, some have proposed that it originated from Roman authorities involved in the judicial proceedings in which adherents of the Jesus-movement came to their attention.[47] But I am not so sure that this follows.

That is, I do not think that the term had to originate in Latin. It is also possible that it was minted by Greek speakers familiar with the Latin practice of using the word endings -ianus/-iani in labels for people linked with named figures. The term "Herodians" (Greek: *Herōdianoi*) noted already shows a similar Latin linguistic influence, and it may be another example of such a term that likely originated in a Greek-speaking milieu.[48] In any case, whatever may be the specific place and circumstances of their initial usage, the terms "Christian" and "Christians" were likely coined by outsiders and apparently were in use to designate followers of Jesus by, or perhaps well before, Nero's brutal action against Roman Christians in 64 AD.[49]

More to the point of this book, the term was distinctively applied to those who were perceived as adherents of the Jesus-movement, and it served to distinguish them from others, whether other Jews or the larger populace. I repeat the point for emphasis: similar to the other terms with similar endings designating adherents or supporters of this or that figure, *Christianoi* designated "Christ-partisans," those, that is, who were identified specifically with reference to "Christ." Indeed, if, as seems likely, the term originally expressed a certain hostility against Christians, it specifies the focus of that hostility as their allegiance to Christ.[50] By the time of the composition of the New Testament writing of 1 Peter (70–120 AD?), however, "Christian" had been taken on by at least some believers as a self-designation. So, for example, in the early second century, Ignatius of Antioch, on his way to a Roman execution, aspires through his death to prove to be genuinely a Christian (Ignatius, *To the Romans* 3.2).

But there are a number of other labels or names as well by which believers refer to themselves in early Christian texts. Indeed, the variety of collective self-designations seems to have been greater in earlier texts than in later ones. In addition to "Christian/Christians," these self-designations include "brothers," "believers," "saints/holy ones," "the assembly" (*ekklēsia*), "disciples," and "the way."[51] Such an accumulation of self-designation terminology is reflective of what in linguistics terminology is called a "social dialect" or a "shared language repertoire" that emerged in earliest circles of the Jesus-movement.[52] Indeed, the multiplicity of such terms probably indicates a vibrant and vigorous sense of a distinctive group identity. Some of these terms were maintained later in regular usage as self-designations, such as "Christian," "believers," and "assembly," and some others fell into disuse, such as "the way" and "saints."[53] But all of these terms exhibit the sense of distinctive group identity that characterized early Christian circles.

Among these terms, *ekklēsia* is particularly noteworthy.[54] Usually translated now in English as "church" and by equivalents in other languages, it remains the most familiar designation for a circle of Christians, from congregational to denominational levels. But the Greek term has an interesting prior usage that prompts questions about what it connoted initially among early Christians. In ordinary Greek usage of that time, the term designated an assembly, especially the formal gathering of the people of a city, comprising typically the free men who were entitled to vote. We see this usage reflected in the account of the Ephesian riot in Acts 19:21-41, which erupts when a certain Demetrius and fellow silversmiths become enraged over Paul's preaching "that gods made with hands are not gods" (v. 26). An angry crowd drags some of Paul's companions into the city theater and threatens mayhem. After some further disturbance, the "town clerk" is depicted as urging the angry crowd that any charges must be brought to the courts and that any further inquiry about matters must be settled "in the regular/lawful assembly" (Greek: *ennomos ekklēsia*).[55]

Some scholars have argued, therefore, that the term *ekklēsia* had a particular and intentional resonance with the use of the term to designate civic assemblies. More specifically, they contend that Paul in particular favored the term to describe the circles of believers as a way of designating their gatherings, at least implicitly, as alternatives to the civic and provincial assemblies.[56] Certainly, the term *ekklēsia* could well have carried this resonance, the Christian "assembly" thus having a similar official character, God's assembly. But it would probably be unwise to confine the early connotations of the term to this one alone.

For we should note that the term is also used in the Greek translation of the Old Testament, often referred to as the Septuagint, in which *ekklēsia* often renders the Hebrew word, *qahal*, in references to the people of Israel as "the assembly of the Lord."[57] In other cases, there are references simply to "the assembly/congregation" where it seems that the word designates followers of God, perhaps gathered liturgically in the Jerusalem temple.[58] In a key text from Qumran, the site of the "Dead Sea scrolls," the Hebrew term *qahal* is used to designate the chosen people of God of the last days.[59] In this instance, the full expression is "the assembly/congregation of God" (Hebrew: *qahal ēl*), which is the exact equivalent of a Greek expression frequently used in the New Testament, "the assembly/church of God" (Greek: *ekklēsia tou theou*).[60]

So, given this interesting varied background of the term *ekklēsia*, and given the frequent use of formal-sounding expressions such as "assembly of God" (or "God's assembly") in the New Testament, it is likely that the early Christian usage of the term typically connoted a special religious significance ascribed to the groups designated by it. In early Christian usage, their "assembly" was not simply a casual social gathering of people, or some sort of club. Instead, by their use of this term, early Christians were claiming a high meaning to their gatherings and their fellowship. Especially in the use of the full expression "the assembly/ assemblies of God," we see this, reflecting their claim that circles

of believers have a special, even unique, religious status and significance. The definite article typically used in these instances
connotes their claim that they comprise God's special people.

The additional point to note is that this *ekklēsia* terminology appears already in our earliest Christian texts, which take
us back to the middle decades of the first century AD, and likely
reflect a still earlier usage in the discourse of the Jesus-movement.
Note, again, for example, that Paul repeatedly refers to his earlier
opposition to the Jesus-movement as directed against "the church
[*ekklēsia*] of God" (Galatians 1:13; 1 Corinthians 15:9) and "the
church" (Philippians 3:6). And in one text, Paul even appears to
divvy up society into three groups: "Jews," "Greeks," and "the
church of God" (1 Corinthians 10:32). In all these instances,
Paul's use of the definite article is also significant, reflecting a special significance of believers as *the* assembly connected with God.
Clearly, from an amazingly early time, the young movement both
focused on Jesus and had a sense of a distinctive group identity.

One type of self-designation is terminology that linked early
believers directly and unambiguously with the biblical and historic significance of the people of Israel. Consider, for example,
instances of this in the Epistle to the Ephesians. This writing is
now widely regarded by scholars as written by someone in Paul's
name posthumously. So, it was composed somewhat later than
Paul's undisputed letters, perhaps sometime roughly 70–90 AD.[61]

Early in the text, the author posits that believers have been
chosen and destined by God for "adoption through Jesus Christ"
(1:4-5). Even though they were "formerly Gentiles in the flesh"
(or "by birth" [2:11]), and so had no inherited standing with
God, their distance from the one true God has now been overcome through Christ (2:11-13). Formerly strangers and foreigners
to God, they are now fully enfranchised among "the saints" and
"the household of God" (2:19). The text also says that, although
Jews and Gentiles were formerly separated by the Jewish law,
this separation has been broken down, and in place of this divi-
sive duality there is now "one new man/humanity" established

in Christ (2:14-15). In these passages we see the notion that the circle of believers incorporates Jews and Gentiles into a new and full unity that is established by Christ, reflective of a group identity that transcends the former ethnic distinctions between them. But their respective ethnic identities are not actually abolished. Instead, what the text depicts is effectively a radical widening of the circumference of God's people, Gentile believers now jointly inheriting with Jewish believers a status as God's favored children.

In 1 Peter, from about the same time and also written posthumously, we see something similar. The author addressees his readers as "exiles of the Dispersion" (1:1), a phrase that could otherwise suggest that they are Jewish. But it becomes clear in the letter that in fact they are, at least largely, non-Jewish ("Gentile") believers (e.g., 1:18-21; 4:3-6). Nevertheless, despite their ethnic origins, the author refers to them as now members of "a chosen race [genos], a royal priesthood, a holy nation [ethnos], God's own people [laos]" (2:9). These terms obviously all derive from biblical/Jewish tradition in which they refer to the Jewish people/nation.[62] So we have here a noteworthy appropriation of these honorific terms to express the group identity of Christians, and recall as well that the letter also gives us one of the few instances of the term "Christian" for believers in 4:16.

We see an earlier expression of something similar in Paul's fiery, and sometimes hard-to-follow, letter to the Galatian churches. From Paul's standpoint, the Galatian churches have been troubled, probably by other Jewish Christians, who likely urged the Galatians to complete their conversion by effectively becoming Jewish proselytes.[63] That is, these figures apparently urged Paul's converts to complement and complete their faith in Christ and their baptism with a commitment to full observance of Jewish law ("Torah"); and for males that included circumcision. This is not the occasion to go further into the details of the situation that prompted Paul's sometimes intemperate letter in which he sought to prevent the Galatians from being "bewitched," to use his term (Galatians 3:1), by these people. The only point I

make here is that one of the lines of argument that Paul lays down
is that in/through Christ even former pagans are now incorporated as descendants ("seed") of Abraham, the great forebear of
the Jewish people (Galatians 3:29), and so are now heirs of the
promise made to Abraham that all the nations would be blessed
through him (Galatians 3:6-14). In short, Paul argued that pagan
converts to Christ did not need to convert also to Judaism and
become Jews. Through their faith in Christ, they were made
additional, and fully valid, children of Abraham, while remaining
non-Jews, "Gentiles."

This readily introduces the tensions that developed between
early circles of Jesus-followers and more traditional Jewish claims
to be God's special people. Certainly, the early group identity
of the Jesus-movement and subsequent "Christianity" often
involved competing claims with larger Jewish tradition of the
time.[64] As early Christianity became more and more comprised
of non-Jews, that and other circumstances led sometimes to sharp
and bitter attitudes on both sides of the controversy. For the present purpose, I simply draw attention to the use of this language
of "people," "nation," and "race," as part of the self-descriptive
vocabulary in early Christian texts.[65]

Use of these terms undeniably reflected and contributed to
tensions, especially with the Jewish tradition of the time, and in
some cases the tensions were expressed in language and actions,
by both sides of the argument, that are regrettable. But we should
remember that the period when this kind of language was first
used by adherents of the Jesus-movement was a time when they
were very much the more vulnerable ones. So, they acted all the
more vigorously to assert the validity of their faith and to secure
for themselves what we might call a cultural space and religious
legitimacy in which they could live out that faith. Unquestionably
also, however, just as many pagans of the time saw early Christianity as offensive, even dangerous to social life as then understood, and as outrageous in its rhetoric and claims, at least some

Jews agreed. The assertion of early Christian religious identity and particularity was by no means a quiet or sedate affair!

Summary

Although much more could be discussed, I hope that the preceding pages suffice to show that early Christianity expressed and represented a distinctive religious identity in the Roman world. Of course, this identity involved claims about the unique significance of Jesus in particular, a matter that I have not directly engaged here at any length.[66] This central place of Jesus/Christ is obviously reflected in the term "Christian." Whether in its likely original usage by outsiders or in its subsequent appropriation by insiders, the term shows that "Christ" was the chief identity marker of the new movement.[67]

The Roman world of the first three centuries was one in which there emerged various competing religious movements that came to define themselves much more intentionally than ever before. Among these was early Christianity, and also Judaism as it came to be known subsequently. Later, especially under Julian the Apostate in the late fourth century, there was the hesitant and not very successful beginning of a new and more monolithic notion of a "paganism" defined very much in contrast to, and influenced by, Christianity. The first three centuries comprised a time of considerable religious ferment. Christians appear to have been active in this, even the initiators in some matters, forcing others to react.[68] Consider again Pliny's actions against Christians in Pontus and Bithynia, for example. It appears likely that the reported success of Christianity in that area provoked among local pagans also a greater sense of their religious identity.[69]

So, this means that in the period that we focus on in this book, we see two interrelated developments: the formation and expression of a distinctive Christian identity, and also the effects of this upon other religious options of the time. It has been common, and justifiable, for scholars to look for influences of the larger

Roman-era environment upon Christianity, but in some matters we should probably also look for influences of early Christianity upon its environment.

Note that pre-Constantinian Christianity took a stance in which political loyalty was disconnected from religious identity and practice. Christians refused to honor the gods on which Roman rulers claimed to base their political authority; but Christians affirmed, nevertheless, a readiness to respect pagan rulers, pay taxes, and in other ways be good citizens. This stance is reflected as early as Paul's letter to Roman believers (Romans 13:1-7) and was then echoed in various Christian texts subsequently (such as 1 Timothy 2:1-3; 1 Peter 2:13-17).[70] Indeed, as this stance was developed by Tertullian in his address to Scapula (the proconsul of Africa, 211–213 AD), we have what may be the first reasoned defense of religious liberty in the ancient world.[71] I cite the key passage in Tertullian's address:

> It is a fundamental human right, a privilege of nature, that everyone should worship according to one's own convictions. . . . It is assuredly no part of religion to compel religion. . . . A Christian is enemy to none, least of all to the Emperor of Rome, who he knows to be appointed by God, and so cannot but love and honor; and whose well-being moreover the Christian must desire, with that of the empire over which he reigns.[72]

Of course, Tertullian's primary aim was to secure religious liberty for fellow Christians. But the principle he enunciated was, for many, a revolutionary one in its time: people, of whatever nation, did not have to subscribe to the religious claims of a ruler, or worship the gods on which the ruler based his claim, in order to accept the ruler.[73] Instead, people such as Christians could have their own reasons, and their own religious basis, for being good citizens.

Moreover, as I have emphasized, early Christian religious identity was distinctive in replacing all others for its devotees.

It was an exclusive religious identity, defined entirely by their standing in relation to the one God, and was not dependent on, or even connected to, their ethnicity. In fact, I contend that this distinctive early Christian group identity is perhaps the earliest attempt to articulate what moderns would recognize as a corporate *religious* identity that is distinguishable from, and not a corollary of, one's family, civic, or ethnic connection.

4

A "Bookish" Religion

Most people today probably presume that sacred books, "scriptures," are central for any religion. That is not actually the case if we look at the longer and wider scope of religions through the ages. It is another notion that we have inherited, and largely from Christianity.

In the context of the Roman-era religious setting, early Christianity was unusual as a "bookish" religion.[1] I do not mean to emphasize the place of texts in early Christianity at the expense of other features, such as worship practices, beliefs, behavioral standards, or social formation. Nor do I ignore the value and effect of the spoken word in the Roman era and so among early Christians also. By calling early Christianity "bookish," I simply assert that reading, writing, copying, and dissemination of texts had a major place—indeed, a prominence—in early Christianity that, except for ancient Jewish circles, was unusual for religious groups of the Roman era.[2] This is not a new observation on my part. Other scholars also have referred to early Christian circles as "constitutionally oriented to texts" and as "textual communities" and have described the early Christian movement collectively as one with "texts at its very heart and soul."[3]

Reading

The subsequent place of books, especially scriptures, in Christian tradition down the centuries is well known, and the biblical texts continue to have a special place in personal piety, in Christian theological reasoning, and in traditional liturgy to the present day. Indeed, the reading of scriptural texts has been a regular component of corporate worship among many/most Christian circles since at least the second century, as seems reflected in a reference to the regular reading of "the memoirs of the apostles or the writings of the prophets" in Christian worship gatherings by the second-century Roman-based Christian teacher and writer Justin Martyr (*First Apology* 67.3). Justin's term "memoirs" (Greek: *apomnēmoneumata*) obviously designates here Christian texts, Gospels in particular, and his term "prophets" here surely designates writings from what Christians came to call the Old Testament.[4] So, at least in the practice of the second-century Roman churches that Justin knew, these texts, Gospels, and Old Testament writings were read as scriptures and as a component feature of the worship gathering.

Probably from still earlier, there is the explicit exhortation in 1 Timothy 4:13 to "give attention to the public reading of scripture" as important among the responsibilities to be fulfilled by the "Timothy" addressed in this text. In another text that purports to be addressed to the same figure, the author commends "all scriptures" as "inspired by God and useful for teaching, reproof, correction, and training in righteousness" (2 Timothy 3:16), which likewise must reflect the place of these texts in early Christian circles. Though both are ascribed to Paul, 1 Timothy and 2 Timothy are widely thought to have been written in his name posthumously, and so the "Timothy" addressed, the name of a member of the apostle Paul's circle of coworkers, is taken as a literary device to give the writings a note of realism.[5] Accordingly, these texts are typically dated after the apostle Paul's execution about 64 AD, and so roughly 70–120 AD. But, whatever their authorship, we can certainly take these writings as reflecting attitudes toward, and uses of, scriptural texts in at least some Christian circles of that time. Unfortunately, the author does not tell us what writings he meant by "all scriptures," but the term likely designates Old Testament writings. As reflected in Justin's statements cited earlier, and as we will confirm shortly, however, other writings composed by early Christians soon came to be treated as scriptures too.

To be sure, earliest references to Christian corporate worship reflect a variety of contributions, including "charismatic" phenomena such as prophecy, tongue speaking, and "revelation" (e.g., 1 Corinthians 14:26-31). But no first-century or second-century Christian text claims to give a complete description of any worship gathering, so we should be cautious in our inferences, neither ascribing nor denying too much.[6] Granted, the earliest explicit references to scripture reading in Christian assemblies are in the texts already noted, which are commonly dated to the late first or early second century AD (such as 1 Timothy) or later (such as Justin). But various factors may account for that, and I suspect that the practice goes back earlier still.

We should note the many citations of, and allusions to, "scripture/s" in our earliest Christian writings, including those writings whose original readers were, at least mainly, former pagans ("Gentiles," non-Jews).[7] I think that this requires us to posit adequate opportunities for those pagan converts to acquire a familiarity with these scripture texts. Otherwise, these many references and allusions would be completely lost on them. Furthermore, the fundamental early Christian claim that scriptural hopes and promises are now being fulfilled through Jesus and the gospel message seems to give us another reason to think that an intense interest in, and acquaintance with, scripture texts was urged and sought, and so also opportunities to read and discuss these texts. I contend, therefore, that it is perfectly plausible that reading and discussing scripture texts ("Old Testament" writings) would have been a frequent activity, both in private and in corporate settings, in Christian circles from the earliest moments. Although the "scripturalization" of Christian worship certainly became more formalized and regularized across time, both the importance and the impact of corporate reading of scripture writings are evident from the outset of the Jesus-movement.

Of course, reading texts in corporate worship required that copies of them were available in any given circle of early Christians, and we should certainly not assume that many early Christian circles had copies of all, or even many, of the writings that came to form part of the Christian Bible. Nevertheless, we should also not underestimate the impressive efforts put into the copying and dissemination of writings in early Christianity. Equally obviously, this widespread use of texts also required individuals who were able to read them out for the benefit of the likely many early Christians who were unable to read.[8] In noting that many/most early Christians could not read and write fluently, or at all, we simply recognize a feature of the ancient Roman setting more generally, a time in which likely the majority of people were functionally illiterate.[9] But although it is likely that only a minority of Roman-era people, perhaps a small minority, could read well enough to handle texts such as those in the Old Testament or those that came to form the New Testament, all that was needed in any given circle of believers was one person able to serve as reader for the others.

One type of evidence, often overlooked, that certain texts were read out in Christian worship gatherings is comprised by the various features of some early Christian manuscripts, features that seem intended to facilitate reading them. These features, which are not typical of Roman-era copies of literary texts, include elementary punctuation, enlarged spaces to signal sense units such as sentences and paragraphs, slightly enlarged initial letters of each line, and other devices as well, such as generous-sized lettering and generous spacing between lines of text. These are found especially often in copies of biblical (Old Testament) texts and those texts that came to form part of the New Testament, and the object of these visual features was likely to assist people in the public reading of these manuscripts.[10]

Indeed, the ancient practice of reading and discussing scripture texts became so much a regular part of early Christian corporate worship that it led in due course to the creation of manuscripts specifically prepared for liturgical usage, with readings arranged in the order of their intended usage, comprising an apparently new literary genre called the "lectionary."[11] Various conventions developed for the regularized reading of scriptures in churches across the early centuries. But, notwithstanding the differences in these schemes, they all indicate that a shared practice of scripture reading as part of Christian corporate worship was, or quickly became, widespread.[12]

Christian and Synagogue Practices

As true of some other early Christian practices, the place of scripture reading in early Christian worship likely derives from and reflects the Jewish matrix in which the earliest Jesus-movement commenced. From at least the first century AD, and likely earlier, the scriptures of Israel, especially the "Torah," the books ascribed to Moses, were read in Jewish synagogues.[13] Among the earliest evidence of this are references to the practice in several New Testament texts that date from the late first century. In Luke 4:16-21, for example, Jesus is portrayed reading from the book of Isaiah in a synagogue. Acts 13:14-15 refers specifically to synagogue readings that include "the law and the prophets," referring to Old Testament writings broadly. Acts 15:21 likewise refers to the regular reading of "Moses," referring specifically to the first five books of the Old Testament traditionally ascribed to him, in synagogues. Note that these early Christian texts posit scenes set in synagogues both in Roman Judaea (Palestine) and in the Jewish Diaspora. Moreover, these New Testament references are consistent with statements by knowledgeable contemporary Jewish writers. Josephus, the Jewish historian from Judaea who wrote in the late first century AD, stated that Jews assembled weekly "to listen to the Law and to obtain a thorough and accurate knowledge of it" (*Against Apion* 2.175), and likewise Philo of Alexandria, a learned Diaspora Jew active in the early first century AD, referred to a similar practice (*On Dreams* 2.127). We also have archaeological evidence in the first-century AD Theodotus inscription that marked the construction of a synagogue in Jerusalem for Greek-speaking Jews from the Diaspora. This inscription includes the "reading of the Law and the teaching of the commandments" among the purposes for which the synagogue was built.[14]

So, the practice of reading sacred texts as a regular part of communal worship was shared by synagogues and the early churches, and in this they were distinctive in the Roman world of religious practice. To be sure, some other Roman-era religious groups as well had sacred writings, but these were reserved for consultation by their priests and were not read as part of the group-worship gathering.[15] We have some other hints that in a few Roman-era cults sacred books may have functioned in one way or another to promote cult beliefs, but there is nothing like the regular place that the scriptures held in the corporate life of Jewish synagogues and in early churches.[16]

Indeed, the regular and prominent place of the reading of certain texts in synagogues and early Christian circles resembles more the ethos of Roman-era philosophical groups than the typical practice of "religion" of the time.[17] The specific textual practices of the various schools of philosophy varied, but they were all "consumers of texts," and, in their gatherings, texts were "part of the everyday business of teaching and learning."[18] Despite the variations in specifics, philosophical groups typically read and studied, collected, distributed, and commented on certain texts that they deemed central to their group identity. Moreover, Roman-era philosophical groups were often concerned with questions about right behavior, including how to think of the gods, and so issues of philosophy and religion, to use our terms, were not mutually exclusive areas of concern in these groups. But even if we grant the similarities with philosophical schools, especially in the role of texts, the ancient synagogues and early Christian gatherings were, nevertheless, "religious" groups. Their discourse and corporate gatherings reflect a primary concern to orient themselves toward their deity, and the behavioral practices that they affirmed were held to be requisite responses to that deity's demands. Their concentration was on their relationship with their deity in worship and behavior, whereas we may broadly take ancient philosophy as primarily concerned with how to live the good life based on the use of reason.

Initially, the "scriptures" read in first-century Christian gatherings were what we typically think of as "Old Testament" texts—that is, the scriptures of the ancient Jewish tradition in which the young Christian movement first emerged.[19] But, as already noted, from an early point there were additional texts read in these settings, newly composed texts that emerged in, and were products of, the early Christian movement. Of course, the inclusion of these Christian writings among those read in corporate worship thereby also distinguished the textual practice of early churches from synagogue scripture-reading practice.

The initial step in this expansion of the texts read in early Christian worship was likely in the corporate reading of Paul's letters (written roughly 50–60 AD). These texts were written to various churches and were clearly intended to be read out in the Christian circles to which they were sent *in the context of their worship gatherings.* Some of these writings, such as Paul's letters to the Corinthian church (1 Corinthians and 2 Corinthians), were addressed to one group of believers in one locale. The same is true for his letters to the Thessalonian church and the Philippian church. His letter to the Romans, however, "to all those in Rome beloved by God" (Romans 1:7), seems to have addressed several church circles in Rome, small groups that were apparently based in the houses of various better-off believers who had space adequate to accommodate such a gathering.[20]

Furthermore, from an early point we have references to Paul's letters being shared among two or more churches translocally, as is reflected in the directions given in Colossians 4:16 to have this epistle read also "in the church of the Laodiceans." Scholars differ over whether the Epistle to the Colossians was written by Paul or by someone in his name after his death, but this is not crucial for my purpose here. Whoever the author, and whatever the precise date of its composition, this statement in Colossians obviously both reflects and promotes the circulation and exchange of Paul's letters among early churches in different cities.

Note also Paul's undisputed letter to "the *churches* of Galatia," the plural "churches" indicating likewise multiple groups, probably in different cities of Galatia, whom he addressed collectively.[21] Paul either sent this letter in multiple copies or perhaps to one church initially, and then the letter made its way around to the other churches, read and perhaps copied as it went from one church to another.[22] So, either immediately or very early, at least some of Paul's letters acquired a translocal usage and recognition.

There are other examples of early Christian texts intended to be read translocally. The book of Revelation addresses churches in seven cities of the Roman province of Asia Minor (2:1–3:21), and so it too was either copied for each church or sent along to each in succession.[23] The Epistle of James is addressed "to the twelve tribes of the Dispersion" (1:1), borrowing the term "dispersion" used by ancient Jews to reflect their dispersal in various lands, and 1 Peter is similarly addressed to "the exiles of the Dispersion in Pontus, Galatia, Cappadocia, Asia, and Bithynia." The question of whether these latter two writings are pseudonymous letters makes it difficult to judge securely whether they were actually sent to these destinations. But, even if they were not, these texts join the others in presupposing and reflecting a vigorous circulation of writings among early Christian groups, a subject that I take up again later in this chapter.

To return to Paul's letters, from this practice of reading them in gathered worship and circulating them translocally, it is likely that they then acquired early on a status as "scripture," at least in some Christian circles, probably before any of the other writings that came to form the New Testament. The authoritative tone of Paul's letters may also have contributed to them acquiring this status. Note, for example, Paul's strong statement in 1 Corinthians 14:37-38 that anyone who refuses to recognize the authoritative nature of his letter is "not to be recognized"![24]

Indeed, even within his lifetime, Paul's letters were intended and functioned as written surrogates for his personal presence.[25] That is, in situations when he could not himself visit a given church, he typically sent one of the companions who travelled with him (such as Timothy or Titus) as his representative and/or wrote a letter in which he dealt with the issues that he wanted to take up with the church. This is rather clearly indicated in 1 Thessalonians 2:17–3:13. After having tried repeatedly and unsuccessfully to visit in person the church that he had founded in Thessalonica (2:17-20), Paul then sent Timothy (3:1-5) to see how the Thessalonian believers were getting along. Upon Timothy's return with an encouraging report about the Thessalonian church, Paul then sent the letter that we know as 1 Thessalonians, affirming his affection and concern and also addressing certain issues of behavior (sexual matters in 4:1-12, and other admonitions in 5:12-22) and questions about the fate of the Christian dead and the future coming of Christ (4:13–5:11). Indicative of Paul's intention that the letter should be treated as an authoritative text, note his command in 5:27 "that this letter be read to all the brothers."[26] That is, the letter should be read in the corporate gathering of the Thessalonian church.

In the case of Paul's correspondence with the Corinthians, it appears that Paul wrote at least one of his several letters to that church because *he did not want to make an in-person visit* at that point. Indeed, he says that he wanted to avoid what he called "another painful visit" (2 Corinthians 2:1), referring to a previous visit and what seems to have been a trying experience for all concerned. This was a rather clear instance in which Paul wrote a letter to function as his voice and presence.

Our earliest clear confirmation that Paul's letters were being treated as authoritative texts—indeed, our earliest explicit reference to any Christian texts referred to as "scriptures"—is in 2 Peter 3:15-16. Note that this passage alludes to a *collection* of Pauline epistles, in the phrase "all his letters," and also counts them among "the other scriptures." That is, the author of 2 Peter includes Paul's letters as having the status of scriptures along with "Old Testament" writings. Further, the formation of a *collection* of Paul's letters that is presupposed in 2 Peter is also interesting and surely itself reflects a high regard for them.[27] Indeed, this Pauline letter collection may have been the earliest step toward the larger collection that we know as the New Testament. We do not know how many letters or what specific letters were included in the collection alluded to in 2 Peter, but I repeat that it is noteworthy that the author refers to a collection of Paul's letters.

Still further, it is striking that both the author of 2 Peter and those whom he regards as "ignorant and unstable" (v. 16) seem to share a high regard for Paul's letters. That is, the author and those other Christians whom he denigrates here disagreed over how to interpret Paul's letters, but they apparently agreed that they are authoritative texts whose interpretation matters. Clearly, the scriptural status of Paul's letters was rather widely affirmed across various Christian groups already by the date of 2 Peter (ca. 70–140 AD?), even among Christians who strongly disagreed with one another over other matters of faith.[28]

A bit earlier in this discussion, I referred briefly to Justin Martyr's description of early Christian worship as including the reading of "the memoirs of the apostles or the writings of the prophets" (*First Apology* 67.3), noting there that the latter expression must refer to texts accepted both by Jews and by Christians as scripture, "Old Testament" writings. I return here to Justin's reference to "memoirs of the apostles," which is commonly taken as referring to the Gospels, as is confirmed by Justin's explicit identification of these apostolic "memoirs" as "Gospels" just a bit earlier (66.3). In his explanation and defense of Christianity, Justin's distinctive and repeated references to the Gospels as "memoirs" (Greek: *apomnēmoneumata*) seem meant to emphasize to his intended readers their significance as authoritative remembrances of Jesus' teaching and acts. The term likely stems from its use by the Greek writer Xenophon (fifth century BC) as the title of his collection of material about Socrates, *Socratic Memoirs* (*Apomnēmoneumata*). So by using this term, Justin also sought to refer to the Gospels in a way that was meaningful in the larger literary/intellectual environment of his day.[29]

But my main point here is that, at least in the church practice that Justin knew and approved in mid-second-century Rome, Gospels were being read in corporate worship and so were being treated as scripture along with "Old Testament" writings. And note that Justin refers to "memoirs" of "apostles" and "Gospels" in the plural. We cannot know for sure how many he included, although studies of the citations in his writings show that Justin knew at least Matthew and Luke, and probably Mark and John.[30] Justin's specific reference to Gospels (plural) written both by "the apostles and by those who followed them" (*Dialogue with Trypho* 103:8) is particularly intriguing. It suggests at least two Gospels ascribed to apostles, and, of course, "Matthew" and "John" would serve nicely. Likewise, Justin's statement suggests at least two Gospels by nonapostolic figures, and here "Mark" and "Luke," who are referred to in early tradition as associates respectively of Peter and Paul, come readily to mind.[31] If these inferences are correct, and they are basically in agreement with studies of citations and allusions in Justin's writings, then we can say that by the mid-second century Justin knew and used the familiar four Gospels as well as other writings that became part of the New Testament.[32]

With particular reference to Gospels, it is noteworthy that Justin reflects a different church practice than that of his Christian contemporary in Rome, Marcion, who found the differences among the multiple Gospels troubling and contended that there could be only one true Gospel account, which, for him, was a version of the Gospel of Luke.[33] For Justin and the churches that he reflects, however, the variations among the Gospels were apparently not as troubling, for it was the *content* of these texts and their value as authentic and multiple remembrances of Jesus that was important to them.[34]

So, to repeat the point for emphasis, by approximately the mid-second century, and quite possibly earlier, letters of Paul and multiple Gospels as well were being read as scripture in many churches along with the "Old Testament" writings that were also accepted as scripture in the synagogue.[35] The composition and circulation of the Christian texts in particular, and the regular practice of reading from them as components of corporate worship (that is, treating them as scriptures), formed the initial developments that led eventually to the familiar New Testament canon.

To underscore an earlier observation, this *corporate* reading of texts in early churches, and in synagogues, also makes less crucial the widely agreed view that in the Roman era only a minority, perhaps a small minority, of people were sufficiently literate to be able to read such extended literary texts.[36] All that was needed was one person in a given church or synagogue able to read out a text, all the others present thereby enabled to have knowledge of the text and be affected by it. That is, whether they were able to read for themselves or not, Christians were able to obtain an acquaintance with the texts read out in their corporate worship gatherings.[37] Romantic notions of a pervasive early Christian "orality" that left little room or need for texts all rest on a body of ill-informed assumptions.[38] The undeniably strong appreciation of the well-spoken word in the Roman era went fully hand-in-hand with an equally strong appreciation for texts of various kinds, both in early Christianity and in the larger culture of that time. To be sure, the Christian texts in view here were intended to be *read out/aloud* to a gathered Christian group, the text "performed" orally—that is, read aloud competently to promote the understanding of them. But the point to emphasize here is that what were thus "performed" were *written texts* read from manuscript copies.

Along with the important practice of the corporate/public reading of texts in early Christian circles, we should also note indications of the private/individual reading of texts by Christians. Indeed, some texts were written expressly to individuals, especially, of course, private letters, but also even some literary texts, such as theological treatises, and likely some "apocryphal" writings.[39] Furthermore, we also have certain copies of biblical texts—including what became New Testament texts—that pretty clearly were made for personal reading and study.

We can tell this by the physical form of the particular copies in question. P.Oxyrhynchus 1228 (cited in lists of New Testament manuscripts as $\mathfrak{P}^{22}$), for example, is a portion of a copy of the Gospel of John preserved on the remains of a reused papyrus roll. The reused roll and the character of the "hand" of the copyist indicate that it was almost certainly a copy made not for public reading but instead for someone's personal study and/or edification.[40] To cite another example, there is P.Oxyrhynchus 655, fragments of a miniature roll dated to the third century AD that contained a copy of the *Gospel of Thomas*.[41] Such miniature rolls and codices were certainly made for individual usage and perhaps also for their portability, allowing them to be read on a journey. The earliest extant examples of these Christian manuscripts for personal usage date to the third century AD, but these are unlikely to have been the first copies of Christian texts prepared for this purpose.

In summary, along with the scriptures inherited from the Jewish tradition, the "Old Testament," early Christian writings as well were read, and read a lot, both in the setting of corporate worship and in private settings by individuals. In this, and especially in the regular reading of texts as part of corporate worship, early Christianity was different from almost any other kind of religious group of the Roman era, synagogue practice being the only close analogy.

Writing

As we have noted, in addition to the Christian texts that at one point or another acquired a scriptural status, there were also many others composed in the earliest centuries. Early Christianity was distinctively "bookish," not only in the place that the reading of certain texts held in their gatherings, but also in the sheer volume of production of new Christian texts. And this composition of texts was a remarkably prominent feature of the young religious movement.[42] If we confine our attention again to the pre-Constantinian period, you can readily get a sense of the efflorescence of early Christian literature by casting your eye over the table of contents of volume 1 of the valuable catalogue of early Christian literature by Moreschini and Norelli.[43] There are at least two hundred individual texts mentioned there dated to the first three centuries.

In addition to the familiar writings that make up the New Testament, there are other gospel-like texts, such as the *Gospel of Thomas*, the *Gospel of Mary*, the *Papyrus Egerton 2*, and numerous others. We also have quasi-official letters to churches (such as *1 Clement*), at least seven more by Ignatius of Antioch, and also Polycarp's letter to the Philippians. There are texts about church order, such as the *Didache* and *The Apostolic Tradition*, and homilies and hortatory texts, such as *2 Clement* and those by Melito and others. There are apocalypse-type writings, such as *Shepherd of Hermas* and the *Ascension of Isaiah*, and so-called "apocryphal" acts, such as the *Acts of Peter* and the *Acts of John*. There are a number of defenses of Christian faith, such as the one by Aristides, Justin's *Apology*, the *Epistle to Diognetus*, Tatian's *Oration to the Greeks*, Athenagoras' *Supplication*, Theophilus' *To Autolycus*, and the *Octavius* of Minucius Felix. Note also poetic/hymnic collections such as the *Odes of Solomon*, and theological treatises such as the *Epistle of Barnabas*, Justin's *Dialogue with Trypho*, Irenaeus' *Against Heresies* and his *Demonstration of the Apostolic Preaching*, Clement of Alexandria's *Christ the Educator* and his other writings, and Tertullian's several large works. Consider the many treatises, homilies, and exegetical works of Origen, and early accounts of Christian martyrs, such as the *Martyrdom of Polycarp*, the *Scillitan Martyrs*, and still other writings.

Some of these texts espouse what came to be regarded as "heretical" doctrines, and some others refute these doctrines. Some seem intended to entertain or to appeal to simple levels of Christian piety, and others are serious efforts to engage imperial authorities and/or the cultural and intellectual world of the time. And there are various other literary purposes served as well. Furthermore, we should recognize that, for all the many texts that have survived in whole or in part, there are others that are known to us only through brief mention of them or by extracts of them in subsequent Christian writers. For example, we know of a defense of Christianity by a Quadratus that was mentioned by Eusebius of Caesarea (*Ecclesiastical History* 4.3.1–2) but is no longer extant. There are likely many others totally lost to us, some without even a mention of them remaining.[44]

But what survives in whole or in excerpts quoted by others makes it amply clear that early Christianity was phenomenally prolific and varied in literary output. The number and substance of the writings produced is all the more remarkable when we remember that all through this early period Christians were still relatively few in number and small as a percentage of the total Roman-era population.[45] In fact, to my knowledge, among the many other Roman-era religious groups, there is simply no analogy for this variety, vigor, and volume in Christian literary output. For other religious movements of the day, such as Mithraism or the cult of Jupiter Dolichenus, for example, there are the remains of numerous shrines and dedicatory inscriptions but no texts.[46] For early Christianity, however, there are no known church structures or inscriptions prior to sometime in the third century AD, but there is this huge catalogue of texts. This is yet another indication that early Christianity was different from at least most other religious groups of the time.

Innovation and Adaptation

We also see interesting innovations and adaptations of literary conventions in this textual output that are observable already in the earliest Christian writings extant. Consider, for example, Paul's letters. If we confine our attention to the seven undisputed ones, all of them are remarkable for their size.[47] One study of the length of ancient Greek letters several decades ago yielded interesting results.[48] Ordinary ancient papyrus letters of the Greco-Roman era (and about 14,000 survive) averaged 87 words each, hardly ever exceeding 200 words. Essentially, these letters served basic and simple communication needs, such as assuring the recipient, "I am well and I trust you are too."

Even if we consider letters by learned figures, some of them more ambitious vehicles for extended discourses on certain subjects, Paul's letters stand out in size. The 796 preserved letters of Cicero range from 22 to 2,530 words, and the 124 extant letters of Seneca range from 149 to 4,134 words. In comparison, Paul's smallest letter, Philemon, is 395 words, extraordinarily large for what looks to be a simple personal letter and well beyond the average length of ancient Greek letters overall. If we consider Paul's larger letters, which have more extended discussion of theological/ethical issues, these are simply off the scale. To cite one count of the Greek texts: 2 Corinthians (4,448 words); 1 Corinthians (6,807 words); Romans (7,101 words). Even the more modest/medium-sized Pauline letters are toward the upper end of the range for literary letters: 1 Thessalonians (1,472 words); Philippians (1,624 words); Galatians (2,220 words).[49] One scholar quipped that, when the Roman Christians first received Paul's letter to them (the New Testament Epistle to the Romans), they were "probably more stunned by the letter's length than by its content."[50]

In short, Paul used the humble and familiar letterform as a major vehicle for serious, often extended, teaching. In fact, in 2 Corinthians (10:10), Paul refers, perhaps with a touch of irony, to what he had heard that some were saying about him, specifically that they deemed his letters more impressive than his person:

> I do not want to seem as though I am trying to frighten you with my letters. For they say, "His letters are weighty and strong, but his bodily presence is weak, and his speech contemptible."

The statement suggests that Paul's physical appearance and rhetorical abilities were not impressive, at least to those for whom these attributes were important; but, even among these ancient critics, Paul's letters were judged much more positively as serious and effective texts.

Granted, Paul's use of the letterform to convey substantial bodies of teaching was not totally unique in its time. The first century AD was a time when philosophers in particular used the letterform as a mode of instruction and dissemination of their teachings.[51] In fact, the contents and literary properties of Paul's letters resemble more the productions of philosophers than of Roman-era religious groups.[52] As well as these non-Christian "philosophical letters," in that same period we see the letterform being used for various other purposes, such as letter essays, novelistic letters (fictional, often pseudepigraphical), and imaginative letters intended primarily to entertain.[53] But I know of no other philosophical or religious group of the time that exhibits an appropriation of the letterform as a serious vehicle for its teaching that is comparable to what we see in letters of Paul and subsequent Christian texts, such as the letters of Ignatius of Antioch and other ancient Christian writers.

The Gospels familiar to us in the New Testament are likewise noteworthy literary products. The Gospels are to be seen in historical terms both as reflecting Roman-era interest in biographical-type writings and as a distinctive adaptation or sub-genre of this type of literature.[54] Mark, generally thought to have been the pioneering Gospel texts, written sometime 65–75 AD, exhibits basic features of *bios* writings of the time (to use Richard Burridge's preferred term), giving a sequenced narrative of Jesus' ministry. But Matthew and Luke, which are generally thought by scholars to have drawn on Mark as a source and basic model, both take the Markan account in a more overtly literary direction. They have more of the features that are characteristic of accounts of great men, who were the typical subjects of Roman-era *bios* literature, such as their respective birth accounts (Matthew 1:18–2:23; Luke 1:26–2:39). The Gospel of John introduces significant amounts of dialogues and other distinctive material, such as the much-studied "prologue" (1:1-18), in which Jesus' ultimate origins are traced back to before the creation of the world. But John, too, retains the basic shape of a *bios* account, mainly focused on Jesus' ministry, death, and resurrection.

At the same time, the Gospels evince distinctive features, most obviously in their subject matter. Their subject is not a ruler or military hero or distinguished philosopher but Jesus of Nazareth, a Galilean of a tradesman's family who was regarded as a prophet by some but executed by the Roman authorities on the charge of sedition. Further, the typical biographical accounts of the day present their subjects as prime examples of previously affirmed cultural values. The figures in these accounts largely serve to illustrate and promote these values, such as heroism. To be sure, the Gospels present Jesus as exhibiting positive qualities such as boldness and courage. But in the Gospels it is Jesus' own person and the particular claims about him as the unique agent of God's purposes that are the focus.[55] In short, the Gospels in their several ways appear to have appropriated the biographical genre but did so for quite distinctive purposes and with innovative results.

I also stress here that we have no analogy or precedent for the number or character of these Gospels' accounts in any religious group of the time. In ancient Jewish literature, there is nothing really comparable.[56] To be sure, the first-century Jewish writer Philo of Alexandria produced accounts of the biblical figures Abraham, Joseph, and Moses. But we have no extended biographical works devoted to Jewish figures of the then-recent past, such as Jesus was.[57] Nor is there any comparable body of multiple works from "pagan" authors, even about any regal or heroic figure. Of course, as we have noted, there are biographical-type writings, typically about royal figures or philosophers of renown, some of these dating from the fourth century BC, and others composed across the first few centuries AD.[58] Some are little more than sketches, such as in Suetonius' collective biographies of *The Twelve Caesars*, though others are more substantial. But I repeat that, even if we were to confine attention to the four New Testament Gospels, they comprise an unprecedented body of texts: four substantial narratives of the one figure, all four written within at most a couple of decades of one another!

Some have cited as a comparable kind of individual work the *Life of Apollonius of Tyana*, by Philostratus. But it was composed circa 217 AD, well over a century later than the New Testament Gospels, and so it can hardly serve as a precedent. Indeed, Philostratus may have taken the Gospels as a basic precedent and stimulus for his work and may even have intended to produce a work to rival the Gospels and the figure of Jesus.[59] We know that some pagan intellectuals of the second century and thereafter, such as Celsus and Porphyry, were familiar with the Gospels. In any case, in comparison to this one account of Apollonius or the various other biographies of kings or other important figures, it is remarkable to have four extended accounts of Jesus' ministry produced by as many authors and all within such a short period.

We should also take note of the ambitious aims of the authors of these particular works. The Gospel of John is widely thought by scholars to derive from a given "community" or circle of early Christians; but at least in its present form it is clearly intended for a much wider circulation, as reflected in the statement of purpose in 20:30-31.[60] The Gospel of Luke, like its sequel, Acts, is formally dedicated to a "Theophilus," but such dedications were often intended to secure the help of the person in publishing the work in question for others to read as well. So, whether Theophilus was a real or fictive figure, the author rather clearly aimed for a wider readership than him. The Gospel of Mark, too, must have circulated rather widely, at least initially, in order for it to have been used so fully as a model and source by the authors of the Gospels of Matthew and Luke. As for the Gospel of Matthew, its contents suggest the aim of providing a major source for Christian teaching; and, if we judge from the many citations and allusions to this Gospel in subsequent early Christian writings, the author's aim was achieved.[61] Indeed, the authors may have succeeded well beyond their aims. For as we have noted, at least by the late second century AD, these Gospels were also being read by pagans as well as Christians.

To cite yet another noteworthy example of an innovation and adaptation in an early Christian writing, consider the book of Revelation. It is striking how prominently references to books, writing, and reading appear in this book.[62] Scholars today commonly refer to the genre of "apocalypse" and to "apocalyptic literature" and refer to Revelation as an example of this genre. But, in fact, it is Revelation from which we derive the term used to label the genre, in the initial words, which were probably intended as the title for the work: "The Revelation [Greek: *apokalypsis*] of Jesus Christ." Revelation was written likely sometime toward the end of the first century AD. Only thereafter did the term *apokalypsis* come to be applied to some other Christian and Jewish texts and then acquire a usage in scholarly discourse as a label for a writing that professes to disclose revelations of heavenly and/or future secrets.[63]

To be sure, there are earlier works commonly cited today by scholars as "apocalyptic" or having apocalyptic elements. The material comprising chapters 7–12 of the Old Testament book Daniel, for example, is typically thought to have been written

sometime in the second century BC, and portions of the extracanonical writing *1 Enoch* are thought to be as old and even older,
especially chapters 1–36 and 72–82.[64] Revelation clearly reflects
similarities to these writings in its worldview, involving a contrast
between a heavenly world of divine order and an earthly world of
evil and rebellion against God, and in other "apocalyptic" literary
features such as the rich use of symbolism. So, Revelation draws
on an ancient Jewish tradition of revelatory writings, but Revelation is also innovative in some noteworthy features.

The author presents Revelation as a prophecy sent in the form
of a letter to seven churches. Although there are ancient Near
Eastern precedents for the use of letters to communicate prophetic oracles, Revelation does not seem to be directly influenced
by them. Instead, the text reflects letter practices specific to early
Christianity.[65] Note, for example, the sender-addressee-greeting
formula in 1:4–5: "John to the seven churches that are in Asia:
Grace to you and peace . . ." (the "Grace and peace" salutation
a distinctive Christian form). Likewise, the "grace-benediction"
that concludes the book in 22:21, "The grace of the Lord Jesus be
with all the saints," is a version of the distinctively early Christian
expression often used as part of the conclusion to letters.[66] Revelation is also unusual in giving us what is commonly taken as
the real name of its author, "John" (1:4, 9; 22:8). "John" (Greek:
Iōannēs) is a Graecized form of the Jewish name Yohanan, which
must mean that the author was a Jewish Christian, perhaps from
Roman Judaea, who had emigrated to the province of Asia (part
of present-day Turkey).[67] Likewise, Revelation is unusual in
giving us the real identities of the original recipients, the seven
named churches addressed in 2:1–3:22. In nearly all other cases,
on the other hand, in both Jewish and Christian "apocalyptic"
texts, the author is fictive, as are the stated recipients.[68]

We may add to this that Revelation is structurally complex
and yet seems to be cohesive and ordered.[69] That is, Revelation seems to have been a single, unified composition, although
it contains a variety of constituent literary forms, and scholars

have proposed various schemes for mapping its structure.[70] This ordered structure, likely entirely the product of the stated author, contrasts with what seems to have been the more complex and multistage literary/composition history of a number of other apocalyptic works.

We should also note again that "John" refers to the work repeatedly as a "prophecy" (1:3; 22:7, 10, 18-19), giving it thereby all the significance of a work conveying divine revelations and directions. That is, the author did not see himself as adding another work to what scholars today think of as a genre of "apocalypses." Instead, he presented himself as giving a distinctive voice to charismatic prophecy received "in the Spirit" (1:9-10), and bearing a solemn authority, as reflected in the stern warning about tampering with his prophecy with which he concludes the book (22:18-19). That is, Revelation very much reflects specifically what we may call the "religious culture" of early Christianity, with its strong sense of urgency and spiritual empowerment.

But it is equally important to note that, unlike the books of the Old Testament prophets, Revelation does not present itself as the secondary written deposit of a set of oracles that were originally declared orally. Instead, in this case, from the first, this prophecy was delivered in *written* form.[71] In fact, the author claims that this was by divine mandate, a heavenly voice ordering him, "Write in a book what you see and send it to the seven churches" (1:11), and early in the book the author pronounces a blessing upon "the one who reads aloud the words of the prophecy" in the context of Christian gatherings and upon "those who hear and keep what is written in it" (1:3). Note again the stern warning in the closing lines against tampering with the wording of the book (22:18-19), which is also clearly expressive of the importance that the author attached to this writing. Revelation is, thus, a particularly strong witness to the place of "textuality" and the "bookishness" of early Christianity.[72]

The Work Involved

In addition to noting various ways in which early Christian texts were distinctive and/or innovative adaptations of literary conventions, we should also take account of the sheer time and effort that was involved in the task of composing them. To my knowledge, the most detailed attempt to imagine how an ancient Christian writer may have gone about composing and preparing a text for distribution is in Randolph Richards' book *Paul and First-Century Letter Writing.*[73] Essentially, and based on ancient descriptions of the compositional process, Richards observes that the process of composing a text such as one of Paul's letters would likely have involved thought, note taking, perhaps some dictation of an initial draft, then editing that draft, and then preparation of the final copy for release to readers.[74] That is, we probably should imagine at least a few days required for these things, and quite possibly more than a few days. Recall the observations made earlier about the size of some of Paul's letters, such as Romans and 1 Corinthians, each of which must have required a considerable amount of time and effort in composing it.

Nor are Paul's letters the only texts that required time and effort. For example, each of the familiar New Testament Gospels as well was a significant literary product. Even the shortest of them, Mark, amounts to about eleven thousand words in Greek; John, some fifteen thousand words; Matthew, over eighteen thousand words; and Luke, over nineteen thousand words. If, as most scholars believe, Acts was written by the author of Luke and as the second of a two-part work giving an account of Jesus and of the emergence of Christianity, we are dealing with quite a substantial literary project. Luke and Acts together amount to nearly thirty-eight thousand words and comprise just over 25 percent of the New Testament. When we also take account of the geographical and chronological coverage of the storyline of Acts in particular, it is clear that the author had impressive aims and a large commitment to his task. He acknowledges predecessors in accounts of "the things fulfilled among us," likely referring particularly to writings about Jesus, and he claims to have done research for his own project (Luke 1:1-4). But in addition, he had to devote considerable thought and effort to the actual composition of it.

There are still other early texts that must have involved much time and effort, such as the "Epistle to the Hebrews," a work of nearly five thousand words, written in accomplished Koine Greek. Though apparently sent formally as a letter, as reflected in the concluding greetings and "grace benediction" in 13:24-25, Hebrews is in fact a sustained treatise intended by the unknown Christian author as "a word of exhortation" urging other early Christians to maintain their commitment in the face of opposition.

We have taken note of Revelation already as a noteworthy text. But I return to it here simply to cite it as another sizable literary project. It comprises over ninety-eight hundred words, making it the sixth largest writing in the New Testament. The author says that he wrote it on the island of Patmos, either having been sent into exile there or having fled there "because of the word of God and the testimony of Jesus" (1:9).[75] In either case, the composition of Revelation involved a major effort, to say nothing of then having to dispatch the text to the seven churches addressed.[76]

If we consider some illustrative Christian texts of the second century, the commitment to composing sizeable and ambitious texts continues to be evident. The several "apologies" (defenses) of Christianity already cited are ready examples. Justin's *First Apology*, for instance, amounts to some 75 pages in the Goodspeed edition, and his *Dialogue with Trypho* is a still larger work of 175 pages.[77] Each of these works, which are quite different in genre, would have required considerable thought, planning, and time spent composing, editing, and preparing the final form to be sent out.

I underscore that this literary output, examples of which date to within the first decades of the Christian movement, is extraordinary. This is especially so for the earliest texts, such as those that make up the New Testament, given that Paul and other early Christian authors were neither professional writers nor of the wealthy and leisured classes with slaves to attend to their needs and with copious free time. Even the second-century writers— such as Justin, who is reported to have styled himself as a Christian philosopher—did not belong to the leisured, wealthy, and well-connected circles of contemporary pagan authors such as Fronto or Celsus. Instead, particularly in the case of Paul and other first-century Christian writers, the impressive body of texts seems to have been composed by their authors amidst other demands on their time.[78] Indeed, in the case of the letters of Ignatius of Antioch, we have writings composed by a Christian en route to execution in Rome! Furthermore, throughout the period that we are focusing on here, the motivation of Christian writers was not so much personal fame, and certainly they had no hope of fortune. This means that there was a strong commitment to producing these texts, and a remarkable readiness to exert the effort involved to do so.

Copying and Circulation

We should also reckon with the process and effort involved in copying and disseminating early Christian texts. In his book cited earlier, Richards judged that simply to make a single manuscript *copy* of Romans, for example, Paul's longest letter, would have required about 11.5 hours, and so, estimating that a copyist might have managed only about 5 hours a day of "actual steady writing," this would mean about two to three days of work.[79] Even for more modest-sized Pauline letters, a copyist would have needed at least a few hours to make a copy. For example, Galatians would have required about 3.6 hours, Philippians about 2.6 hours, and 1 Thessalonians about 2.4 hours.[80] Of course, the actual times will have varied somewhat, depending on factors such as the skill and speed of the copyist and whether it was a formal copy prepared for public reading or a more informal and private copy. We for whom information technology has made the production and copying of texts so easy should recognize that copying these ancient, often sizeable, texts required significant time and effort. It had to be done one pen stroke at a time.

Nevertheless, it is clear that early Christians were heavily invested precisely in this activity. References in early Christian texts, and early manuscript evidence as well, indicate that Christian texts obtained a wide and ready circulation translocally. For example, early copies of texts composed in Rome and elsewhere appear to have made their way to the Egyptian provincial town of Oxyrhynchus, some 120 miles south of Alexandria, Egypt, with impressive promptness.[81]

I noted earlier the collecting and dissemination of Pauline letters among various churches translocally, and we have other evidence of similar activities for other early Christian writings. For example, in his *Letter to the Philippians*, the second-century Christian teacher Polycarp mentions his intention to send with it "the letters of Ignatius [of Antioch] that were sent to us by him, together with any others that we have in our possession" (13.2). We do not know with certainty which or how many letters of Ignatius that Polycarp possessed and sent, but his letter indicates that, not long after Ignatius wrote his letters to several churches, Polycarp had some sort of collection of them and so was able to send copies to the Philippian church. This dispatch of Ignatius' collected letters comprised "a de facto publication of the collection as such."[82] In short, Polycarp's letter gives us a textual snapshot of the dedicated process of collecting and disseminating early Christian writings within a very short time after their composition.

We have another explicit indication of how an early Christian text was disseminated in the fascinating second-century work known as the *Shepherd of Hermas*. The author, Hermas, claims to have made a copy of a "little book" (Greek: *biblaridion*) that he saw in a vision of an elderly woman (*Vision* 2.1). Later, in another vision, the same elderly woman directs Hermas to prepare two copies of this book and to send one copy to Clement and one to Grapte, who were both leading figures in Hermas' Roman church. Clement is then to send the book "to the cities abroad," and Grapte (a woman) is to "instruct the widows and orphans" in the church in Rome. As for Hermas, he is to "read it to this city, along with the elders who preside over the church" (*Vision* 2.4).

Whatever you make of Hermas' claims about his visions, it is likely that the basic procedure that he says he was directed to follow reflects the process and resources by which Christian texts were often disseminated. The Clement to whom Hermas was to give a copy of the book in question may be the same Roman church figure whose name was given to the early Christian text known as *1 Clement*, typically dated toward the end of the first century AD, which was sent by the Roman church to the church in Corinth.[83] In any case, the mention of his role in *Shepherd of Hermas* suggests that Clement acted as a kind of corresponding secretary for the Roman church, with a responsibility to make and send copies of writings composed for dissemination.[84] From such references as these in early Christian texts of the second century, it appears that, already by that point, churches in several major cities such as Rome, Antioch, Caesarea, and Alexandria were both producing texts and copying and disseminating them to Christians elsewhere.[85] Of course, this is further indication of the strong sense of translocal connections among early Christian circles.

There is also rich physical evidence in second- and third-century Christian papyri reflecting "extensive and lively interactions" between Christians in various parts of the Roman world that included the wide circulation of various texts.[86] As the papyri and textual references confirm, the texts that circulated included both scriptural writings and a variety of others as well, such as letters (e.g., *1 Clement*), hortatory treatises (such as *Shepherd of Hermas*), homilies (such as those by Melito), and theological treatises (such as Irenaeus' *Against Heresies*). And, again, these are only the writings for which there is extant evidence. Who knows how many other texts were composed and circulated similarly? Certainly, by all indications, early Christians were very much involved in what we would call a committed "networking" with one another and across considerable distances.

Note that in this period, there was no public postal system, and so Christians had to invest their own personal and financial resources in disseminating their texts. Their readiness to do so is both impressive and without parallel among religious groups of the time. In view of how much time and resources early churches devoted to communicating with one another, in the process developing their own system for doing so, we may ask what it tells us about how early Christian groups regarded one another.[87] Well, I think that it certainly shows that Christians thought of themselves as connected with other believers translocally and that they thought it crucial to share texts with one another as constitutive of their faith. There was, for example, "a busy, almost hectic traffic of messengers and letters between the churches" of Asia Minor.[88] In sum, early Christians not only sent letters; they also copied and disseminated their scriptural writings and various other Christian literary texts, and in this intense activity we have another distinctive of Roman-era Christianity.

But Christians also prepared copies of some texts for still wider circulation and reading than among churches. The obvious examples are the "apologies," defenses of Christianity by writers such as Justin, each of which was formally addressed to the emperor of the day. Scholars wonder whether any of the emperors actually took the time to read them. But we must assume that the authors actually sent these works to the emperors addressed in them and perhaps also sent copies for circulation among Christian groups and/or the general public. In any case, it is rather clear that at least some of these works were read by at least some non-Christians, perhaps particularly by some among learned pagan circles. The pagan critic Celsus, for example, gives evidence of having read Justin's *Apology* and seems also to have read a slightly earlier Christian apology known as *The Dialogue of Jason and Papiscus* (written about 140 AD, ascribed to Aristo of Pella).[89] Whatever their actual success, clearly some Christians made impressive efforts to disseminate their works, not only among fellow believers, but more widely as well. Here again, it is difficult to find an equivalent effort by other religious groups of the day.[90]

Physical and Visual Distinctives

Early Christians were not only a distinctively "bookish" religious movement; they also were distinctive in some preferred physical and visual features of their books, particularly copies of their scriptural texts.[91] Let us start with the bookform that they preferred, especially for these scripture texts: the codex, the ancestor of the modern leaf book.[92]

Christian Preference for the Codex

In the larger Roman cultural environment of the first few centuries AD, the overwhelmingly preferred bookform for literary texts was the bookroll, or scroll. The codex was certainly also known but was in limited usage, and mainly for work-a-day texts, such as tables of astronomical data or lists of medical remedies. From some comments by the Roman writer Martial, however, we know that by the late first century AD there were also a few experiments with producing copies of his poems and perhaps a few other literary texts by others as well, in the form of small codices intended for informal usage and portability. Illustrative of these experiments, the catalogued ancient manuscripts of the second and third centuries AD include the remains of a small number of codex copies of pagan literary texts.[93] But, indicative of the general preference for the bookroll, there is the professional opinion of the Roman jurist Ulpian, around the beginning of the third century AD, as to what could be counted as "books" (Latin: *libri*), when the term appears in a will or bequest. Ulpian makes it clear that he regards the bookroll (Latin: *volumen*) as the proper reference, "whether of papyrus or parchment or other material." Ulpian also granted, with a slight reluctance, that codices—whether papyrus, parchment, or even waxed tablets—should be included in the legal meaning of "books"; but he implied that, properly speaking, the term really designates bookrolls.[94] Certainly, in Roman-era book culture generally, especially throughout the first two centuries AD, the codex seems to have been regarded as not really an appropriate bookform for literary texts, too informal, probably, and the bookroll reigned supreme.[95]

Christians, however, with an equally firm attitude, preferred the codex. Let us look at some figures for comparison purposes.[96] For example, about 95 percent of extant second-century AD non-Christian copies of literary texts are bookrolls, and about 5 percent are codices. But at least 75 percent of all second-century Christian manuscripts of any text are codices.[97] Marked differences in bookform preferences between Christians and the wider Roman culture continue to be evident also in the third century AD.[98]

Further, if we focus more closely on the kinds of texts copied in Christian manuscripts, we see something else interesting. Christians preferred the codex generally, to be sure, but they preferred the codex particularly for the copies of texts that they regarded and read as scripture. As the prime evidence, it is clear that the great majority of Christians in the second and third centuries regarded what came to be called the "Old Testament" writings as scripture. Of the approximately seventy-five extant Christian copies of Old Testament writings dated to the second or third century, only about 4–7 percent are bookrolls.[99] As for the writings that came to form the New Testament, many of which likewise were being read widely in churches as scripture, to date we have no clear example of any of these writings copied on an unused bookroll.[100] By contrast, of the nearly sixty copies of other Christian literary texts, such as theological treatises, homilies, and "apocryphal" gospels, dated to the second or third century, about one-third of these are bookrolls. This obviously still represents a strong Christian preference for the codex, but not nearly as strong as is exhibited in the early copies of texts that we know were coming to be treated as scripture.[101]

Let me clarify the point about what we can infer as to likely Christian usage of texts from the forms of their books. There is not a simple one-to-one relationship between the codex book-form and the status and usage of a text. As noted, Christians seem to have preferred the codex generally for all their literary texts in this early period. But this preference is exhibited with particular strength for copies of certain texts, and these happen to be "Old Testament" writings and those Christian texts that we know were also being treated as scriptures, writings that are now part of the New Testament. We see a somewhat greater readiness to use both codex and roll bookforms for other texts. So, in summary, a given text in codex form does not automatically mean that it was a copy treated as scripture. But a copy of a Christian text in bookroll form suggests either that the text was *not* regarded and used as scripture by which I mean read in worship gatherings of churches, or at least that this particular copy was not prepared for such use. It was probably someone's personal copy of that text.

Scholars have offered various putatively practical advantages of the codex as reasons for why Christians so strongly preferred this bookform. But they are illusory and irrelevant.[102] In an earlier book, I reviewed proposals about the supposedly obvious practical advantages of the codex and found them all dubious.[103] The only practical advantage noted by ancient writers is that *small* codices were handy to read while travelling. But the overwhelming number of Christian codices are not such miniature ones. Furthermore, to underscore the point, Christian preference for the codex was not uniformly strong for all texts but, instead, particularly strong *precisely for texts that they most highly valued, those that they treated as scriptures.* Any explanation for why Christians preferred the codex must take account of this.

In my view, the early Christians' preference for the codex, especially for their most highly regarded texts, must have been conscious and deliberate. Given the prominence of the bookroll for literary texts generally in the Roman era, early Christians must have been well aware that in preferring the codex they were at odds with the larger book culture of the time. The bookroll was the prestige bookform of the day, and so, if Christians wanted to commend their texts to the wider culture, especially the texts that they read as scripture, it would seem an odd and counterintuitive choice to prefer the codex bookform for these texts. Indeed, it would seem like a deliberately countercultural move. If not in intention, at least in effect it was counterintuitive and, I would say, countercultural. It certainly had the effect of distinguishing early Christian books physically, especially Christian copies of their sacred books.[104]

Some scholars have contended that a shift toward the codex was slowly taking place in the wider book culture of the second through fifth centuries AD. Perhaps, although this is not actually clear from the evidence. But, even if we grant this, we have to judge Christians as well ahead of any such process, at least proceeding in a much faster pace. Indeed, Christians seem to have been "pushing the envelope" of book technology of the second and third centuries. We see this in the several methods of codex construction that they experimented with in copying Christian texts of this period.[105]

We have codices comprising a single stack of papyrus sheets, such as the Chester Beatty codex of Pauline epistles ($\mathfrak{P}^{46}$, early third century), which originally was made up of fifty-two folded papyrus sheets stitched together in a single "gathering." The Chester Beatty Gospels-Acts codex, however ($\mathfrak{P}^{45}$, about the same date or a bit later), was constructed by stitching to one another fifty-six individually folded sheets. Still other early Christian codices were constructed of "multiple gatherings," each gathering comprising three or four or more folded papyrus sheets stitched together, these gatherings then stitched to one another to form the completed codex.

If the development of the codex bookform for serious literary purposes was already under way by the third century, why would Christians still be experimenting with these various techniques? The more likely scenario is that, in the second and third centuries

AD, it was actually Christians who were at the leading edge of codex developments. The impetus among early Christians for experimenting with these various techniques of codex construction was clearly to accommodate larger bodies of text into one physical book, as illustrated in the two Chester Beatty codices mentioned. In short, Christians took up the humble codex bookform and sought to develop it to serve their own needs, thereby preferring and developing this bookform distinctively. Their commitment to copying texts and to the codex bookform drove their efforts to develop codex technology.

Furthermore, we should recognize that the preference for the codex demanded a commitment to developing the particular steps and skills necessary in codex construction. To make a bookroll essentially required only the skill of copying a text in tall, narrow columns onto a continuous length of papyrus writing material, just as it came from the manufacturing process, made up of successive sheets of papyrus glued together. But to produce a codex involved first estimating the length of a papyrus writing material necessary for a given text, then cutting the papyrus into sheets for folding, then writing the text on these sheets (careful to keep them in proper order), and then assembling the sheets in some manner. Also, copyists had to write on both sides of the papyrus material, whereas in a bookroll only the side with horizontal fibers was used.[106] Further, the writing column was typically wider, running most of the width of the pages, requiring all four margins to be calculated.

Nevertheless, despite the extra skills and steps needed, and despite the wider cultural preference for the bookroll, and whatever the originating impulse for the early Christian preference for the codex, it quickly became the distinctively preferred bookform for Christian texts, especially Christian copies of scriptural texts. Given that our earliest evidence comes almost entirely from Egypt, however, you may well ask whether it is representative of preferences in the wider Roman Empire. With other scholars, I think that "it seems reasonable to take the Egyptian evidence as roughly indicative" of bookform preferences more widely.[107] The brisk circulation of early Christian texts noted earlier is an important factor in making this judgment. Christians were sharing texts translocally, and that included sharing the physical forms of the copies of these texts as well, all through the early period that we are focusing on in this book. So, the preference for the codex exhibited in extant copies of Christian texts found in Egypt likely reflects a wider general Christian preference.

The *Nomina Sacra*

Another striking feature of early Christian manuscripts—and again, particularly in copies of Christian scriptural texts—is called the *nomina sacra*.[108] This term refers to a Christian scribal practice of writing certain words in a distinctive abbreviated way, usually the first and final letters of the word, yielding a "contracted" form of it, and with a horizontal stroke placed over this abbreviated form. As with the Christian preference for the codex, this scribal practice began so early that it was already a convention by the time of our earliest extant fragments of Christian manuscripts, a few of which take us back into the mid-/late second century AD.

It is noteworthy that certain words were more consistently treated as *nomina sacra*, particularly the Greek words for "God," "Lord," "Jesus," and "Christ." This makes it likely that the practice began with one or another of these words. Thereafter, at an early point, copyists began treating certain other words as *nomina sacra* as well, and by the Byzantine period some fifteen words were often written this way.[109]

In earlier publications, I have supported the view that the practice may have begun with an abbreviated form of *Iēsous* (the Greek word for "Jesus").[110] For reasons posited in these earlier publications, this proposal accounts in particular for the origin of that curious horizontal stroke typically placed over the abbreviated forms of these words, which was not typical of Greek or Latin abbreviations. Positing that the practice began with *Iēsous* also accounts for the distinctive way this particular word is abbreviated in some early manuscripts. For, in addition to the "contracted" first-letter and last-letter forms of the Greek word ΙΗΣΟΥΣ (e.g., ΙΣ, ΙΥ) in most manuscripts, in some other early manuscripts we find a "suspended" form, the first two letters as the *nomina sacra* abbreviation: ΙΗ. That is, the word *Iēsous* distinctively was written in two different *nomina sacra* forms, some manuscripts using the "contracted" forms, and other manuscripts having this "suspended" form. So it appears that the *nomina sacra* treatment of Jesus' name has a history somewhat distinguishable from the other words. But it is not essential here to engage further the question of which word may have initiated the *nomina sacra* practice. Instead, I want to make briefly a few broader points more relevant to this particular discussion.

First, whatever the origin of the *nomina sacra* practice, it seems to be a Christian scribal innovation that had the effect of setting off the words in question visually from the surrounding texts in which they appeared. The horizontal stroke in particular has this effect. Even if you cannot read Greek, you can immediately spot the *nomina sacra* on the page of ancient manuscripts. Second, the originating motivation for writing these particular words in this manner was likely reverential, the copyist practice visually expressive of early Christian piety. That is, writing these words, especially the words referring to God and Jesus, in this special manner was a way of registering a certain reverence for them, and in particular a way of doing so *visually*.

In ancient Jewish copies of biblical texts, scribes often wrote the sacred name of God (*YHWH*) in special ways.[111] Sometimes, they wrote the name in a different script. For example, in some Greek manuscripts *YHWH* was written in Hebrew characters. Sometimes, in Hebrew manuscripts, ancient scribes substituted for *YHWH* a set of dots, and sometimes they replaced *YHWH* with a substitute word, such as *Elohim*, the Hebrew word translated "God."[112] These Jewish copyist practices, too, were expressive of reverence, in this case reverence for God and God's sacred name. With most scholars who have considered the question, I support the view that this reverential attitude and purpose gives us a certain similarity between the Jewish scribal treatment of the divine name and the early Christian practice of the *nomina sacra*.

But the respective scribal practices are also distinguishable. I repeat that the specific *nomina sacra* practice seems to have been a Christian innovation and so is another distinguishing feature of early Christianity.[113] There is no instance of *nomina sacra* forms in pre-Christian Jewish manuscripts. The *nomina sacra* practice also differed in "mechanics" from the comparable Jewish copyist practices that exhibited reverence for *YHWH*. For example, the use of the horizontal stroke over an abbreviated form seems to have been a Christian innovation. Also, there was a difference in what readers were expected to do with the various scribal devices. From various evidence, it appears that many or most devout Jews of the early Roman period typically avoided pronouncing God's name (*YHWH*), even when reading their scriptural texts in which *YHWH* was written.[114] So, for example, in reading their scriptures aloud in Hebrew, when they came to where *YHWH* stood in the text they might have substituted the word *Elohim* or *Adonay*. If reading a Greek scriptural text, they would typically have used *Kyrios* ("Lord") in place of pronouncing the divine name. So, it appears that one function of the Jewish copyist devices that we have noted was to signal to readers to use an appropriate oral substitute for *YHWH*.

But, so far as we know, when early Christian readers came to the *nomina sacra* forms in their texts, they simply pronounced the words as if they were written in full and in ordinary form. This in turn means that the *nomina sacra* were exclusively *visual* phenomena. So, on the one hand, if you were an ancient Christian simply listening to a text read out and did not, or could not, read the text for yourself, you might not know that these words were written in any special way.

On the other hand, as purely a visual phenomenon, the *nomina sacra* comprise what are probably our earliest extant attempts by

Christians to register their faith/piety visually in an early symbolic manner. Recall that this copyist practice is evidenced in the earliest fragments of Christian manuscripts, which are paleographically dated as early as sometime in the mid-/late second century AD. This makes these manuscripts chronological rivals to the catacomb paintings and other material that are more typically cited in histories of early Christian art.[115] So, I have urged that the *nomina sacra* attest the emergence of an identifiable early Christian "visual culture" and, indeed, may well be the earliest evidence of this.[116] Thereafter, by the Byzantine period, *nomina sacra* were also used outside of texts—for example, on icons—especially to refer to God, Jesus, and Jesus' mother.

Summary

Any adequate analysis of early Christianity must reckon with its "bookish" nature.[117] In the foregoing pages, I have surveyed the main expressions of this bookishness, which was another of the distinguishing features of early Christianity in its Roman setting. We have noted the central place of reading texts (both in corporate and in private settings), the extraordinary composition of an abundance of new texts, the considerable energies and resources devoted also to copying and dissemination of texts, and the distinguishing physical and visual features of early Christian books. These phenomena all combine to make the young Christian movement distinctively text oriented in the context of the varied religious environment of that time. In short, "textuality" was central, and, from the outset, early Christianity was, indeed, "a bookish religion."

5

A New Way to Live

Today people tend to think of "religion" as typically involving a set of behavioral requirements, "do's and don'ts" about how to live; but in the ancient world that was not the case. Here again, early Christianity was unusual in its emphasis on social and behavioral practices as central in the religious commitment required of adherents, in some of the specifics of what was required of adherents, and in the seriousness with which this emphasis was pursued in what must be judged a noteworthy social project. But before we look at those practices more closely, it will be helpful to take brief account of some features of the wider cultural setting in which early Christians sought to live out this commitment.

The Roman-Era Setting

In ascribing a distinctiveness to early Christianity in certain social and behavioral practices, I intend no stereotype of the Roman era—for example, as one of simple decadence and a moral wasteland. Certainly, there was cruelty and decadence then, as (with variations in specifics) in pretty much any other time, including our own. But we should not imagine the ordinary people of the Roman period as depraved and cruel.[1] Instead of such assumptions, we should presume with good reason that, whatever their individual lapses in behavior, most ordinary people likely tried to take care of their families as they saw best how to do it; professed and hoped for fair play, honest dealings, and justice; admired generosity and self-restraint; and in general held these and some other values not all that different from the best of our time.

Infant Exposure

But, all the same, it was also a time when people legally and without qualms, it appears, engaged in some practices that, hopefully, we would regard as abhorrent today. Consider, as one particularly striking example, the practice of discarding unwanted babies and the reasons they were discarded.[2] This practice, often referred to in scholarly studies as "infant exposure," typically involved casting the unwanted newborn baby on a trash-heap site or some abandoned place, the infant left to die or be collected by someone, usually to be reared for slavery. Although today it will be difficult to consider the practice without revulsion, in the Roman period it was apparently not a source of great moral outrage, at least not widely. As an illustration, let us note an oft-cited letter from a man named Hilarion, who was probably serving in the Roman army, to his wife, Alis, written in 1 BC. His letter reflects the apparent frequency of, and casual attitude toward, infant abandonment. Moreover, the letter shows that it was practiced by people who otherwise seem to have had recognizably humane feelings.

After greeting his wife and other relatives with her at their home, Hilarion begs her to "take care of the little one," their child, promising to send money as soon as he is paid. Then, referring to Alis expecting another child very soon, he writes, "if it is a boy, let it be, if it is a girl, cast it out." But then after this rather blunt order, he continues by expressing his unaltered tender affection for Alis: "How can I forget you? I beg you then not to be anxious."[3] Obviously, the man was not a monster and was capable of tender feelings. Nor was he unusual for the time in his attitude about infant exposure. That is precisely the point to note: the practice of discarding infants shortly after birth, and before they had been accepted by the father as family members, was so much a feature of the culture of the Roman period that many otherwise caring people seem to have felt little reluctance about it.[4] This contrasts with Roman-era attitudes toward killing or discarding children after they had been accepted into their families.[5] That was condemned.

Scholars have explored the various reasons why infant exposure was so widely practiced. One proposal is that, in some cases, it may have been prompted by poverty. Perhaps some parents, living in straightened circumstances, may have felt that they could not afford another child. Perhaps in other instances parents may simply have preferred to focus their limited resources on providing more fully for a small number of children. We hear of similar cases of poor people disposing of unwanted infants occasionally today, but they tend to make the headlines. In the Roman era, however, it would hardly have received attention.

In Hilarion's case, poverty does not seem to have been the factor. The letter suggests that he was happy enough to have another child, so long as it was a son. He just did not want a daughter. He was likely not unique in this view, and scholars suspect, therefore, that many more female than male infants were discarded.[6] Indeed, one of the reasons that infant exposure was practiced so widely was probably that, in contrast to the contraception and abortion techniques of that time, it allowed parents such as Hilarion to choose the sex of the children whom they wanted to rear.[7]

Whatever the parents' reasons, as noted already this "exposure" of infants would have meant either their death, widely assumed to be the fate of many, or being picked up by people who often reared such abandoned infants for subsequent sale as slaves. Indeed, exposed infants seem to have provided a ready source supplying a large continuing demand for slaves.[8] One estimate is that some 500,000 new slaves were needed annually in the Roman Empire and that slaves reared from discarded infants may have supplied over 150,000 of these.[9] The second-century Christian author of the *Shepherd of Hermas* was apparently an instance of this. Hermas says that he had been brought up as such a foundling and was then sold to Rhoda, the Christian woman who features among the characters in this text.[10] More ominously still, exposed infants, both females and males, were also often picked up and reared to serve their masters or to be sold to others, as enslaved prostitutes in brothels.[11] In a scathing attack on this practice, the second-century Christian writer Justin Martyr actually claimed that this was the fate of most abandoned infants, both males and females (*First Apology* 27.1).

Justin is representative of the revulsion at the practice of infant abandonment that is expressed in early Christian writings.[12] As one recent scholar has observed, "With abortion and abandonment, we come to a distinct parting of the ways between Christians and general Graeco-Roman practice."[13] Of course, this attitude echoes and was inherited from the Jewish tradition.[14] The early first-century Jewish writer Philo of Alexandria, for example, condemns infant exposure at some length as prohibited by the laws of God and nature and as "the worst abomination of all" (*On the Special Laws* 3.112).[15] Indeed, Philo's attack on the practice gives us one of the most extended references to it. Philo claims that parents sometimes strangled newborn infants, or threw them into the sea, or took them to some deserted place, where they might be devoured by beasts or carnivorous birds, or perhaps taken in by "passing travellers" (*On the Special Laws* 3.110–16, citing 116). Flavius Josephus, another first-century Jewish writer, likewise insisted that Jewish law requires that all offspring should be brought up and forbids either abortion or infant exposure (*Against Apion* 2.202). Some pagan writers of the time thought the Jews unusual in not abandoning unwanted babies.[16]

To be sure, among pagans of the time as well, there were some voices raised against the practice, warning us, again, against simplistic characterization of attitudes. Among these is the impressive first-century Stoic philosopher Musonius Rufus, who contended that having children was a civic duty and that infant exposure was contrary to nature and comprises disrespect for the gods, especially Zeus, whom Musonius portrays as the "guardian of the family, from whom wrongs done to the family are not hidden." He specifically cites as "most monstrous of all" those who, although prosperous, abandon their infants that are born later, so that those born earlier might inherit greater wealth. In response to those who might invoke their poverty as a reason for infant exposure, Musonius responds, in imagery similar to that in a saying ascribed to Jesus, "From where do the little birds, which are much poorer than you, feed their young?"[17] Another pagan voice, the Roman historian Tacitus, writing in the late first or early second century about the Germanic tribes, appreciatively referred to the chastity of their wives and noted that they do not cast off their infants (*Germania* 19).

Nevertheless, beyond expressing such pronouncements and sentiments, neither these pagan moralists and philosophers nor others of the early imperial period made any serious effort to bring infant abandonment to a halt or sought actively to dissuade the wider populace from it. Although there were occasional local policies designed to promote multiple children and discourage abortion and infant exposure, there were no Roman imperial laws specifically against infant exposure.[18] There was, one modern historian judged, "disapproval, and there was grief—but perhaps not very much shame."[19] But neither disapproval, by some, nor grief, perhaps especially in mothers, was enough to stop or even hinder the widespread exposure of evidently healthy and legitimately conceived infants, particularly females, at least many of whom might otherwise have been accommodated by their families. So far as we know, the only wide-scale criticism of the practice, and the only collective refusal to engage in infant exposure in the first three centuries AD, was among Jews and then also early Christians.

Gladiator Contests and Other Spectacles

I turn now from this problematic feature of the private sphere of behavior to consider an example of a comparably striking feature of the public sphere, the prominent place of gladiatorial contests and other blood-sport public spectacles in the early Roman era.[20] The essence of gladiatorial shows was two men equipped with mortal weapons and placed in an arena for combat that was expected to involve wounding and that could, and often did, lead to the death of one of them, with an enthusiastic audience hoping in any case to see blood. Originally, and at times thereafter, the contestants were captured enemies, forced to fight for their lives in an arena before a Roman crowd. The crowd, thereby, were able to share in the Roman triumph over their enemies. By the first and second century, however, the continuing popularity of gladiatorial contests led to the use of slaves who were trained for this combat in gladiatorial schools and managed by their owners.[21] But also sometimes freedmen and even a few freeborn individuals willingly trained as gladiators, hoping to survive and win prize money sufficient to move on at some point to some other way of life.

The major place of gladiatorial contests in public entertainment is reflected in the various kinds of combatants, each giving the contests a particular twist. For example, there was the *hoplomachus*, who wore armor and fought mainly with a lance, and the *murmillo*, equipped with a large shield and who was often pitted against a *retarius*, equipped with a net and trident. And there were still other types of gladiators. But the common characteristic among them was that they were all stylized as foreign types; a gladiator did not fight with the armor and weapons of the Roman soldier. So, part of the enjoyment for the crowds was watching them fight, and perhaps die violently, with some symbolic and cultural distance from the spectators and the emblems of their own culture.[22] And each spectacle program might involve scores or even hundreds of gladiators, the various contests extending over perhaps several days.

We should also note that there was a particular association of gladiatorial contests with the emperor. In Rome, the emperor sat in a reserved box, and he rewarded the victorious combatants. Prominent images of the emperor adorned the sites of such contests elsewhere as well, symbolically making the association with him evident wherever they were held. Thus, at least indirectly, gladiatorial contests reflected the power of the emperor and the empire that he presided over and represented in his person. Illustrative of this, in his list of achievements and contributions to the people and institutions of the Roman world, Caesar Augustus included these:

> I gave three gladiatorial games in my own name and five in that of my sons or grandsons; at these games some 10,000 men took part in combat. . . . I gave beast-hunts of African beasts in my own name or in that of my sons and grandsons in the circus or forum or amphitheater on twenty-six occasions, on which about 3,500 beasts were destroyed.[23]

But, in addition to gladiatorial fights, there were other kinds of violence-as-entertainment on offer to the public.[24] A placard that was found in the ruins of Pompeii promised thirty pairs of gladiators in combat, and wild animal hunts as well, across four successive days in April of a given year.[25] Wealthy sponsors, including the emperor, often made free tickets available for the lower orders of society, which helped assure a large attendance and also allowed the benefactors to win favor with the general populace.

Such events held in the huge Colosseum in Rome could attract fifty thousand spectators. In numerous other cities, the venues were somewhat smaller, but the contests were still a prominent feature of civic life. The varied program could involve animal fights and wild animal hunts in the morning, the execution of criminals and fugitive slaves at lunchtime (which, for noncitizens, might be by crucifixion, fire, or wild animals), perhaps then comic presentations and athletic contests, and in the afternoon the main event: gladiator fights.

Fitting In and Being Different

To reiterate a point made early in this chapter, my purpose in citing the practice of infant exposure and violent public spectacles is not to repeat the Hollywood stereotypes of the Roman era as simply violent and morally debased.[26] Instead, I simply offer a couple of examples of practices that were prominent and widely condoned in that time but that were treated as objectionable by Christians. The key emphasis, again, is that on these and some other matters there were differences between early Christianity and aspects of the wider culture of the time. It would, however, be misleading to portray the relationship of early Christians and their cultural setting as simply consisting of differences, just as it would be erroneous to downplay differences. But we must take some care to characterize these differences. As we have seen in considering the practice of infant exposure, early Christian writers often expressed a view held also by at least some pagans. What made the early Christian stance in such matters different was not always the sentiment itself but that it was openly expressed and was intended to shape social behavior, certainly among Christians, and also even the wider public. This could result in social tensions, however, and even antagonism from non-Christians.

Especially in the first three centuries, therefore, when Christianity was regarded widely as a strange and dubious new religion, Christians had to avoid drawing the ire and accusations of non-Christians, while also advocating and living out their own beliefs and practices. This likely involved frequent, sometimes complicated, decisions about what Christians felt that they could or could not do, what social events they could take part in, and what roles in society they could accept, requiring them to negotiate their existence as best they could. The most frequent and painful tensions may have been not from governing officials but with family members, friends, and other associates.

In chapter 2, for example, we noted briefly Paul's directions to Corinthian Christians about what they could and could not do in response to invitations from their pagan families and/or acquaintances to participate in various social occasions. Recall that, on the one hand, Paul flatly opposed believers accepting any invitation to join in the open worship of the various pagan deities—for example, by taking part in meals held as part of a sacrificial rite in honor of a deity. For to take part in such meals, he insisted, would comprise "idolatry" (1 Corinthians 8:1-13; 10:14-22). On the other hand, Paul permitted his converts to purchase and eat whatever meat was available in the city market "without raising any question" as to whether the meat might have originated from some animal sacrifice to a pagan deity (10:23-26). Furthermore, he also allowed that believers could accept a dinner invitation from non-Christians and could eat whatever was put on the table, likewise "without raising any question" (10:27), provided that the host did not explicitly declare the meal a participation in a sacrificial feast to a pagan deity (10:28). If the host did pronounce the meal to be dedicated to a pagan god, then believers should not partake of the food.

We see in Paul's discussion just one example of how complex things could get for the former pagans who embraced Christian faith and, nevertheless, sought to remain part of their families and the wider social fabric of their city. Paul's summarizing statement with which he concludes the matter in 1 Corinthians shows the combination of religious commitment and a desire to avoid social conflict: "So, whether you eat or drink, or whatever you do, do everything for the glory of God. Give no offense to Jews or to Greeks or to the church of God" (1 Corinthians 10:31).

In a relevant Christian text mentioned in a previous chapter, likely composed sometime in the late second century, known as the *Epistle to Diognetus*, we have another witness to early Christians seeking both to be and to be taken as participants in their social/cultural context and yet also maintaining and articulating things that made them different.[27] The text addresses three main questions (*Diognetus* 1.1): What God do Christians believe in and worship? What is the nature of the strong affection that they have for one another? Why has "this new race" and way of life come into the world now and not before?

In addressing the first question, the author begins by defending Christians' refusal to worship the traditional deities, disdainfully referring to them as mere objects of stone, wood, bronze, or other material (2.1–10). Then, the author also distinguishes Christian practice from that which he ascribes to Jews, whom he portrays as misguided in making sacrificial offerings to God (3.1–4) and as also observing what the author characterizes as ridiculous customs about food, Sabbath, circumcision, fasting, and calendrical observances (4.1–6). Clearly, the author was unhesitating in declaring what he presents as a distinctive Christian stance about religious beliefs and worship.

But then, in what is for us the more important section, the author sketches how Christians are "not distinguished from the rest of humanity by country, language, or custom" (5.1). They follow "the local customs in dress and food and other aspects of life," and yet also they "demonstrate the remarkable and admittedly unusual character of their own citizenship" (5.4). Christians "participate in everything as citizens," but, he complains, they have to "endure everything as foreigners" (5.5). Furthermore, Christians "marry like everyone else, and have children, but they do not expose their offspring" (5.6), here again reflecting the Christian rejection of infant abandonment. Also, obviously responding to rumors of Christian orgiastic practices, the author memorably states, "They share their food but not their wives" (5.7).[28]

The text goes on then to assert that Christians certainly live on earth, "but their citizenship is in heaven." This phrase likens Christians to people who are citizens of one country but live in another. Christians, the author insists, obey the laws of the lands in which they live. Indeed, he claims that they exceed the demands of laws in their private lives (5.9–10), apparently meaning that they live by higher standards than the earthly laws require. Though dishonored, slandered, insulted, and cursed, they bless in return and offer respect (5.14–15). When unjustly punished, "they rejoice as though brought to life" (5.15), perhaps alluding to Christians martyred for their faith.

Then, in an extended analogy, the author compares the relationship of Christians to the world as like "what the soul is to the body" (6.1–10). Christians are dispersed "throughout the cities of the world," dwelling in the world, but they are "not of the world." Though hated and wronged, "Christians love those who hate them." Moreover, he declares, just as the soul becomes all the stronger when denied food and drink, for instance, through fasting, "so Christians when punished daily increase more and more," likely meaning an increase in numbers, a claim echoed also in 7.8.

Following this, the author then returns to matters of religious belief, laying out some basics of the Christian gospel. He declares that the one true God who created all things sent his Son "as a human to humans," to save them "by persuasion, not compulsion" (7.4). In God's "beloved child," God and God's redemptive purpose are now fully revealed (8.1–11).[29] This Son became "a ransom for us," for only "in the Son of God alone" can sinners find themselves put right with God (8.4–5). Given this demonstration of God's love for humanity, the author urges, what response can anyone make other than to love God in return and also to imitate God in loving others, sharing their burden, seeking to benefit those who may be worse off, and providing for their needs (10.1–6). The one who understands this, he declares, will not ridicule Christians but instead admire those who suffer for their faith, and "will condemn the deceit and error of the world" (10.7).

This text is addressed to a "most excellent Diognetus," phrasing that posits the named person in an elite position; but it is not clear whether he was an actual or a fictional/symbolic figure.[30] In any case, although this writing is cast as an explanation and defense of Christianity for outsiders, the preservation of the text is certainly down to it being read and circulated among Christians.[31] Such "apologetic" works, for whatever religious cause, were, and are still, often intended as much or more to bolster adherents in their commitment. In the case of this particular text, therefore, the claims about Christian beliefs and behavior addressed to this Diognetus are also likely indicative of what was advocated and urged within various Christian circles of the time. And what the text shows is an effort by Christians to remain a productive influence in their respective cultural settings while also maintaining their own distinguishing beliefs and behavior.

A "Religion" with Behavioral Demands

In chapter 2, I noted the view that early Christianity can seem more like a philosophy than a religion, if assessed by the features that typically marked what we could call "religion" and philosophy in the Roman period. I also indicated why I think that it is valid, nevertheless, to refer to early Christianity as a "religious" movement, although, to be sure, of a different kind.[32] One of the ways it was different was in the early Christian emphasis given to shaping the everyday behavior of believers, which is the focus in this chapter. Recall that what we mean by "religion" in the Roman period typically focused on ritual actions and responsibilities involving sacrifice, altars, shrines, and observances of appropriate days of the month or year. Roman-era religion did not typically have much to say on what we might term "ethics," "dos and don'ts," which I will refer to here more simply as "behavior" or "conduct."[33]

To see this unusually firm early Christian linkage of "religion" with everyday behavior, note how much space is given to teaching and exhortation in early Christian writings about how to live, right from the earliest extant texts onward. Paul's letters, for example, reflect this. A major part, and arguably most, of each of his letters is typically given over to teaching and exhortation about Christian behavior. Granted, these exhortations are usually and explicitly grounded in theological convictions and claims, and the strong theological bases for behavior in early Christian texts comprise a distinguishing feature in comparison with most philosophical texts of the day. With occasional exceptions such as our old friend Musonius Rufus and his student Epictetus, philosophical writers of the time tended simply to present virtues of self-control and the avoidance of social shame as main motivations for the behavior they advocated.

Consider again as an illustration of this theologically based behavioral emphasis Paul's letter known as 1 Thessalonians. Paul begins the letter by congratulating the Thessalonian believers for their enthusiastic embrace of his gospel message (1:1-10) and by recounting his own conduct in his mission to them and others (2:1-16). Then he expresses his strong but frustrated wish to visit them in person again (2:17–3:13). After this, Paul turns to exhortations about how believers "ought to live and to please God," beginning with a reminder of the "instructions we gave you through the Lord Jesus" (4:1-2), alluding to teaching that he had delivered when he established the Thessalonian church.

Paul commences this part of the letter by reminding the Thessalonian believers that God's will for them is "sanctification" (or "holiness"; Greek: *hagiasmos*), here specifically meaning "that you abstain from fornication [*porneia*]," each of them (particularly the males) exhorted to order their sexuality "in holiness and honor," and not "like the Gentiles who do not know God" (4:4-5).[34] The concern here is clearly not an ascetic avoidance of sex altogether but instead the avoidance of what he labels *porneia*, which seems to designate illicit sex. We will see this concern expressed also in passages in 1 Corinthians, which we will consider shortly. Here in 1 Thessalonians, Paul specifically urges the (male) believers to avoid adultery—that is, sex with another man's spouse—which Paul refers to here as wronging their brothers (4:6), for otherwise they set themselves against God (4:7-8).

It is interesting to note that in pagan Greek texts, the term *porneia* simply designates prostitution, the sale of women's bodies for sex. But as a recent study of the usage of the term shows, in Jewish and then Christian texts, *porneia* designated "a wide subset of extramarital sexual activity" that was tolerated in the broader Roman-era culture. Specifically, this included sex with prostitutes, courtesans, and slaves, and, of course, many/most prostitutes of the time were also slaves.[35] Paul's usage here in 1 Thessalonians and in some other texts reflects this broader meaning, which could include "adultery" (having sex with another man's wife) but extended to other forms of illicit sex as well.[36]

Of course, the male-oriented nature of Paul's exhortation will be somewhat embarrassing for more gender-egalitarian readers today. For instance, consider again Paul's direction to men in 1 Thessalonians 4:6 not to wrong a Christian brother by having sex with his wife. This obviously reflects the ancient emphasis that adultery was a violation of the rights of a husband. Similarly curious sounding to moderns is Paul's use of the Greek term *skeuos* ("vessel, utensil, tool"), likely as a metaphor referring to a man's own wife, in the command that "each of you [men] know how to keep his *skeuos* in holiness and honor" (4:4).[37] This modern embarrassment with these gendered exhortations may be reflected in the NRSV translation of verse 4, which renders the exhortation as "that each of you know how to control his own *body* in holiness and honor" and renders Paul's statement in 4:6 as "that no one wrong or exploit a brother *or sister* in this matter."

But Paul's male-oriented rhetoric may well have been intentional, and even more it may have been particularly appropriate in his context. In the larger Roman-era cultural setting of this letter, the double standard in sexual practice was fully in force. Wives were generally held to one standard of behavior, strict marital chastity, and husbands to quite another one. Men, husbands included, were allowed considerably more freedom to have sex with other women, particularly women deemed not to possess status and honor. So, although sex with the wives of other men or with freeborn virgins was not approved, other kinds of sexual activities were openly tolerated, and even encouraged. These included sex with courtesans and prostitutes and also sex with boys, typically slave boys. An oft-cited statement of the fourth-century BC Greek orator Demosthenes, but indicative of later attitudes as well, is illustrative of the sexual latitude allowed to men: "We [men!] have *heterai* [concubines, courtesans] for pleasure, female slaves for our daily care [a sexual euphemism] and wives to give us legitimate children and to be guardians of our households."[38] Quite simply, in the ethical conventions of Roman society, a married woman's sexual behavior was a matter of great concern, but men, single or married, were allowed great latitude in their sexual activities.[39]

Paul's male-oriented exhortations were, thus, very likely intended specifically to project a very different standard of male sexual behavior in particular among Christian husbands. This involved the unusual move of positing the same standards of "holiness and honor" that were expected of women, especially wives, in that culture more generally, thereby challenging the dominant "double standard" morality of the time. Essentially, in 1 Thessalonians, Paul commands husbands to confine their sexual relations to their own wives, treating them honorably, which probably means, or at least includes, not using their wives simply to have children while then enjoying sex with other women.[40] The term translated here "holiness/sanctification" typically described something, such as an altar or other cultic object, or someone such as a priest, as separated from ordinary use and reserved for the service of a deity. In this context, it is Christian men in particular whom Paul summons to act out this attribute in their sexual life, not by refraining from sex altogether, but by sexual behavior that shows that they are obedient to their God and set apart in this matter for God's service.

After this brief passage dealing with sexual behavior, Paul continues his exhortation to take in other matters. He commends more generally fraternal love among his converts (Greek: *philadelphia*) and congratulates the Thessalonian believers that this also is something that they have already learned and, indeed, commendably practiced (4:9-10). Then, he follows this by urging them to "aspire to live quietly, mind your own affairs, and work with your hands, as we directed you, so that you may behave properly toward outsiders and be dependent on no one" (4:11-12).

Thus far in these exhortations, Paul reaffirms things that he says he had taught during his initial ministry when he founded the church in Thessalonica. It is not entirely clear whether there were also problems in the church—such as specific sexual shenanigans or interpersonal frictions—that may have prompted these particular statements, or only some of them, or whether Paul simply sought here to illustrate the distinctive "in-group" behavior expected of Christians. In any case, Paul was clearly aiming to reinforce a sense of particular Christian group identity, his rhetoric in this letter positing an "us and them" differentiation between the collective behavioral obligations of believers and the contrasting behavior that Paul imputed to those who were not believers.[41]

Then, in the immediately ensuing paragraphs of 1 Thessalonians, Paul turns to what more clearly appear to be questions that had arisen in the Thessalonian church about the future coming/return of Jesus (4:13–5:11). Specifically, there seems to have been some anxiety about what might be the fate of "those who have died," likely meaning fellow believers, while awaiting Jesus' return from heaven (Greek: *parousia*), and so Paul addresses this concern first (4:13-18).[42] He assures the Thessalonians that the Christian dead will not be left out. Instead, together with those alive at the time of Jesus' return, they "will be with the Lord

forever"; and he urges the Thessalonian converts to "encour-
age one another with these words." Again, Paul's aim here is
not simply doctrinal clarity but also reinforcement of social and
collective behavior, including in this case mutual encouragement and steadfastness in the distinctive hope that he projects
for believers.

This concern for collective behavioral effort is even more
transparent in the next section of the letter, where Paul engages
the question of when Jesus will return (5:1-11). His answer to
the chronological question is essentially to dismiss it. The "day
of the Lord will come like a thief in the night," with no advance
notice and no way of calculating it. So, instead of worrying about
when it will happen, believers are to live as those who know that
the event will happen, fully awake to the consequences of Jesus'
return, not "drunken" or "asleep." In a series of metaphors drawn
from the accoutrements of the soldier, Paul also urges believers to
don "the breastplate of faith and love, and for a helmet the hope of
salvation," and he reiterates his plea that believers should encour-
age and "build up" one another (5:11).

Then, in the following lines (5:12-28), Paul urges respect
for "those who labor among you, and have charge of you in the
Lord," and he gives a string of exhortations to be at peace with
one another; to give mutual help; to avoid retribution; to rejoice,
pray, and be thankful; and to exercise critical judgment with
regard to oracles of Christian prophets. Paul ends the letter with
his prayer-wish for the Thessalonian believers that they be kept
"sound and blameless," an appeal for their prayers for him, and the
commands that they greet one another with "a holy kiss" and that
this letter be read out to the whole church.

We could trawl through Paul's other letters and then on into
many other early Christian texts and find a similarly strong stress
on the behavioral consequences of Christian faith. The specifics
of the activities exhorted vary from one Christian text to another,
often in response to certain issues or problems that prompted
the composition of the various texts. But there is also a broadly

consistent body of behavior that they promote, and all the texts reflect the view that participation in Christian faith entails a significant commitment to the collective effort that is required of believers.

Sex and Marriage in 1 Corinthians

Before we move on to other matters, I want to return to the topic of sex and marriage, because they formed such a large area of concern in early Christian texts. We noted earlier Paul's brief exhortations against *porneia* and urging sexual "holiness" in 1 Thessalonians, and I now turn to a couple of passages in 1 Corinthians, where Paul also discusses this and related matters. This letter is Paul's response to communications from the Corinthian believers in which they had posed to him a string of problems and issues, most of which I will not try to address here. I confine myself to how Paul engages Corinthian questions concerning sex and marriage in a couple of key passages. Neither these questions nor Paul's responses in 1 Corinthians amount to a full-scale view of either topic, however, for Paul focuses on the specific issues posed to him. But his responses are interesting, nonetheless, and are at least further illustrations of how, at this very early point in the emergence of what became Christianity, he sought to shape the relevant behavior in the churches that he founded.

The first reference to issues of sexual activity in 1 Corinthians comes in 5:1-13. Here Paul addresses a situation that he calls *porneia*—in this case, a situation so wrong that, he says, even among pagans it is not approved. A man in the church was in a sexual relationship with "his father's wife" (5:1-2). This interesting expression, which seems to draw on prohibitions about sex with near kin in some Old Testament texts, may mean that the woman was actually the man's stepmother. If so, she quite possibly could have been much younger than his father and closer to the man's own age, making a sexual relationship/attraction more plausible.[43] In any case, Paul appears to portray the rest of the church, or at least a goodly portion of it, as fully tolerant of this situation. Paul, however, orders the Corinthian believers to meet as a church and "hand this man over to Satan for the destruction of his flesh, so that his spirit might be saved on the day of the Lord" (v. 5). We cannot linger over the various specifics of this passage, nor can we consider here Paul's reasons for his emphatic condemnation of the sexual relationship in question.[44] The point I emphasize is that Paul's treatment of matters in this passage clearly makes "moral" behavior, specifically in this case proper sexual behavior, an integral part of being a member of the church. Believers are expected to live by certain standards, and the church collectively is to be involved in disciplining believers who violate those standards.

Then, in 1 Corinthians 6:9-20, after a set of warnings about various kinds of activities that he declares are incompatible with "inheriting" the kingdom of God (6:9-11), Paul again refers to *porneia* in responding to what commentators commonly see as another of the issues on the boil in the Corinthian church: Did it matter if Christian men had sex with prostitutes? As noted already, men having sex with prostitutes was not a particular problem in the wider Roman attitudes of the day, and it appears that some of the Corinthian believers continued to treat such sexual activity as compatible with their new status as members of the church.[45] Were they simply insufficiently converted from their pagan attitudes, or perhaps had they even developed some notion that allowed them to think that sex with prostitutes was not incompatible with their Christian faith? For example, perhaps they thought that their inner/true spiritual sanctity as Christians was unaffected by what they did with their bodies.[46]

Whatever the case, it is now widely agreed that at points in this passage Paul cites slogans that were bandied about by those believers who approved of sex with prostitutes, such as "all things are permitted" (6:12) and "foods for the belly and the belly for foods" (6:13).[47] Modern translations such as the NRSV typically indicate that these are slogans of people in the Corinthian church, and not Paul's own statements, by putting them inside quotation marks. A major reason for seeing these statements as expressing the views of those whom Paul corrects is that, in each instance where he cites one of these slogans, Paul then takes issue with it. So, in 6:12, he follows the slogan "all things are permitted" by responding, "but not everything is beneficial"; and, after repeating the slogan again, he urges, "but I will not be dominated by anything." Likewise, after quoting the slogan in 6:13 about "foods for the belly, etc.," he responds with this correction: "But the body is meant not for fornication [*porneia*] but for the Lord, and the Lord for the body."

Indeed, all through 1 Corinthians 6:12-20 Paul's emphasis is very much on believers' *bodies* as the crucial venue, so to speak, in which they are to live out their faith commitment.[48] "Your bodies are members of Christ," he declares, and so believers must not have illicit sex—with a prostitute, for example (6:15). Indeed, in an astonishing move, citing a statement from the Genesis creation account—"the two shall be one flesh," which was typically seen as referring to the physical/bodily union effected in marriage— Paul applies this biblical statement to having sex with a prostitute! Even such casual sex, he says, is a *bodily* union, which is precisely what makes it all the more seriously wrong. He proceeds then to emphasize further the bodily nature of the sin of *porneia* (6:18) for believers, declaring that their bodies are individually "a temple of the Holy Spirit within you, which you have from God." Paul then ends this passage by urging, "You were bought with a price [alluding to Jesus' sacrificial death for them]; therefore glorify God *in your body*" (6:19-20).

As we noted earlier, *porneia* is not the term that Roman-era men used typically for their extramarital sexual activity.[49] Instead, they used the term specifically to refer to what prostitutes did, "prostitution." Paul's usage of the term, however, reflects ancient Jewish, and then Christian, usage, in which the term designated a wider variety of *male* sexual activities that appear to have been tolerated commonly in the wider society, including men having sex with prostitutes, courtesans, and slaves. By referring to these activities collectively as *porneia*, Paul labels them as sinful and completely off-limits for believers. In doing so, I repeat, he asserted and reflected a stance diametrically opposed to the prevailing attitudes of the time, and he intended to distinguish sharply what should be the sexual behavior of believers, particularly males.

But Paul did not simply forbid such practices. He presents in this passage a distinctive new basis for doing so and for framing appropriate sexual activity for believers. Recall that, in 1 Thessalonians, Paul simply made sexual behavior something for which believers are answerable to God. But in 1 Corinthians 6, Paul cites the bodily resurrection of Jesus as an emphatic affirmation of embodiment and so underlines the importance of what believers do with/in their bodies. As Paul makes clear a bit later in 1 Corinthians 15, Jesus' resurrection is the pattern and basis for the future resurrection of believers, which is their ultimate hope. So, in keeping with his understanding of Jesus' resurrection, Paul held that the future resurrection of believers will mean the transformation of their mortal body into a new and glorious one, to be sure, but nevertheless an embodiment, not some other kind of bare "spirit" existence.[50]

In Paul's thought, this means that, even now, what believers do with their mortal body has significance, and so he insists that, precisely because it is unquestionably a bodily activity, sexual behavior is a crucial matter. The bottom line in the passage is that the diverse sexual activities covered in Paul's use of *porneia*, though they may have been approved in the wider culture and even among some Corinthian believers, are to be completely off-limits for them.

In still another passage in 1 Corinthians (7:1-16), Paul addresses what appear to be several more questions posed to him, these about marriage, and here also his response is very interesting.[51] It is now widely recognized that Paul opens the topic by quoting what again appears to have been a slogan, this one expressing the sexual asceticism of some in the Corinthian church: "It is well for a man not to touch [sexually] a woman" (7:1). Then, as with the slogans he cites in 6:12–13, Paul immediately posits his own view over against this one in 7:2–5. The sentiment expressed in the slogan that Paul corrects here seems to have been that married Christians should refrain from sexual relations, even, or perhaps especially, with their Christian spouses. So, as curious as it may seem to find both views held in the one church, Paul's discussion in 6:12–20 corrects some who considered it acceptable to have sex with prostitutes, and then in 7:1–40 he engages others who advocated a sexual asceticism, at least so far as conjugal sex is concerned.[52]

Paul's initial response in 7:1–5 is to counter the slogan with a robust affirmation of conjugal sex in marriage, and the specifics of his response are worth noting. First, he posits that marriage, and marital sex in particular, can help believers to avoid temptations to various illicit sexual activities, which are designated here with the plural, *porneias*. That was not a novel idea, as there are similar sentiments about marital sex as helping to avoid temptations to illicit sex expressed in some other ancient texts, particularly Jewish ones (e.g., Proverbs 5:15–23; Tobit 4:12). More typically, however, in these other texts the exhortation is directed to men only and is intended solely to shape their sexual behavior. But in 1 Corinthians 7:1–2, Paul implicitly makes marriage a hedge against illicit sex *for wives as well as husbands*: "Let each man have his own wife; *and let each woman have her own husband*."[53] He reinforces this in what follows, urging both husbands and wives to respect the conjugal rights of their respective spouses (v. 3), and Paul declares that, just as the husband has a valid claim on the wife's body, meaning sexually, so the wife has an equally valid sexual claim on her husband (v. 4).[54]

Then, going still farther, Paul urges spouses not to "deprive" their marital partners (v. 5), here meaning that they are not to abstain unilaterally from conjugal sex. The term "deprive" (*apostereō*) is a strong way of referring to the matter, as it generally refers to stealing or defrauding someone (as in 1 Corinthians 6:7; Mark 10:19). Paul goes on to stipulate that any abstaining from conjugal sex must be only by mutual consent and only for a limited time that is to be dedicated mutually to prayer. Thereafter, the couple should return to regular marital sex with each other, and Paul again notes that otherwise there is the danger of temptation toward illicit sexual activities.[55]

The particular points to underscore in these verses are that Paul rather strongly affirms marital sex, rejecting what appears to be the ascetic attitude of some in the Corinthian church; that he also posits marriage as involving sexual rights for *both* partners (not only men); and that he affirms marital sex as a hedge against temptations to other sexual activities (*porneias*). Further, in addition to the mutuality in his discussion here, wives as well as husbands acknowledged as having sexual rights and demands on each other, Paul firmly confines the sexual activity of married Christians to their own spouses. The plural *porneias* clearly designates a breadth of sexual activities with anyone other than one's spouse that are, again, forbidden. In light of the Jewish and early Christian usage of *porneia* noted earlier, the plural form of the term makes it particularly likely that it includes here not only sex with prostitutes but also other extramarital sex—for example, with courtesans or slaves.[56]

I emphasize again that, more typically in the Roman era, sex with prostitutes and courtesans, and with young boys as well, was not only tolerated but even affirmed *as a hedge against adultery*—specifically, sex with another man's wife or with a freeborn virgin. It is noteworthy, therefore, that Paul, with some other ancient Jewish voices, condemns a far wider spectrum of sexual activities, labelling them all as *porneias*, and that he posits marital sex as *a hedge against these various temptations to extramarital sex of any kind*.[57] In short, Paul reflects a broadening of prohibited sex well beyond adultery. This alone represented a major shift in comparison to the attitudes of the larger Roman world.

"Husband of One Wife"

For another illustration that early Christianity worked against the "double standard" so prominent in Roman-era attitudes toward sexual behavior, note the curious requirement in 1 Timothy 3:2 that a "bishop/overseer" (Greek: *episkopos*) must be "husband of one wife." This requirement is also laid upon those who served as "deacons" (Greek: *diakonoi*) in verse 12. Commentaries regularly note that this in some way resembles a moral trope familiar in the ancient setting, specifically the praise of a woman who remained married to one man, the "wife of one husband." Indeed, both in Latin and in Greek there was even a special term of praise applied to such a woman: *univira* (Latin), or *monandros* (Greek), indicative of how much this marital loyalty was prized and thematized in a male-dominated culture in which divorce was common.[58] These terms often appear in burial tributes to women, such as grave inscriptions. Actually, in 1 Timothy 5:9, this trope is more directly reflected, where one of the attributes to be required of a widow who is enrolled on the list of those to be supported by the church is that she be "wife of one husband/man."

But the noteworthy point typically missed is that in 1 Timothy this sexual loyalty is required of *men* as well as women, at least men who are to serve as leaders and so, in some sense, as behavioral models in churches of the time. It bears remarking that in Latin and Greek there was no term equivalent to *univira* or *monandros* that applied to men, which tells us something! In the culture of the day, loyalty to one spouse was idealized specifically as female behavior. So, in making this behavioral requirement of male leaders, the author of 1 Timothy had no choice but to compose a Greek phrase for the purpose: *mias gynaikos andra* (literally, "husband of one wife/woman," or "a one-woman man/husband").[59] Here again, we see that the decisive step taken in early Christian sexual teaching was to bring males under the same sort of behavioral requirements that in the larger cultural setting were expected of "honorable" women. In the matter of marital fidelity and chastity, it seems that for early Christians what was good for the goose was also thought good for the gander![60]

Sexual Ab/use of Children

I consider now a related and still more sensitive topic. Especially in recent years, the sexual abuse of children has become a widely noted and justifiably condemned vice, and, perhaps consequently, it has also received some increased recent attention by scholars of the ancient world.[61] We must remember, however, that in the Roman era the sexual use of children, including young adolescents and also younger children, was widely tolerated and even celebrated lyrically by some pagan writers of the day, such as Juvenal, Petronius, Horace, Strato, Lucian, and Philostratus.[62] Indeed, there was a whole vocabulary in Greek referring to the practice, including *paiderastēs* (a lover of boys/children), the verb *paiderasteō* (to engage in sex with boys/children), and *paiderastia* (the practice itself). Indicative of the widely shared acceptance of sex with children, these words typically carried no connotation of disapproval but were simply descriptive.[63] In an important study, however, John Martens has shown that early Christian condemnation of the practice even led to what appears to be a distinctive Christian terminology coined to refer to it. It appears that Christians invented the verb *paidophthoreō* and the noun *paidophthoros* used in their condemnations of the practice, and Martens persuasively contends that these terms should be rendered respectively as "to sexually abuse/corrupt children" and "one who sexually abuses/corrupts children."[64] These terms reflect an emphatic Christian rejection of "pederasty," relabeling it as "child corruption/abuse," and relabeling a man who has sex with children as not a "(sexual) lover of children" (*paiderastēs*) but "a destroyer/corrupter/seducer of children" (*paidophthoros*).[65]

The earliest instances of this new verb, "to corrupt children," are in two Christian texts of the second century— the *Didache* and the *Epistle of Barnabas*—and in both texts the term appears in a list of behavioral prohibitions.[66] In *Didache* 2.2, the command "you shall not corrupt [sexually] children" (Greek: *ou paidophthorēseis*) appears right after prohibitions against murder and adultery, and it is immediately followed by further prohibitions against being "sexually immoral" (*ou porneuseis*), stealing, practicing magic and sorcery, and abortion and infanticide (infant exposure), and then by a further list of other vices to avoid (2.3–7). In the *Epistle of Barnabas* 19.4, the term appears in a list of prohibitions introduced as "the Lord's commandments," the "Lord" here likely referring to Jesus, and it is part of a trio of prohibitions against various forms of sexual promiscuity (*ou porneuseis*) and adultery as well. Clearly, the "corrupting" of children in the word used in these early Christian texts is the sexual exploitation/abuse of them.

Given the appearance of these distinctive terms in both of these texts, neither of which seems dependent on the other, it is likely that these words originated earlier still in Christian discourse. Likely, they were framed as part of the effort to distinguish Christian behavior from practices of the wider culture and also to warn against these practices among Christians.[67] Again, we see the effort to form a distinguishable group identity expressed in a strong and distinctive behavioral commitment.

These distinctive terms that were developed to express condemnation of child sexual abuse appear also in the texts of other early Christian writers such as Justin, Tatian, Theophilus, Clement of Alexandria, and Origen, all from the second and third centuries AD. Sometimes they serve to illustrate "Gentile/pagan" depravity, and they form "a part of the apologetical battery thrown up at the Greco-Roman opponents of the Christians."[68] But the earliest uses in *Didache* and *Barnabas* show that the originating purposes in relabeling "pederasty" as "child (sexual) corruption" included also the concern to discourage the practice among Christians. In short, the terms are not simply ancient Christian propaganda against outsiders. They also reflect a collective effort to shape Christian behavior over against the practices tolerated in the wider culture, an effort that even included innovations in the vocabulary of sexual behavior.

Pagan Philosophical Voices

As noted briefly earlier, there were also "pagan" figures who, at least in some matters, advocated behavior similar to what was urged in early Christian circles and who likewise sometimes invoked the gods in their exhortations as a basis for them. For example, Musonius Rufus urged that men should be held to similar standards of virtue as women in abstaining from adultery and avoiding "gluttony, drunkenness, and other related vices" (4.15). Indeed, he contended that, for men and women, sex should be confined to marriage and then only for procreation (12.1–10), insisting that sex for pleasure was wrong, even in marriage. In this latter emphasis, he clearly seems to differ from Paul's view of marital sex, although some later Christian writers, such as Clement of Alexandria, took a position closer to Musonius.[69] As part of his strict stance about sex, Musonius exhorted specifically against husbands having sexual relations with a courtesan (*hetaira*) or their own female slaves.[70]

Note, however, that Musonius' reasons for his stance were that sexual desires and indulgences (Greek: *aphrodisioi*) demonstrate a lack of self-control (*sōphrosyne*) and so are shameful for the man/husband. This was an effective point in the Roman culture in which honor and shame were so important. But Musonius makes no reference to any obligation that a husband might have to his wife in these matters, nor did Musonius express any concern about how female slaves might feel about being used for sex. As also noted earlier, however, Musonius sometimes posited religious concerns as bases for his exhortations. Recall, for example, that he condemned abortion and infant abandonment as "sins against the gods . . . and against Zeus."[71]

But I think that there are some crucial differences between what we see in early Christian texts and what we find in these philosophers.[72] Commendable though their exhortations are, and in some matters advocating behavior similar to that urged in early Christian texts, there is a difference, especially in social impact.

Musonius and his like essentially directed their efforts at a few dedicated students who were willing to commit themselves to the lengthy and rigorous demands of training to live by the principles of their teachers of philosophy. There is no indication that Musonius or other philosophers of the time invested in serious efforts to effect changes in the behavior of wider circles of people at large. It would be an exaggeration to portray Musonius and other Roman moralists, therefore, as forerunners who prepared the way for Christians in behavioral teaching. In some modern scholarly portrayals of sexual attitudes and practices of the Roman era, "the gloomy tribe of Stoic brethren have been allotted too much say."[73]

By contrast, the early Christian texts reflect a rather strong effort to promote widely in circles of believers a collective commitment to the strict behavior that these texts advocate. That commitment was laid upon adherents immediately upon their baptism, whatever may have been their consistency in observing it thereafter. These texts, therefore, which come from various locations and across the early Christian centuries, represent a historically noteworthy social project. It was probably novel in its time, comprising the formation of *groups* of believers translocally in the *collective* observance of certain behavior that was held to be *essential* to their distinctive group identity. Even though the total numbers involved were initially small, there is an evident seriousness and ambition to promote this project reflected in the Christian texts. And this effort obviously succeeded measurably, both in terms of the growth in numbers of Christian adherents and, apparently, in general effects on their behavior.

Furthermore, early Christian discourse proffered a different basis for the behavioral aims advocated. As noted already, Musonius and philosophical traditions in general appealed to the individual's sense of honor and the avoidance of personal shame, shame in the eyes of others and so also internally, as the basis for the demands of living by their principles. But early Christian texts typically invoked divine commands, appealed to the divine calling laid upon believers to exhibit holiness, and, notably, invoked the mutual responsibility of believers to one another in their behavioral efforts, reflecting an emphasis placed on the formation of a *group ethos*. That is, early Christian teaching made everyday behavior central in one's religious responsibility to the Christian God and thereby replaced social shame with a theological basis for life. In place of worries about possible embarrassment socially, Christians posited the judgment of God. The difference was profound. Indeed, it is fair to judge that the impact of the distinctive stance of early Christian teaching involved "a transformation in the deep logic of sexual morality."[74]

Furthermore, I repeat that believers were to take on the demands of Christian behavior immediately upon their initiation as Christians, with the promise given that they could be enabled for this behavioral effort by divine gift. In the language of early Christian texts, God's Spirit was at hand to infuse them with a new moral resolve and energy. To cite one important text, in his letter to the Romans (6:1-23), Paul urges believers to make a thoroughgoing behavioral commitment—indeed, to undergo a transformation—regarding themselves in a radical manner as "dead to sin and alive to God in Christ Jesus," no longer allowing sin to exercise dominion over their bodies (6:11-12). And a bit later in Romans (8:1-17), Paul emphasizes the empowerment of God's Spirit in believers for this endeavor. Whatever you make of this notion of divine empowerment, it is at least a major distinctive of earliest Christian discourse about the behavioral requirements incumbent upon believers and the basis for the requisite effort to observe those requirements.

Some other early Christian texts, however, simply set forth the behavior required of believers as divine demands, as in the second-century writing known as the *Didache*. The first major section (1.1–4.14) lays out "the way of life" for believers in a long series of exhortations issued as having divine authority and organized under the two capital commands to love God and to love one's neighbor (2.1). But, in fact, although stated as a religious obligation, this whole body of exhortation concerns social and interpersonal behavior. For example, believers are to love even those who hate them, to refuse retaliation, and to show generosity to all. They must not murder, commit adultery, or pederasty, or theft, or engage in magic or infant abandonment, or covet another's possessions, or commit perjury, or give false testimony. They should practice humility and associate with the humble, and not cause divisions but promote peace among their fellow believers. There are even commands to discipline and teach one's children "the fear of God," and against giving orders to one's slaves "who hope in the same God as you" in anger "lest they cease to fear the God who is over you both" (4.9–10). Also, illustrative of the corporate and collective nature of the behavior exhorted, believers are to confess their transgressions to fellow believers in church (4.14), so that their prayers may be offered with a clear conscience.

Recall from chapter 1 of this book Galen's grudging admiration of the behavior of Christians, particularly because he conceded that Christians included many from subelite social levels and those who were not trained in philosophy.[75] Galen's comments reflect the point I am making. Early Christianity was not always distinctive in the specific behavior advocated. Instead, in historical terms I think that the key distinctive was that Christianity represented a strong effort to promote this behavior in all adherents, of all social levels, among men as well as women, and as characteristic of and defining Christians as a particular kind of religious group. That is, early Christianity represented *a distinctive kind of social effort* to reshape behavior.

Religion and Morality in a Pagan Religious Group

In taking account of the Roman-era context of earliest Christianity, noting shared and distinctive features, I point to a religious cult group in Philadelphia, Lydia (Philadelphia Neokaisareia, in modern-day Turkey), from which we have an interesting inscription dated to the late second or early first century BC.[76] The inscription refers to a revelatory dream/vision of the house-holder, a certain Dionysius, in which Zeus ordered him to set out the ordinances in the inscription. These include the setting up of altars to a number of gods, all of them familiar Greek deities except for Agdistis, a local one. The shrine was to be presided over by Zeus Eumenes and Hestia, and the ordinances also required the performance of purifications and cleansings and other rites "in accordance with ancestral custom." Monthly and annual sacrifices to these various gods were to be conducted accordingly.

Among its features that have made for interesting comparisons with early Christian groups, however, are the behavioral requirements set out in the inscription for those who are members of this cult group. These requirements specify that both men and women, free persons and slaves, are to take oaths to the gods that they will not practice deceit or use poisons, harmful spells, love potions, abortion drugs, contraceptives, or "any other thing fatal to children," nor are they to conspire with anyone else in the use of such things. Further, apart from his own wife, the free man is not to have sexual relations with any married woman, whether she be free or slave, "nor with a boy nor a virgin girl."

There is then a more extended set of stipulations about the behavior of free women members of the group. A free woman is to be chaste, having sexual relations solely with her own husband. Any wife who violates this rule is thereby rendered impure and so unworthy to take part in the cult sacrifices and related rites. The gods will inflict powerful curses upon her, and will hate and punish any who transgress the behavior set out in the inscription, but will be kind and generous to those who observe its requirements.

There are certain obvious and interesting points of similarity to some features of early Christian groups. The Philadelphia cult was a household, comprising its free persons and slaves, adults and children, similar to the household-based nature of many early Christian churches, especially in the first century. Also,

the behavioral requirements of the Philadelphia cult are strin-
gent, similar in some respects to the requirements laid upon early
Christians. In particular, note a similar emphasis on regulating
sexual conduct.

But the similarities may have been exaggerated in some
scholarly discussion of the inscription.[77] For example, the inclusion of free persons and slaves, men and women alike, does not
indicate some new universalism or democratization in religion
but simply reflects the variety of people who made up this ancient
well-to-do household, all of the members expected to take part
in its cultic activities, as led by the master of the household. Nor
does the inscription reflect some sort of radical egalitarian innovation. In the typical pagan house cult of the time, the roles of
men and women were strictly differentiated. For example, only
men performed the sacrifices in such household cults, and slaves
took part, but they served in the cult as slaves. There is no indication in the inscription that this cult operated any differently.

As for the behavioral strictures set out in the inscription, their
very specificity invites questions about what is omitted. For example, the inscription specifically forbids a man to have sex with a
married woman or with boys or a virgin girl, which leaves one
to wonder why there is no mention of prostitutes or courtesans.
This suggests that the particular concern is actually about dis-
ruptive sexual activities *among the members of the household*, and so
the inscription does not address what sexual activities a man may
engage in with other kinds of individuals outside the household.

Also, we should note that the Philadelphia inscription represents one local, household-based, cult group. It was not an
expression of a larger translocal religious movement. Indeed,
there is no indication that Dionysius even sought to recruit followers from beyond his own household. By contrast, early Christianity appears to have been energetic in declaring its beliefs and
practices and aggressive in seeking converts in the larger society,
largely through the social networks of Christians. Further, the
initially small early Christian circles seem to have thought of and

conducted themselves very much as linked to believers in other locations and very much as part of a translocal movement.[78] So, if we consider closely the Philadelphia household cult as to its likely social and historical intentions and impact, there is no real comparison.

The Social Location of Early Christian Behavioral Exhortation

In assessing early Christian exhortation about behavior in the Roman-era context, it is important to take account of a prime social location in which that exhortation was typically communicated, particularly in the first two centuries: the house-based church gathering.[79] For my purpose, the physical structure of the house is not as important as the nature of the groups that comprised these early gatherings. In some cases, similar to the pagan house cult in Philadelphia, they were likely all or mainly members of a given household, which could include family members of two or more generations, plus any household slaves. In other cases, however, the Christian circles likely also included individuals from other households as well. If we survey the social and economic strata represented in earliest Christian churches, it now seems clear that there was a certain diversity that included both slaves and free persons, and people of varying economic and social levels as well, although Christians from the highest social levels were apparently few until perhaps sometime in the late second and/or third centuries.[80]

The first observation to make about the setting of early Christian behavioral exhortation is that it was typically given and heard in such close *groups*, and by all members of the group. We have noted how much of early Christian exhortation is about what we might call interpersonal relations—and comparatively little to do with ritual or cultic practices. There was particularly a concern with how believers were to treat one another. For example, Paul's lists of "works of the flesh" and the contrasting "fruit of the Spirit" in Galatians 5:16-26 are, respectively, various forms of bad and good interpersonal behavior. The corporate delivery and affirmation of such exhortations by believers had the effect of enforcing these demands as constitutive for the Christian circle of which they were a part. It was not down to individuals to pursue their own private improvement and development. Instead, early Christian behavioral exhortation was presented as a corporate commitment and a social project to which believers were summoned collectively.

Recall also that from the earliest years onward Christian circles included men and women, free and slave persons, adults and children. Granted, Musonius Rufus contended that daughters and wives should learn philosophy, but there is little indication that he actively recruited women as his philosophical students.[81] By contrast, early Christian circles typically were socially complex in the gender, age, and social status of participants.

That is especially relevant in considering the early Christian exhortations directed to specific social groups, particularly in certain New Testament passages often referred to as "household codes": Colossians 3:18–4:1; Ephesians 5:21–6:9; 1 Timothy 2:8-15; 3:4-5; 6:1-2; Titus 2:1-10; and 1 Peter 2:17–3:7.[82] These passages have been the focus of scholarly attention for over a century now, and it is neither practical nor necessary here to try to review all the contours and complexities of that body of work.[83] Essentially, these texts address three major social pairs: wives and husbands, parents and children, and slaves and masters. The texts all presume and accept the social structures reflected in these pairings and basically exhort members of each set of relationships about how to conduct themselves within these structures. So, for example, Colossians 3:18–4:1 urges wives to be submissive to their husbands, and husbands to love their wives and not treat them harshly. Children are urged to obey their parents, and fathers are not to provoke their children. Christian slaves are to obey their "earthly masters" with diligence, and Christian masters are ordered to treat their slaves "justly and fairly" in the knowledge that they also have "a Master in heaven." The other "household code" texts have basically similar exhortations.

There are certain similarities to teachings about household management in ancient philosophical texts, particularly by Aristotle, but also Plutarch and Xenophon; and there are partial parallels in ancient Jewish texts such as Sirach 3:1–16.[84] So, one general observation is that these early Christian texts reflect a concern that Christian household life should match or even exceed the ideals affirmed in the larger Greco-Roman culture.[85]

But, along with these similarities, there are some interesting distinctive features of the early Christian exhortations. Of course, the references to "the Lord" (Jesus) in these texts readily mark them off as Christian. Perhaps the most extended example of this is in Ephesians 5:25-33, an elaborated exhortation to husbands to love their wives with a devotion and self-sacrificial concern that is patterned after Christ, who "loved the church and gave himself up for her" (v. 25). But also noteworthy is the extended exhortation and encouragement to Christian slaves in 1 Peter 2:18-25, where the author likens any unjust sufferings that they may bear, likely as Christian slaves of pagan masters, to the sufferings of Christ (vv. 21-25). This linkage of the suffering of slaves with Christ effectively ennobles the situation of slaves, at least at the level of the discourse, a striking step in a world in which slaves typically counted for little as to dignity. Of course, this did not amount to the abolition of slavery or even securing the freedom of slaves, at least at that point. But this sort of compassionate rhetoric addressed to slaves was unusual, if not unique, in the Roman world.

My main concern here, however, is a couple of other features that reflect the social location in which these various exhortations were heard. For one thing, note that the advice on household management found in the various "pagan" philosophical texts was written for the males in charge of households, exhorting them how to manage their wives, children, and slaves. In contrast, these early Christian texts directly address each of the parties concerned in these relationships, not simply the dominant males. As noted already, the Christian texts exhort wives directly to subject themselves to their own husbands and advise them how to conduct and attire themselves honorably (Colossians 3:18; Ephesians 5:22-24; 1 Peter 3:1-6). The texts also address children directly, urging them to obey their parents (Colossians 3:20; Ephesians 6:1-3). Slaves, likewise, are addressed directly, the texts exhorting them to serve their masters conscientiously (Ephesians 6:5-8; Colossians 3:22-25; 1 Peter 2:18-25). This sort of direct address to these various subordinate groups is a distinctively Christian innovation in these household codes, apparently unique in the ancient setting. So, along with noting the similarity of the early Christian "household codes" and the household management advice in the wider ancient setting, we must also recognize that there is no parallel to the direct address to the subordinate members in the various social pairings.[86]

This direct address treats these subordinate parties as moral agents, who are capable and responsible to respond to the exhortations to them. To be sure, the nature of their response is circumscribed by their respective situations and social status. The texts do not advocate an overturning, or even a questioning, of the social structures of the day. But, for that matter, there is scant indication that anyone in the ancient world seriously contemplated any such social revolution. For example, those enslaved likely wished that they were not and were glad if the opportunity came to be manumitted; but there was no notion among slaves or others that slavery itself would or could be abolished as such.[87] In fact, as soon as they were able to do so, freed slaves often acquired slaves of their own.[88] So, although it may seem to comfortable moderns that the early Christian texts are morally deficient in failing to summon slaves to rise up in revolt and in failing to demand that Christian masters immediately free all their slaves, neither was actually a realistic option at the time. But the point to underscore is that, despite the various limits on the scope of their actions imposed by their social situation, Christian wives, slaves, and children were addressed as moral agents in early Christian texts and, perhaps just as importantly, as fellow members of the body of believers in which these various exhortations were delivered. We should not discount too hastily what this, even this modest conferral of dignity, could have meant in that ancient setting to those who were otherwise unable to change their situation.

Furthermore, there is another important and distinctive feature of early Christian "household code" exhortations. As members of a body of Christian believers, those in the various subordinate social categories also heard the exhortations given to those in the corresponding dominant positions: husbands, parents, and masters. So, for example, in those circumstances in which the Letter to the Colossians was read in church gatherings, Christian wives were fully a part of the gathering and heard their Christian husbands exhorted to love their wives and "never treat them harshly" (3:19). Likewise, Christian children heard fathers ordered not to provoke their children (3:21), and slaves heard masters warned to treat their slaves "justly and fairly," in the knowledge that they also had a heavenly Master to whom they were responsible for their conduct (4:1).

Similarly, the direct address to those in various social positions in 1 Peter reflects the presence of believers in all of them. This means that, as well as the exhortation directed to believers in any one social position, they would all have also heard the instructions given to believers in various other social positions. For example, Christian masters would have heard Christian slaves exhorted to serve faithfully (2:18), but also both slaves and masters heard the references to unjust sufferings inflicted on slaves (2:18-20). The notion that any treatment of slaves could be *unjust* suffering was a rather unusual one in the Roman period. Also, all would have heard the likening of the suffering of Christian slaves to Christ's redemptive suffering (2:21-23). In the early Christian discourse context, this gave to their sufferings a distinctive meaning and even an honor. Christian wives heard the instructions to husbands in 1 Peter to treat their wives considerately and "also as heirs of the gracious gift of life" (3:7-8).

This discourse situation, this group social setting comprising believers of these various social categories, each of them addressed directly in the hearing of all the others in the group, is another distinguishing feature of early Christian behavioral exhortation. To emphasize the point, the setting of early Christian exhortation is certainly different from a circle of elite male students gathered with a teacher/philosopher discussing how best to order their individual lives. The setting of the communication of the early Christian household codes is also different from the transmission of advice from one dominant/free male to others of the same social category, as in the household management texts of Greco-Roman antiquity.

Granted, the early Christian household-code texts give general directions to the various categories of believers addressed, and their actual day-to-day situations likely would often have required adaptation, careful negotiation of relationships, and perhaps compromises, some of which may have been uncomfortable or even distasteful. For example, slaves were often expected to provide sexual services for those who owned them, male and/or female. So any such demands would have produced intense moral tensions for Christian slaves, for whom such sexual service would be *porneia*. Christian wives married to non-Christians, and Christian children under the rule of non-Christian parents likewise, would have had particular tensions to deal with and difficulties in their efforts to live out their faith while avoiding some activities that they regarded as idolatry. For example, they would have had to deal with the typical expectation of all members of a household to take part in reverencing the household gods. But, all such difficulties and compromises included, the various behavioral exhortations and the particular efforts to actualize them in life comprise a major way in which early Christianity was distinctive in the ancient Roman-era setting.

Summary

The behavioral expectations placed on early Christians were demanding and represented at a number of points sharp departures from what was tolerated and even approved in the larger Roman culture. In some emphases, early Christian behavioral demands resembled some ideas advocated in some philosophical circles of the day. But, even considering these resemblances, we can see that there is a major difference in the historical effects of early Christian behavioral exhortation. Christian adherents of all social positions were called, and from the point of initiation onward, to live up to the behavioral demands of their faith. Early Christianity "took it to the streets," generating a novel social project in that time.

Obviously, as with some other features, early Christian convictions about behavior reflected the Jewish context in which the Jesus-movement initially emerged. Likewise, there was a similarity in the effort to make certain behavior indicative of group identity. But also early Christian exhortation took on particular discursive features that reflected distinguishing beliefs, especially beliefs about Jesus. Furthermore, some early Christian teachings, especially in sexual matters, seem to reflect the generation of some distinctive emphases, the challenging of the sexual double standard of the day in particular, and even what appears to be the formation of new words to express revulsion at the sexual exploitation of children.

Finally, the programmatic incorporation of adherents of various social positions gave a particular kind of group setting in which early Christian behavioral exhortation was delivered. Christians of whatever social position were well aware of the behavioral demands made on all others in whatever social position. This surely reinforced a sense of collective behavioral responsibility.

Conclusion

Early Christianity of the first three centuries was a different, even distinctive, kind of religious movement in the cafeteria of religious options of the time. That is not simply my historical judgment; it is what people of the time thought as well. In fact, in the eyes of many in the Roman era, Christianity was very odd, even objectionably so. There were, of course, the rumors of orgies and cannibalism, which we could write off as the ignorant prejudice of the masses. But even among those who took the time to acquaint themselves more accurately with Christian beliefs, practices, and texts, the response was often intensely negative.

Consider, for example, the time and effort involved in something like Celsus' full-scale critique of Christianity—researching, organizing thoughts, composing the critique—and you get a sense of that negativity. Sophisticated pagans such as Celsus and Marcus Aurelius apparently regarded Christianity as not simply unbelievable but, it appears, utterly incompatible with religion as they knew it. For them, Christianity was, we may say, "a clear and present danger" that had to be opposed.

When considered as a religion in that time, the most obvious oddity was Christianity's "atheism"—that is, the refusal to worship the traditional gods. Yes, of course, as we have observed, Christians shared this exclusivist stance with Judaism. But pagans could write off the well-known Jewish refusal to worship the gods as an ethnic peculiarity. The aggressively transethnic appeal and spread of early Christianity, however, gave it no such character and made Christianity seem much more "in your face." Other religious movements of the time had their oddities too. But early Christianity was not simply odd; it was deemed dangerous to traditional notions of religion and, so it was feared, also for reasons of social stability.

Recall, for example, that Celsus railed against and ridiculed how early Christians spread their faith among children, slaves, and others of low status. We know that he exaggerated and that Christianity also made a successful appeal to at least some individuals of somewhat higher status. But Celsus' ridicule also likely reflected a certain unease on his part that this antisocial and worrisome religious movement was spreading among the sort of people who should simply take their religious beliefs and practices from their betters and from tradition. Recall also Pliny's rather determined efforts to exterminate—literally!—Christian faith in the area that he was assigned to govern. We noted as well his claim that the spread of Christianity had led to a decline in the economic activities associated with the traditional gods, and his severe treatment of Christians who refused to obey his demands to renounce their faith. I repeat: in characterizing early Christianity as dangerously different, we are only reflecting the views of informed pagans of the time.

It could also be dangerous in those early centuries to be a Christian. Christian tradition subsequently has tended to focus on martyrs, those Christians who were put to death for their faith.

Early on, these included James Zebedee (executed by Herod Agrippa [ca. 42 AD]), the many Christians who suffered Nero's cruelties in 64 AD, the Antipas killed in Pergamum sometime in the late first century, and those unnamed Christians executed by Pliny in the early second century.[1] Even so, your actual chances of being executed as a Christian were probably limited. But, even if not all that frequent, the killing of any Christian would surely have had frightening effects on all other Christians who knew of it. For a small movement made up of little circles of believers well aware of their dissonance with the larger culture and sensing their vulnerability, it would not have taken many deaths to make them feel threatened.[2] Surely that would have served as a disincentive for at least some.

But there were other and much more frequent costs as well for being a Christian in the first three centuries. For example, you might receive harassment and ostracism from family members, friends, and associates. Christian slaves of pagan masters might well have suffered corporal punishment, and wives of pagan husbands might well have received verbal and physical abuse. Scrupulous Christian members of professional guilds who demurred acknowledging the guild deities would have found themselves the object of scorn and worse. Indeed, these and other social costs were such that it prompts the question why people chose to become Christians in that period.

Most attempts to answer that question seem to me facile, but this is not the place to go into the matter further.[3] I confine myself here to making the observation that the social costs of becoming a Christian in the first three centuries comprise another way in which early Christianity was distinctive. It was unlike the consequences of joining practically any other religious group or voluntary association. Becoming a Christian in that time involved something more demanding. For in requiring the renunciation of the traditional gods, adherence to early Christianity differed from participation in any other voluntary association.[4]

Early Christianity was distinctive, but not absolutely so or in every respect. At a certain level of generalization, we could note, for example, that a common meal as part of their gatherings was also a feature of many, or perhaps most, other religious groups of that time. The early Christians put on their sandals one at a time, so to speak, just like everyone else. Recall the emphasis in the *Epistle to Diognetus* that Christians were part of their society in many matters, such as food, dress, and some other customs. We have also observed similarities with Jewish tradition and/or with some philosophical schools in some teachings about proper behavior.

Nevertheless, even in these matters early Christianity was distinguishable, especially when assessed as a social phenomenon. For example, Roman-era Judaism never really tried to enforce, or even promote very aggressively, its religious and behavioral teachings among non-Jews. Similarly, in the main, philosophical teaching was intended to have effects on those individuals who committed themselves to the rigors of internalizing the attitudes proffered by their teachers. Granted, there were also wandering, "popular" teachers, especially in the Cynic-Stoic camp, who advocated their way of life "on the stump" in public places. But there is little evidence that this activity generated a recognizable social movement of any significance.

From earliest years, however, what became Christianity went transethnic and translocal, addressing males and females of all social levels and generating circles of followers who were expected to commit to particular beliefs and behavior from the point of initiation into the young religious movement. Though initially small and insignificant in the first centuries, the movement continued to grow and spread geographically, quickly obtaining a salience and having an impact well beyond its numbers, as reflected by the repeated expressions of antipathy for it from non-Christians.

In short, even if we allow for similarities with other groups of the day, when considered as what I have termed "a social project," early Christianity was distinctive. Certainly, Christianity did not fall from the sky like some foreign object. It was a historical phenomenon and can be studied as such. But it would be facile, and poor historical analysis, to ignore the very real ways in which early Christianity was a novel and distinctive development, several of them explored in the preceding chapters.

To turn from the ancient to our period, at the outset of this book I stated that one of my purposes was to address, though only briefly, our cultural amnesia. The point is that each of the distinguishing features of early Christianity discussed in this book has become for us a commonplace assumption about religion. For example, whether we align ourselves with any religious faith or not, we likely think and speak in terms of a single deity, "God." We may profess some kind of faith in "God" or deny that "God" exists. But we typically assume that there is one "God" to consider. That this is so is largely due to the impact of Christianity.

We also tend to think of ethnicity and religious affiliation as, in principle, distinguishable, with religious affiliation typically thought of as a voluntary choice. In this also, we see the impact of Christianity, already observable at the earliest stages in the first three centuries that are the focus of this book. Granted, in European Christendom all through the Middle Ages and into the early modern period, people typically regarded themselves as Christians by virtue of being citizens of this or that European nation. So, for example, most Greeks, Danes, Italians, and other nationalities tended to think of themselves as nominally Christians simply by birth. For many Europeans, therefore, genuine religious "freedom," meaning the opportunity to make a choice about one's religious affiliation, may be associated with modernity, and in immediate chronological terms that is so. But, as we have seen in an earlier chapter, early Christianity actually introduced effectively the notion of a religious identity separate from one's national/ethnic identity. Further, even at the height of European Christendom, Christianity was not tied to any one national identity. Instead, even then, Christianity was transethnic, and so at least distinguishable from one's ethnicity, if not fully separable from it.

The place of books in early Christianity, so remarkable in the ancient Roman setting, is another example of influence upon notions that we take for granted today. We expect religion to involve some sort of scriptural writings, and we assume that the practice of religion will typically include reading these writings, whether in corporate worship or in private devotion. As to why this assumption is so taken for granted in our culture, this, too, is down to the influence of Christianity. Indeed, we might even wonder whether the triumph of the codex over the bookroll, yielding thereafter our familiar leaf book, was, at least in some significant measure, a reflection of the influence of Christianity, especially in the post-Constantinian centuries.

The early Christian emphasis on, and teaching about, everyday behavior as central to Christian commitment is yet another distinctive feature that has had a profound subsequent impact. In the ancient Roman period and down through human history, what we call "religion" tended to focus more on honoring, appeasing, and seeking the goodwill of deities through such actions as sacrifices and the performance of related rituals. "Religion" did not typically have much to say about what we call "ethics," how to behave toward others, how to conduct family or business, and the formation of character. If we assume today, however, that religion is concerned with such matters, with ordering behavior, this again is likely down to the influence of Christianity in particular. Whether you approve of Christianity's influence in shaping behavior or not is another question. My point is that our unquestioned assumption that religions are all concerned with teaching about "ethical" behavior almost certainly derives from Christianity.

In pointing out how early Christianity of the first three centuries was distinctive, I hope to sharpen our historical understanding of that exciting ancient period and particularly our appreciation of the remarkable religious movement that, alone of the many new religious movements of that time, has survived as a living force down the centuries. In underscoring how certain distinctive features of early Christianity have also shaped our world, I hope that we who are so very conscious of our own time will perceive better the importance and influence of this remarkable religious movement of the ancient Roman world.

Appendix
The History of Early Christianity
in Scholarly Perspective

An historical approach to early Christianity, and accompanying controversies over how early Christianity resembled and/or differed from the larger Roman-era setting, began in earnest in the nineteenth century. In his 1888 Hibbert Lectures, *The Influence of Greek Ideas and Usages upon the Christian Church*, Edwin Hatch described himself as "a pioneer" venturing into "comparatively unexplored ground," and he referred to "the science of history marching . . . almost for the first time, into the domain of Christian history."[1] Hatch's book exhibits a combination of impressive historical work along with a particular theological concern, in his case a concern to distinguish between the originating impulses and character of earliest Christianity (which he affirmed) and the subsequent developments that drew upon Greek philosophical ideas (which he regarded less positively). Indeed, indicative of his theological concern, Hatch expressed the hope (rather ambitiously) that as a result of his study there might even be a rebirth of Christianity. Reflecting the Liberal Protestant Christianity affirmed by many of his time and cultured class, Hatch hoped that this rebirth would focus on the ethical values that he saw reflected in the Sermon on the Mount and would jettison (or at least downplay) what he regarded as the regrettable emphasis on "metaphysical creed"—that is, doctrines such as enshrined in the Nicene Creed so central in traditional Christianity of his day.[2]

In the following decades, this effort to situate early Christianity historically developed further, among scholars of various nationalities, and particularly in the influential early twentieth-century works of German scholars in the so-called *religionsgeschichtliche Schule* (history-of-religion school).[3] They produced a prodigious body of work; but theirs, too, was not simply a historical project pursued dispassionately for its own sake. As several scholars subsequently have shown, the work of these figures was prompted and shaped by theological interests of their own time and setting.[4]

In particular, whereas Hatch was concerned with the influence of Greek ideas, the German history-of-religion scholars portrayed early Christianity as heavily influenced by "oriental" religious ideas and practices. I should explain that by "oriental" they meant what is now called the "Middle East," positing influences from what is now Iran and Syria, for example. As Suzanne Marchand showed in her excellent study of "German Orientalism," however, these Protestant scholars were also churchmen of their time and shared a strong practical concern for German society. The larger aim of these history-of-religion scholars was to promote the reformulation of Christian faith and practice stripped of these putative "oriental" elements. That is, they hoped to produce a form of Christianity that could be embraced by "modern" and cultured people and, in particular, that could promote the moral renewal of the German *Volk*.[5]

The various early efforts by Hatch and subsequent scholars were chiefly concerned to identify "influences" (whether Greek or "oriental") upon early Christianity. Also, whereas Hatch focused on developments in the second to fourth centuries, the German history-of-religion scholars concentrated more on the first century, indeed on the first few decades of the young Christian movement. This made their claims all the more controversial, for they carried the alleged influence of "foreign" ideas and practices right back into the New Testament itself and into the earliest years of the young Christian movement. Moreover, as with Hatch, the German history-of-religion scholars regarded these influences and the resulting Christian beliefs and practices as largely regrettable and (for their program of a modern form of Christian faith) disposable.

Although strictly speaking Richard Reitzenstein was not a member of this scholarly group, he was perhaps its most influential sympathizer.[6] He contended that oriental "mystery religions" provided precedents and parallels for the young Christian movement and had even been influential upon early Christian beliefs and rituals such as baptism and eucharist.[7] Reitzenstein's views, however, have not held up well under subsequent critical scrutiny, especially his almost obsessive concern to find evidence of a supposed pre-Christian "gnostic redeemer myth."[8] The putative similarities to early Christian practices that he posited are often not persuasive, and he tended to convert any surface similarities too simplistically into causal connections.

For example, consider supposed "oriental" parallels to early Christian baptism. On the one hand, various ceremonial washings for ritual purification were widespread in the ancient world; but, on the other hand, they typically functioned quite differently. In pagan contexts (such as the so-called mystery cults), these immersions were typically part of the preparation for an initiation ceremony into the cult, whereas in early Christian circles baptism was the crucial ritual part of the initiation process itself.[9] Moreover, whereas in pagan settings the washing/immersion could function to remove ceremonial impurity, early Christian baptism was connected with the divine remission of "sins" (i.e., ethical/moral behavior). Furthermore, there is simply no "mystery cult" parallel to Paul's treatment of baptism as expressing a union with Jesus in his death and resurrection that involves a believer's "death" to sinful practices and a "rebirth" to new and empowered moral effort (especially Romans 6:1-14).[10]

But perhaps the most influential and controversial work of this group of scholars was Wilhelm Bousset's classic book, *Kyrios Christos* (1913).[11] Bousset portrayed belief in Jesus as divine Lord as essentially one of the regrettable and disposable products of those putative "oriental" influences. He insisted that in the faith of the earliest circles of the emergent Christian movement (which Bousset termed "The Primitive Palestinian Community") Jesus was identified as the "Son of Man," the title of a supposedly well-known heavenly, messianic figure who would execute God's redemptive program in the near future. God had designated Jesus for this role by raising him from death.

Per Bousset, however, this "primitive" view of Jesus was quickly and early superseded in what he called "The Gentile Christian Primitive Community."[12] These were putative circles comprised (at least mainly) of converted pagans in non-Jewish cities such as Antioch and Damascus, among whom Jewish monotheistic concerns were supposedly not so influential. So, Bousset contended, in these settings pagan religious beliefs about divine heroes and demigods were influential factors. Under the influence of such beliefs, these converted pagans shaped a different view of Jesus, not as "the Son of Man," but as the divine "Lord" (Greek: *Kyrios*) to whom they offered worship. This treatment of the risen Jesus effectively as a deity (which Bousset called the "*Kyrios*-cult") was, Bousset claimed, reflective of the many pagan deities of the time and was the decisive, major step in the whole wider history of earliest Christianity. But, he granted, it happened early, indeed so early that this was the version of early Christian faith into which Paul was immersed after his "conversion" from strenuous opponent of Jewish circles of Jesus-followers to perhaps the most well-known advocate of their faith, an event commonly placed within the first couple of years after Jesus' crucifixion.[13]

I will not proceed further here into the details of Bousset's classic study or other works of the history-of-religion school. I have offered appreciative critiques of Bousset in particular in previous publications over a number of years.[14] These scholars posed important historical questions, and I admire their great learning, but their judgment too often seems to have been skewed by presuppositions and what were in fact theological aims.

The point I wish to emphasize is that the history-of-religion scholars contended that in major points of belief and religious practices, early Christianity was influenced (indeed, heavily shaped) by "oriental" currents in the larger Roman-era religious environment. In order to support this contention, however, Bousset and his history-of-religion colleagues alleged and emphasized putative similarities of early Christianity to its setting and showed less interest in noting differences. They also tended to ignore chronology in their use of sources. For example, they used Mandaean texts from several centuries later as supposedly indicative of the background of early first-century Christianity.[15] But this is obviously dubious in method. They also seem to have shown less interest in exploring connections and influences from the Old Testament and Jewish traditions, preferring to posit "oriental" (pagan) sources and going to great lengths to do so.

Understandably, the claim that almost from its earliest years Christianity had been heavily influenced (and so corrupted) by "oriental" forces generated a considerable reaction. This reaction came especially from scholars who recognized (rightly) that the aims of the history-of-religion scholars were not simply historical but also theological. Indeed, as I have noted, Bousset and his colleagues overtly sought to challenge the validity of key components in the traditional Christian confession. For example, one of my eminent predecessors in New College (Edinburgh), H. A. A. Kennedy, wrote a substantial study grappling with Reitzenstein's claims about the influence of "mystery religions," in which Kennedy contended (cogently in my view) that the claims were dubious.[16] Numerous other scholars addressed Bousset's work critically. Indeed, only three years after its initial publication, Geerhardus Vos released a valuable review of scholarly responses that comprised nearly seventy pages.[17] And in the following years, this critical engagement with Bousset continued, generating, for example, book-length studies by the American scholar J. G. Machen and the British scholar A. E. J. Rawlinson.[18] These works combined close analysis of Bousset's work with a concern to rebut its challenge to traditional beliefs about Christ.

That is, the obvious and undisguised religious/theological aims of the "history-of-religion" scholars understandably generated responses prompted by contrary religious theological concerns. I repeat the point for emphasis, however: the exploration of similarities or differences between early Christianity and its Roman-era environment is a valid historical project in its own right. It need not be linked to some larger theological aim of one kind or another.

Notes

Introduction

1 Wayne A. Meeks, *The Origins of Christian Morality: The First Two Centuries* (New Haven: Yale University Press, 1993), 1.

2 I use the terms "Christianity" and "Christians" well aware of the scholarly debates about them. In this book, the terms simply designate respectively the movement, with due allowances for its varied nature, with the figure of Jesus at its center that came to be called "Christianity" and adherents of that movement. Similarly, I use the word "pagan(s)" in the sense used by historians of the Roman period, simply as a shorthand way of designating the non-Jewish and non-Christian traditional religious outlook and practices of the time.

3 The term "Christians" is said to have been used initially in Antioch (Syria) according to Acts 11:26, in events placed sometime in the 30s of the first century AD. The accuracy of this report is disputed,

but the issue is not crucial for my purposes. The earliest use of the term "Christianity" is in the letter of Ignatius of Antioch to the Romans (3:3), written sometime in the early second century AD. I discuss questions about these terms in connection with early Christian religious identity in chapter 3.

4   The execution of James Zebedee and the arrest of the apostle Peter are reported in Acts of the Apostles (12:1-5) as enjoying the support of "the Jews" (probably the temple authorities). The death of Jesus' brother, James, is reported by the first-century Jewish writer Josephus (*Jewish Antiquities* 20.197–203).

5   Earliest depictions of open conflicts set in various cities are in the New Testament book Acts of the Apostles: e.g., Iconium (14:1-7), Philippi (16:16-40), Thessalonica (17:1-9), Corinth (18:1-17), Ephesus (19:21-40). But note also less specific references to sufferings of early believers, such as 1 Thessalonians 2:14-16 (where Paul compares them to the suffering of Jewish believers in Judaea), Hebrews 10:32-36 (looking back to a previous time of sufferings that involved public abuse and plundering of possessions), 1 Peter 4:12 (exhorting steadfastness in "the fiery ordeal that is taking place among you"), and the stark warnings about various hardships in passages such as Mark 13:9-13 (which refers to being brought before civic councils, synagogue authorities, betrayal by family, and being "hated by all because of my [Jesus'] name").

6   In recent years, several substantial multi-author works have appeared that give helpful reviews of the spread of early Christianity, including the following: Philip E. Esler, ed., *The Early Christian World*, 2 vols. (New York: Routledge, 2000); Margaret M. Mitchell and Frances M. Young, eds., *The Cambridge History of Christianity,* vol. 1, *Origins to Constantine* (Cambridge: Cambridge University Press, 2006); William Tabbernee, ed., *Early Christianity in Contexts: An Exploration across Cultures and Continents* (Grand Rapids: Baker Academic, 2014); and Susan Ashbrook Harvey and David G. Hunter, eds., *The Oxford Handbook of Early Christian Studies* (Oxford: Oxford University Press, 2008), 283–386.

7   Tacitus (*Annals* 15.44) says that the cruelties inflicted upon Christians by Nero were such that they generated "a sentiment of pity" among the populace. Josephus (*Jewish Antiquities* 20.183–84) portrays Nero as also hostile to Jews and posits Nero's annulment

of the civic rights of Jews in Caesarea as what led in time to the Jewish revolt and war of 66–70 AD. Some scholars recently have questioned the veracity of the ancient reports about Nero as tyrant and megalomaniac: Jas Elsner and Jamie Masters, eds., *Reflections of Nero: Culture, History and Representation* (London: Duckworth, 1994); but the accounts of Nero's pogrom against Christians continue to be treated as valid by most scholars. The recent challenge by Brent D. Shaw, "The Myth of the Neronian Persecution," *Journal of Roman Studies* 105 (2015): 73–100, seems to me flawed and ultimately unpersuasive. Christopher Jones offers an incisive critique of Shaw's article in "The Historicity of the Neronian Persecution: A Response to Brent Shaw," *New Testament Studies* (forthcoming).

8   E.g., these are used as rough estimates by Rodney Stark, *The Rise of Christianity* (Princeton: Princeton University Press, 1996); and Keith Hopkins, "Christian Number and Its Implications," *Journal of Early Christian Studies* 6 (1998): 185–226. Hopkins gives a handy chart of the projected growth of Christianity across the first three centuries, along with a list of "interstitial numbers of Christians" at various dates along the way (193).

9   Hopkins, "Christian Number," 206. For the most comprehensive and detailed catalogue of the geographical spread of early Christianity, see Roderic L. Mullen, *The Expansion of Christianity: A Gazetteer of Its First Three Centuries* (Leiden: Brill, 2004); he focuses on the period prior to Constantine. This work includes a number of helpful maps. A summary account is given by Frank Trombley, "Overview: The Geographical Spread of Christianity," in *The Cambridge History of Christianity,* vol. 1, *Origins to Constantine,* ed. Margaret M. Mitchell and Frances M. Young (Cambridge: Cambridge University Press, 2006), 302–13.

10 In his brief and approving reference to Nero's actions against Christians (*The Twelve Caesars* 16.2), Suetonius refers to them as adherents of "a new and wicked superstition" (*superstitionis novae ac maleficae*). In his more extended account of the same incident, Tacitus (*Annals* 15.44) refers to Christianity similarly as "a dangerous/ destructive superstition" (*exitiabilis superstitio*).

11 These early Christian writers include Justin Martyr, Athenagoras, Tatian, Theophilus, and the anonymous author of "The Epistle to Diognetus," plus others whose works survive only incompletely or

in references to them by others. For introductions and descriptions of these works, see, e.g., Johannes Quasten, *Patrology,* vol. 1, *The Beginnings of Patristic Literature* (Westminster, Md.: Christian Classics, 1986; original publication 1950), 186–253; and Claudio Moreschini and Enrico Norelli, *Early Christian Greek and Latin Literature: A Literary History,* vol. 1, *From Paul to the Age of Constantine,* trans. Matthew J. O'Connell (Peabody, Mass.: Hendrickson, 2005).

12 I borrow the phrase from Eric Osborn, *The Emergence of Christian Theology* (Cambridge: Cambridge University Press, 1993), 3.

13 Christians who are uneasy about state involvement in promoting a particular religion might well wonder whether Constantine's adoption of Christianity can really be seen so simply as a "triumph." It certainly meant some changes for Christianity as well as the empire.

14 Ramsay MacMullen, *Christianizing the Roman Empire A.D. 100–400* (New Haven: Yale University Press, 1984), viii.

15 Robin Lane Fox, *Pagans and Christians* (New York: Alfred A. Knopf, 1987), 271.

16 Jan N. Bremmer gives a lively account of several noteworthy efforts in *The Rise of Christianity through the Eyes of Gibbon, Harnack and Rodney Stark* (Groningen: Barkhuis, 2010).

17 The flood of subsequent scholarly work notwithstanding, it would be difficult, for example, to improve on the classic discussion of how early Christianity reflected its Roman-era religious and philosophical setting and how it differed, by A. D. Nock, *Conversion: The Old and the New in Religion from Alexander the Great to Augustine of Hippo* (Oxford: Oxford University Press, 1933), esp. 187–253.

18 Note, e.g., Gillian Clark, *Christianity and Roman Society* (Cambridge: Cambridge University Press, 2004), who acknowledges both parallels with other Roman-era religious groups and also "some distinctive features" (22), such as the more central place of texts, Christian circles networking translocally, and collecting funds to help fellow Christians.

19 Rodney Stark, "Why Religious Movements Succeed or Fail: A Revised General Model," *Journal of Contemporary Religion* 11 (1996): 133–46. In this article, Stark revises somewhat his earlier proposal: "How New Religions Succeed: A Theoretical Model," in *The Future of New Religious Movements,* ed. David G. Bromley and Phillip E. Hammond (Macon, Ga.: Mercer University Press, 1987), 11–29.

20 For the list of features, Stark, "Why Religious Movements Succeed," 144.

21 See Stark, "Why Religious Movements Succeed," 137–38, for discussion of this, which he calls "strictness."

22 "Shakers," in *Oxford Dictionary of the Christian Church*, 2nd ed., ed. F. L. Cross and E. A. Livingstone (Oxford: Oxford University Press, 1983), 1268. See also this recent interview-based news story: http://bustedhalo.com/features/the-last-of-the-shakers (accessed 6 January 2016).

23 There is a good introduction, along with the Greek text and English translation on facing pages, in Michael W. Holmes, ed., *The Apostolic Fathers: Greek Texts and English Translations*, 3rd ed. (Grand Rapids: Baker Academic, 2007), 686–719.

24 See the appendix.

25 We look at examples in the next chapter.

26 Alan F. Segal (*Rebecca's Children: Judaism and Christianity in the Roman World* [Cambridge, Mass.: Harvard University Press, 1986]) presents rabbinic Judaism (in varied forms the Judaism that we know today) and Christianity as twins that developed from the "mother" tradition, Jewish tradition of the Hellenistic and Roman period.

27 See a similar judgment by Rodney Stark, "Antioch as the Social Situation for Matthew's Gospel," in *Social History of the Matthean Community: Cross-Disciplinary Approaches to an Open Question*, ed. David L. Balch (Minneapolis: Fortress, 1991), 190 (189–210). More pertinent to interest in the eventual "triumph" of Christianity is another comment: "Since paganism had served the religious needs of the Greco-Roman world for centuries, its demise must have involved extraordinary factors" (190). In "Why Religious Movements Succeed," Stark observed that, although hundreds of new religious movements appear annually, "virtually every new group will have one thing in common: eventual failure." He estimated that "probably no more than one religious movement out of 1000 will attract more than 100,000 followers and last for as long as a century," and he noted, "Even most movements that achieve these modest results will become no more than a footnote in the history of religions" (133).

28　For one brief attempt recently, see Jan Bremmer, "The Social and Religious Capital of the Early Christians," *Hephaistos* 24 (2006): 269–78.

29　"History walks a tightrope between the unique and the typical. If we explain everything by analogy, we deny to our forebears the individuality we take as a basic feature of our own humanity." Edwin Judge, *Social Distinctives of the Christians in the First Century: Pivotal Essays by E. A. Judge*, ed. David M. Scholer (Peabody, Mass.: Hendrickson, 2008), 134. I take "history" in Judge's statement to refer to the efforts of historians to attempt reconstructions of the past.

30　See, e.g., Karen L. King, "Which Early Christianity?" in *The Oxford Handbook of Early Christian Studies*, ed. Susan Ashbrook Harvey and David G. Hunter (Oxford: Oxford University Press, 2008), 66–84.

31　"Valentinians" were linked to the early Christian teacher Valentinus, and "Marcionites" to another early Christian teacher, Marcion, both active in the second century AD. The scholarly emphasis today on the diversity of early Christianity is often attributed to the influential book by Walter Bauer, *Orthodoxy and Heresy in Earliest Christianity* (Philadelphia: Fortress, 1971), which achieved this influence only after its translation into English well after its initial appearance in German (1934) and through advocacy of it by influential scholars, especially in North America. For a handy collection of primary texts reflecting the diversity of early Christianity, see Robert M. Grant, *Second-Century Christianity: A Collection of Fragments*, 2nd ed. (Louisville, Ky.: Westminster John Knox, 2003). On "gnostic" Christianity, see Pheme Perkins, *Gnosticism and the New Testament* (Minneapolis: Fortress, 1993). But also note the critique of the "gnostic" category by Michael A. Williams, *Rethinking "Gnosticism": An Argument for Dismantling a Dubious Category* (Princeton: Princeton University Press, 1996).

32　For recent and accessible treatments of Marcion, see the complementary articles in *Expository Times* 121 (2010): Paul Foster, "Marcion: His Life, Works, Beliefs, and Impact," 269–80; Sebastian Moll, "Marcion: A New Perspective on His Life, Theology, and Impact," 281–86; Dieter T. Roth, "Marcion's Gospel: Relevance, Contested Issues, and Reconstruction," 287–94.

33 Larry W. Hurtado, *Lord Jesus Christ: Devotion to Jesus in Earliest Christianity* (Grand Rapids: Eerdmans, 2003), 563–648, esp. 563.

34 Paula Fredriksen ("Christians in the Roman Empire in the First Three Centuries CE," in *A Companion to the Roman Empire*, ed. David S. Potter [London: Blackwell, 2006], 587–606) rightly noted that with Constantine certain forms of early Christianity were able to enforce their stance as "orthodoxy" with power (588). But the form of Christians/Christianity that Constantine adopted had already become dominant, and that is why he adopted it. He was not a fool.

1: Early Christians and Christianity in the Eyes of Non-Christians

1 L. W. Hurtado, "Early Jewish Opposition to Jesus-Devotion," *Journal of Theological Studies* 50 (1999): 35–58; republished in L. W. Hurtado, *How on Earth Did Jesus Become a God? Historical Questions about Earliest Devotion to Jesus* (Grand Rapids: Eerdmans, 2005), 152–78. See also Claudia J. Setzer, *Jewish Responses to Early Christians: History and Polemics, 30–150 C.E.* (Minneapolis: Fortress, 1994). Stephen G. Wilson (*Related Strangers: Jews and Christians 70–170 C.E.* [Minneapolis: Fortress, 1995], 169–94) surveyed second-century evidence.

2 In the New Testament book Acts, he is introduced as "Saul" and as a violent opponent of the young Jesus movement (Acts 8:1-4). In the succeeding narrative in Acts, he continues to be referred to by this name, until 13:9, with the transitional statement, "Saul, also known as Paul." Thereafter, he is consistently referred to as Paul. In his letter to the Philippians, he claimed to be of the Israelite tribe of Benjamin, from which came the Old Testament King Saul. So, he was probably named "Saul" after that figure but used "Paul" (Greek: *Paulos*; Latin: *Paulus*) as a public name, esp. among non-Jews. Indicative of the use of the name by others, in Acts 13:7, the proconsul of Cyprus is named Sergius Paulus. Acts repeatedly says Paul was born in Tarsus (Acts 9:11; 21:39; 22:3), in what is now south-central Turkey.

3 In an article published some years ago now, I reviewed issues about Paul's dramatic religious move from opponent to proponent of the young Jesus-movement: Larry W. Hurtado, "Convert, Apostate

or Apostle to the Nations: The 'Conversion' of Paul in Recent Scholarship," *Studies in Religion/Sciences religieuses* 22 (1993): 273–84. As reflected in that article, scholars debate whether Paul's experience is best labeled a "conversion," for he never indicates that he ceased being Jewish or that he thought he had left one religion for another. Instead, he refers to being "called" by God, similar to Old Testament prophets, and to experiencing God's "revelation" of Jesus' high significance (Galatians 1:15–16). So if we use the term "conversion" for Paul, it can only be to signal what he regarded as a momentous change in how he saw Jesus and the will of his God. Paul shifted from being a Pharisee opposed to the early Jesus-movement to an ardent advocate for it. But he did not change religions. He came to a radically new view of what his ancestral God required of him.

4 As noted by Martin Hengel, *The Pre-Christian Paul* (London: SCM Press, 1991), 71–72.

5 For a fuller discussion, see Martin Hengel, *The Zealots* (Edinburgh: T&T Clark, 1989), 149–77; and Torrey Seland, *Establishment Violence in Philo and Luke: A Study of Non-conformity to the Torah and Jewish Vigilante Reactions* (Leiden: E. J. Brill, 1995).

6 In addition to the texts cited here, note also Psalm 106:30 and 4 Maccabees 18:12.

7 Philo, *Special Laws* 1.54–57; and in 2.252–57 also note a similar stance. In others of his writings as well, Philo treats Phinehas' actions positively as allegorical lessons: *On Drunkenness* 73–76; *On the Confusion of Tongues* 57; *On the Posterity of Cain* 182–83.

8 See, e.g., Hengel, *Pre-Christian Paul*, 63–86; although on some points—e.g., his rather strict distinctions between "Hellenists" and Aramaic-speaking parties in the Jerusalem church—I am not persuaded. On this latter topic, see Craig C. Hill, *Hellenists and Hebrews: Reappraising Division within the Earliest Church* (Minneapolis: Fortress, 1992). For other views of Paul's persecution, cf. Arland J. Hultgren, "Paul's Pre-Christian Persecutions of the Church: Their Purpose, Locale and Nature," *Journal of Biblical Literature* 95 (1976): 97–111; Paula Fredriksen, "How Later Contexts Affect Pauline Content; or, Retrospect Is the Mother of Anachronism," in *Jews and Christians in the First and Second Centuries: How to Write Their History*, ed. Peter J. Tomson and Joshua Schwartz

(Leiden: Brill, 2014), 17–51, esp. 42–47. In my view, however, she errs in assuming that the reason Paul was flogged (five times) in diaspora synagogues was the same as the reason that he had earlier persecuted Jewish believers. I think that Paul's own actions against Jewish believers was both more severe in intent and prompted by more serious concerns.

9 Those who propose this notion typically point to the speech ascribed to Stephen in Acts 7:1-60. But it is actually not all that clear that the speech expresses an "anti-temple" stance. Instead, the emphasis is on the persistent disobedience of his Jewish people to God's revelations, culminating in their rejection of Jesus.

10 Hultgren ("Paul's Pre-Christian Persecutions," 102–3) expresses something similar, but he focuses more on the beliefs and claims about Jesus promoted by Jewish believers, whereas I suggest that the place that Jesus held in their devotional practices may also have been judged problematic.

11 This is a fairly uncontroversial summary of earliest claims about Jesus in the aftermath of his followers' experiences of him as raised from death by God. For fuller discussion, see, e.g., my book *Lord Jesus Christ: Devotion to Jesus in Earliest Christianity* (Grand Rapids: Eerdmans, 2003), esp. 155–216.

12 So also, e.g., Hengel, *Pre-Christian Paul*, 83–84; Dieter Sänger, "'Verflucht ist jeder, der am Holze hängt' (Gal 3,13b): Zur Rezeption einer frühen antichristlichen Polemik," *Zeitschrift für die Neutestamentliche Wissenschaft* 85 (1994): 279–85.

13 See, e.g., G. N. Stanton, "Jesus of Nazareth: A Magician and a False Prophet Who Deceived God's People?" in *Jesus of Nazareth, Lord and Christ: Essays on the Historical Jesus and New Testament Christology*, ed. Joel B. Green and Max Turner (Grand Rapids: Eerdmans, 1994), 164–80.

14 Josephus also says (*Jewish Antiquities* 20.201–2) that Ananus' execution of James was not approved by "the most fair-minded and who were strict in observance of the law [Torah]," quite likely referring to Pharisees. At least in part this may reflect tensions between Pharisees and Sadducees over the administration of the Jerusalem temple. Josephus posits Ananus as aligned with the Sadducees, a Jewish religious party that he portrays as "more heartless than any of the other Jews . . . when they sit in judgement" (20.199).

15 These and many other texts relating to early Christianity in English translation are gathered in J. Stevenson, ed., *A New Eusebius: Documents Illustrative of the History of the Church to A.D. 337* (London: SPCK, 1974). For fuller discussions of the individual figures, see Robert L. Wilken, *The Christians as the Romans Saw Them* (New Haven: Yale University Press, 1984); Stephen Benko, "Pagan Criticism of Christianity during the First Two Centuries A.D," in *Aufstieg und Niedergang der römischen Welt,* series 2, vol. 23.2, ed. H. Temporini and W. Haase (Berlin: De Gruyter, 1980), 1055–1118; and, more recently, the extended discussions by Jeffrey W. Hargis, *Against the Christians: The Rise of Early Anti-Christian Polemic* (New York: Peter Lang, 1999); Xavier Levieils, *Contra Christianos: La critique sociale et religieuse du christianisme des origines au concile de Nicee (45–325)* (Berlin: De Gruyter, 2007); and Jakob Engberg, *Impulsore Chresto: Opposition to Christianity in the Roman Empire c. 50–250 AD,* trans. Gregory Carter (Frankfurt am Main: Lang, 2007).

16 Indicative of the sometimes fragile process by which such ancient works survived, books 11–16 of the *Annals* are preserved in one manuscript from the eleventh century. See, e.g., Ronald Haithwaite Martin, "Tacitus," in *Oxford Classical Dictionary,* 3rd ed. rev., ed. Simon Hornblower and Antony Spawforth (Oxford: Oxford University Press, 2003), 1469–71.

17 As I indicated in the Introduction, I don't find Brent Shaw's recent attempt to challenge Tacitus' report, "The Myth of the Neronian Persecution," persuasive.

18 So, e.g., David G. Horrell, "The Label Χριστιάνος: 1 Peter 4:16 and the Formation of Christian Identity," *Journal of Biblical Literature* 126 (2007): 366 (361–81). The most recent discussion of the origins and early meaning(s) of the term "Christians" (Greek: *christianoi;* Latin: *christiani*) is in Paul Trebilco, *Self-Designations and Group Identity in the New Testament* (Cambridge: Cambridge University Press, 2012), 272–97; he judges that the term originally designated both Jewish and Gentile adherents of the Jesus-movement. Cf. Philippa Townsend, "Who Were the First Christians? Jews, Gentiles and the *Christianoi,*" in *Heresy and Identity in Late Antiquity,* ed. E. Iricinischi and H. M. Zellentin (Tübingen: Mohr Siebeck, 2008), 212–30; she argues that the term originally designated only pagan converts. In

chapter 3, I return to questions about the origin and earliest usage of this term.

19 In this same text, Tacitus also gives us one of the earliest pagan references to Jesus' execution, referring to him as "Christus, from whom the name [Christian] had its origin," who "suffered the extreme penalty during the reign of Tiberius at the hands of one of our procurators, Pontius Pilatus." (I cite the translation in Stevenson, *New Eusebius*, 2.)

20 See, esp. Engberg, *Impulsore Chresto*; Engberg emphasizes that opposition initially came mainly from family, neighbors, etc., not so much from government authorities.

21 John Scheid, "*Superstitio*," in *Oxford Classical Dictionary*, 3rd ed. rev., ed. Simon Hornblower and Antony Spawforth (Oxford: Oxford University Press, 2003), 1456; and more fully Richard Gordon, "*Superstitio*, Superstition and Religious Repression in the Late Roman Republic and Principate (100 BC–AD 300)," in *The Religion of Fools?* ed. Stephen Anthony Smith and Alan Knight (Oxford: Oxford University Press, 2008), 72–94.

22 1 Peter 1:1 refers to Christians in Pontus and Bithynia as among the addressees, and other ancient sources refer to Christians in Pontus (e.g., Lucian, *Alexander* 25.38). Marcion (a Christian teacher who relocated to Rome and was branded a heretic) came from Sinope, a city in Pontus.

23 English translation with notes in Stevenson, *New Eusebius*, 13–15. For a full discussion, see esp. A. N. Sherwin-White, *The Letters of Pliny: A Historical and Social Commentary* (Oxford: Clarendon, 1966). He finds it "noteworthy that Pliny had trouble with Christians only in Pontus," and he insists that scholars' references to the events as set in Bithynia are "misleading" (694). See also the discussion of Pliny in Wilken, *Christians*, 1–30.

24 Pliny's claim not to be sure of how Christians should be handled seems to me a bit coy. As Horrell observed, Pliny seems to have been fully confident in the actions he took, his only possible uncertainty being about how to handle those who had once been Christians but now renounced their faith: "Label Χριστιάνος," 375.

25 See also, e.g., Keith Hopkins, "Christian Number and Its Implications," *Journal of Early Christian Studies* 6 (1998): 189 (185–226).

26 Pliny does not identify who his informants were about this.

27   Pliny, *Epistles* 10.97. English translation in Stevenson, *New Eusebius,* 16.

28   Cf. Hopkins, "Christian Number," 190; Hopkins suspected that Pliny exaggerated the number and impact of Christians in his province.

29   Irad Malkin, "Votive Offerings," and H. S. Versnel, *"Votum,"* in *Oxford Classical Dictionary*, 3rd ed. rev., ed. Simon Hornblower and Antony Spawforth (Oxford: Oxford University Press, 2003), 1612–13.

30   As noted also by Craig de Vos, "Popular Graeco-Roman Responses to Christianity," in *The Early Christian World*, vol. 2, ed. Philip F. Esler (New York: Routledge, 2000), 872 (869–89).

31   Scholars debate the historicity of events in Acts, but, whether or not this specific event happened as described in Acts, the early Christian readers were clearly expected to recognize the event as credible in light of their own experiences.

32   See the discussion in "Attitudes to Foreign Cults," in Craig Steven de Vos, *Church and Community Conflicts: The Relationships of the Thessalonian, Corinthian, and Philippian Churches with their Wider Civic Communities*, Society of Biblical Literature Dissertation Series 168 (Atlanta: Scholars Press, 1999), 56–84, citing 59.

33   Leonard V. Rutgers, "Roman Policy toward the Jews: Expulsions from the City of Rome during the First Century CE," in *Judaism and Christianity in First-Century Rome*, ed. Karl P. Donfried and Peter Richardson (Grand Rapids: Eerdmans, 1998), 93–116; Eric Gruen, *Diaspora* (Cambridge, Mass.: Harvard University Press, 2002), 29–36, 38–41.

34   Ramsay MacMullen, *Enemies of the Roman Order: Treason, Unrest, and Alienation in the Empire* (New York: Routledge, 1992 [orig. ed. 1966]). On the persecution meted out occasionally to philosophers, see 46–94.

35   In 249 AD, Emperor Decius issued a decree requiring all citizens to participate publicly in sacrifice to the Roman gods, and to be able to produce a certificate indicating that they did so. Examples of these documents (*libelli*) survive (e.g., Stevenson, *New Eusebius,* 228–29). Decius conducted a persecution of Christians, and this empire-wide requirement to sacrifice was likely prompted, at least in part, by the perception of a growing threat of Christianity. If so,

this would be another indication that Christianity prompted developments in Roman judicial procedures. Cf., e.g., J. R. Knipfing, "The *Libelli* of the Decian Persecution," *Harvard Theological Review* 16 (1923): 345–90; Reinhard Selinger, *The Mid-Third Century Persecutions of Decius and Valerian*, 2nd rev. ed. (Frankfurt: Peter Lang, 2002); P. Siniscalco, "Decius," in *Encyclopedia of Ancient Christianity*, ed. Angelo Di Berardino, 3 vols. (Downers Grove, Ill.: IVP Academic, 2014), 1:682–83. But J. B. Rives ("The Decree of Decius and the Religion of Empire," *Journal of Roman Studies* 89 [1999]: 135–54) proposed that Decius' decree was not solely (or even particularly) directed against Christians but was simply a clumsy effort to promote a greater religious unity in the empire.

36   T. D. Barnes, "Legislation against the Christians," *Journal of Roman Studies* 58 (1968): 37 (32–50); reprinted in his book *Early Christianity and the Roman Empire* (London: Variorum Reprints, 1994), chap. 1. Compare the more recent discussion of the matter by Paul McKechnie, *The First Christian Centuries: Perspectives on the Early Church* (Downers Grove, Ill.: InterVarsity, 2001), 58–64; he judged that "from the 60s Christianity was illegal" (63), and posited Nero's pogrom of 64 "a defining moment" (64), a more controversial position.

37   Among the many studies of this interesting figure, there is the recent work by Thomas A. Robinson, *Ignatius of Antioch and the Parting of the Ways* (Peabody, Mass.: Hendrickson, 2009).

38   The key work remains Richard Walzer, *Galen on Jews and Christians* (London: Oxford University Press, 1949). Wilken, *Christians*, 68–93, is also an excellent fuller discussion of Galen's references to Christians.

39   Walzer, *Galen*, 43. But cf. Loveday Alexander, "Paul and the Hellenistic Schools: The Evidence of Galen," in *Paul in His Hellenistic Context*, ed. Troels Engberg-Pedersen (Minneapolis: Fortress, 1995), 64–68 (60–83); Alexander contends that Galen's reference to Christians is more ironical and was intended to liken certain philosophical schools to Christians in what he regards as their irrational beliefs.

40   See the provocative discussion of possible bases for these rumors in Stephen Benko, *Pagan Rome and the Early Christians* (London: Batsford, 1985), 54–78; but contrast Jan N. Bremmer, "Early Christian

Human Sacrifice between Fact and Fiction," in *Sacrifices humains: Dossiers, discours, comparaisons; Actes du colloque tenu à l'Université de Genève, 19–20 mai 2011*, ed. Agnes A. Nagy and Francesca Prescendi (Turnhout: Brepols, 2013), 165–76.

41   The passage I refer to here is from Galen's now-lost summary of Plato's *Republic* and is preserved only in Arabic quotations. For Arabic text and English translation, see Walzer, *Galen*, 15–16.

42   Walzer, *Galen*, 68.

43   Citing the translation of Galen's statement in Walzer, *Galen*, 15.

44   His "Meditations" is available in many editions, including this one online: http://classics.mit.edu/Antoninus/meditations.html (accessed 7 January 2016).

45   For an English translation: http://www.earlychristianwritings .com/text/peregrinus.html (accessed 7 January 2016). Benko (*Pagan Rome*, 30–39) gives a summary along with discussion of other pagan references to Christians and appears to treat the story of Peregrinus as reflective of a real person (albeit caricatured by Lucian), as does Jan Bremmer, "Peregrinus' Christian Career," in *Flores Florentino: Dead Sea Scrolls and Other Early Jewish Studies in Honour of Florentino Barcìa Martìnez*, ed. Anthony Hilhorst, Èmile Puech, and Eibert Tigchelaar (Leiden: Brill, 2007), 729–47.

46   Lucian, *The Passing of Peregrinus* 13. Translation, slightly modified, from A. M. Harmon (http://www.earlychristianwritings.com/ text/peregrinus.html).

47   For text and introduction, see Henry Chadwick, trans., *Origen: Contra Celsum* (Cambridge: Cambridge University Press, 1965); and for further discussion, see Wilken, *Christians*, 94–123; and Peter Van Nuffelen, *Rethinking the Gods: Philosophical Readings of Religion in the Post-Hellenistic Period* (Cambridge: Cambridge University Press, 2011), 217–30.

48   Johannes Quasten (in *Patrology*, vol. 2: *The Ante-Nicene Literature after Irenaeus* [Westminster, Md.: Newman, 1953], 52–57) focuses on Origen's refutation.

49   Michael Bland Simmons, "Graeco-Roman Philosophical Opposition," in *The Early Christian World*, ed. Philip F. Esler (New York: Routledge, 2000), 844 (840–65). Simmons devotes a large part of his essay to major themes in Celsus' critique (851–60).

50   Quasten, *Patrology*, 52.

51 Simmons, "Graeco-Roman Philosophical Opposition," in Esler, *Early Christian World*, 847.

52 Benko, *Pagan*, 148 (see 147–58 for his fuller discussion of Celsus' views, on which I draw particularly in the following paragraphs).

53 Celsus seems to have obtained these claims from a Jewish critic of Christianity. These sorts of claims (and others) are also found in later Jewish sources, as reviewed by Peter Schäfer, *Jesus in the Talmud* (Princeton: Princeton University Press, 2007).

54 Information about Porphyry comes mainly from Christian sources, esp. Eusebius, *Ecclesiastical History* (6.19). An interesting character, Porphyry at one time had apparently been an acquaintance of the Christian scholar Origen but then became antagonistic to Christianity. See, e.g., P. F. Beatrice, "Porphyry," in *Encyclopedia of Ancient Christianity*, 3 vols., ed. Angelo Di Berardino (Downers Grove, Ill.: IVP Academic, 2014), 3:257–60; it has copious further bibliography.

55 See, e.g., Rodney Stark, *The Rise of Christianity* (Princeton: Princeton University Press, 1996), 4–13.

56 Minucius Felix, *Octavius* 9.6, and more fully the bitter tone of the speech of Caecilius in this work (8–9). For full discussion of Minucius Felix, see Harry James Baylis, *Minucius Felix and His Place among the Early Fathers of the Latin Church* (London: SPCK, 1928); and an excellent commentary by G. W. Clarke, *The Octavius of Marcus Minucius Felix* (New York: Newman, 1974). Among the other Christian texts of the time that answer such pagan accusations are the *Epistle to Diognetus* and Justin Martyr's *Apology.*

57 Phrasing taken here from Adolf von Harnack's excursus "Christians as a Third Race, in the Judgment of Their Opponents," in *The Mission and Expansion of Christianity in the First Three Centuries* (London: Williams & Norgate, 1908; repr., New York: Harper & Bros., 1961), 269 (266–78).

58 Bremmer, "Early Christian Human Sacrifice," 175 (165–76).

59 Benko, *Pagan*, 158.

60 The text of Justin's defense (Greek: *apologia*) in English is available online here: http://www.earlychristianwritings.com/text/justinmartyr-firstapology.html (accessed 7 January 2016). Of the many publications on Justin, I mention a recent multiauthor volume that arose from a conference on Justin held in New College

(Edinburgh): Sara Parvis and Paul Foster, eds., *Justin Martyr and His Worlds* (Minneapolis: Fortress, 2007).

61   Eric Osborn, *The Emergence of Christian Theology* (Cambridge: Cambridge University Press, 1993), citing 1 and 9.

62   In comments on an earlier draft of this chapter, Jan Bremmer characterized Osborn's statement as "rather hyperbolic." I agree.

63   According to the *Scriptores Historiae Augustae* (ca. 400 AD), Emperor Elagabalus included "the religions of the Jews and the Samaritans and the rites of the Christians" among those acknowledged in a temple he built on the Palatine Hill, and there are also several references to Emperor Alexander Severus expressing a positive attitude toward Christians. For example, he is said to have included images of Apollonius, Christ, Abraham, and Orpheus, along with statues of deified emperors, in his private chapel. Scholars have raised serious questions about the reliability of this rather late source. For references, see Menahem Stern, *Greek and Latin Authors on Jews and Judaism*, 3 vols. (Jerusalem: Israel Academy of Sciences and Humanities, 1974–1984), 2:612–42 (esp. #518, #522).

64   A. D. Nock, *Conversion: The Old and the New in Religion from Alexander the Great to Augustine of Hippo* (Oxford: Oxford University Press, 1933), 207.

65   I cite an emailed comment by Jan Bremmer on an earlier draft of this chapter: "Indeed, interestingly, Judaism never received such major intellectual critiques from Roman elite, presumably because they were seen as an ethnic group whereas Christianity cut through social and ethnic categories."

66   In an earlier publication, I addressed this question, briefly and in a very preliminary manner: Hurtado, *How on Earth*, 56–82 ("To Live and Die for Jesus: Social and Political Consequences of Devotion to Jesus in Earliest Christianity"). In a more recent publication, I address this matter more fully: *Why on Earth did Anyone Become a Christian in the First Three Centuries?* (Milwaukee: Marquette University Press, 2016).

67   Attentive readers will perhaps note my hat being tipped to "rational choice theory" here. But I intend no firm, or adequately informed, allegiance, and it may be a bit pretentious even to mention the matter. Stark, *Rise of Christianity*, 167–72, gives a brief explanation of the theory.

68 Some have proposed, for example, that early Christianity offered adherents a circle of people to whom they could relate closely—true, along with many other "voluntary associations" of the time that did not, however, involve any equivalent social cost. On the whole, I think that the attempts to engage the question have produced rather inadequate, even banal, answers.

2: A New Kind of Faith

1 Of course, in some parts of the world, Islam has contributed to the "one God" viewpoint, too. But by the time it became influential, after the seventh century AD, Christianity's influence was already widespread.

2 Although there are now many discussions pertaining to the matter, I think that a now-classic study remains essential reading: A. D. Nock, *Conversion: The Old and the New in Religion from Alexander the Great to Augustine of Hippo* (Oxford: Oxford University Press, 1933), esp. "The Spread of Christianity as a Social Phenomenon" (193–211) and "The Teachings of Christianity as Viewed by a Pagan" (212–53).

3 I borrow the notion of religion "a la carte" from the Canadian sociologist Reginald Bibby, who in various publications has charted the eclectic nature of the religion espoused by many people today in Canada.

4 Consider, e.g., the first two definitions in the entry on "religion" in the *Collins English Dictionary*, 3rd ed. (Glasgow: HarperCollins, 1992), 1309: "1. Belief in, worship of, or obedience to a supernatural power or powers considered to be divine or to have control of human destiny. 2. Any formal or institutionalized expression of such belief: *the Christian religion*" (emphasis original).

5 See, e.g., Brent Nongbri, *Before Religion: A History of a Modern Concept* (New Haven: Yale University Press, 2013).

6 In the nineteenth century, as part of a Hindu renaissance in India (in response to British colonial rule), these various traditions came to be reinterpreted as comprising a common semi-unified national religion, alongside Islam and Christianity.

7 For a good overview of the phenomena that characterized Roman-era religion, see David Frankfurter, "Traditional Cult," in *A*

Companion to the Roman Empire, ed. David S. Potter (London: Blackwell, 2006), 543–64.

8 See, e.g., the entries on the Greek word *eusebeia* in standard dictionaries such as Henry George Liddell and Robert Scott, *A Greek-English Lexicon*, new ed., rev. Henry Stuart Jones (Oxford: Oxford University Press, 1940), 731. But it is interesting to note that in the Greek Old Testament and in early Christian writings, the term is used more clearly to refer to reverence or piety toward a deity.

9 *Epistle to Diognetus* 1 (dated variously 150–225 AD). For the text, see Michael W. Holmes, ed., *The Apostolic Fathers: Greek Texts and English Translations*, 3rd ed. (Grand Rapids: Baker Academic, 2007), 686–719.

10 Nongbri, *Before Religion*, 7.

11 From texts such as Romans 9:1-11; 2 Corinthians 11:22-24; and Philippians 3:4-6, it is clear that Paul remained in his own mind a member of the Jewish people and loyal to the God of his people. Granted, he says that he experienced a divine "revelation" of Jesus' true significance as God's "Son" and so felt himself "called" by God to become a proponent of the gospel (Galatians 1:13-15). But he did not describe himself as a "convert" who had forsaken his Jewish past for a new religion called "Christianity."

12 The term *ioudaïsmos* seems to have been coined to designate the committed observance of Jewish customs and law, in contrast to the term *hellēnismos*, designating the practice of Greek culture (in language, customs, etc.)—i.e., to "hellenize." Earliest uses of *ioudaïsmos* are in 2 Maccabees 2:21; 8:1; 14:38; and 4 Maccabees 4:26, and in all these places it connotes Jewish religious/cultural practices.

13 E.g., the excellent work by Mary Beard, John North, and Simon Price, *Religions of Rome*, 2 vols. (Cambridge: Cambridge University Press, 1998).

14 Nongbri, *Before Religion*, 156.

15 "For the average inhabitant of the cities of the Empire, east or west, 'religion' meant something public, something to do with sacrifices and processions and festivals, and something that carried the sanction of long practice in a particular locality. It was not a private affair, and it did not normally demand exclusive loyalty." Loveday Alexander, "Paul and the Hellenistic Schools: The Evidence

of Galen," in *Paul in His Hellenistic Context*, ed. Troels Engberg-Pedersen (Minneapolis: Fortress, 1995), 61 (60–83).

16 Charles King, "The Organization of Roman Religious Beliefs," *Classical Antiquity* 22 (2003): 275–312.

17 *Social Distinctives of Christians in the First Century: Pivotal Essays by E. A. Judge*, ed. David M. Scholer (Peabody, Mass.: Hendrickson, 2008), 130; this essay is also published in E. A. Judge, *The First Christians in the Roman World: Augustan and New Testament Essays*, ed. James R. Harrison (Tübingen: Mohr Siebeck, 2008), 404–9.

18 I draw here on an observation by Alexander, "Paul and the Hellenistic Schools," in Engberg-Pedersen, *Paul*, 62.

19 In an earlier publication also, I sketched briefly the nature of "the religious environment" of earliest Christianity: L. W. Hurtado, *At the Origins of Christian Worship* (Grand Rapids: Eerdmans, 1999), 7–38.

20 Keith Hopkins, *A World Full of Gods: Pagans, Jews, and Christians in the Roman Empire* (London: Weidenfeld & Nicolson, 1999).

21 Ramsay MacMullen, *Paganism in the Roman Empire* (New Haven: Yale University Press, 1981), 1.

22 MacMullen, *Paganism*, 2.

23 Mark S. Smith, *God in Translation: Cross-Cultural Recognition of Deities in the Biblical World* (Grand Rapids: Eerdmans, 2010).

24 Robert Turcan (*The Cults of the Roman Empire*, trans. Antonia Nevill [Oxford: Blackwell, 1996]) focuses on the various deities imported into, or newly refashioned in, the Roman Empire—e.g., Isis (75–129), and Mithras (195–247); and now particularly Jan N. Bremmer, *Initiation into the Mysteries of the Ancient World* (Berlin: De Gruyter, 2014), 110–41. There is an open-access online version: http://www.degruyter.com/view/product/185838 (accessed 7 January 2016).

25 E.g., in the famous second-century AD story the *Metamorphoses* of Apuleius (also known as *The Golden Ass*), there is a prayer to Isis (19) that identifies her with various other goddesses, including Ceres, Venus, and Proserpine: Robert Graves, trans., *The Transformations of Lucius Otherwise Known as the Golden Ass by Lucius Apuleius* (Harmondsworth: Penguin Books, 1950), 243.

26 Studies of various Roman-era cites show this: e.g., John E. Stambaugh, *The Ancient Roman City* (Baltimore: Johns Hopkins University Press, 1988).

27   Terry M. Griffith ("ΕΙΔΩΛΟΝ as 'Idol' in Non-Jewish and Non-Christian Greek," *Journal of Theological Studies* 53 [2002]: 95–101) contends that the term was very occasionally used by pagans to refer to cult *images*, not the deities themselves, and with no pejorative connotation. But contrast the conclusions reached by Jan Bremmer, "God against the Gods: Early Christians and the Worship of Statues," in *Götterbilder der mittleren und späten Kaiserzeit*, ed. D. Boschung and A. Schaefer (Munich: Wilhelm Fink, 2015), 139–58. Whatever the case, the term certainly came to be used much more commonly by Jews and Christians, and consistently in a strongly pejorative sense.

28   Hans Hübner, "ειδωλειον, *et al.*," in *Exegetical Dictionary of the New Testament*, ed. Horst Balz and Gerhard Schneider, 3 vols. (Grand Rapids: Eerdmans, 1990–1993), 1:386–88.

29   Seven of the eleven New Testament uses of *eidolon* are in Paul's letters: 1 Thessalonians 1:9; 1 Corinthians 8:4, 7; 10:19; 12:2; 2 Corinthians 6:16; Romans 2:22. For further references and discussion, see, e.g., Hübner, "ειδωλειον, et al."

30   The stern condemnations of the teachings of "Nicolaitans" and "that woman Jezebel" in Revelation 2:14-15, 20-23, who are accused of approving "fornication" and eating "food sacrificed to idols," suggests that there were, at least in some early Christian circles, people who took a less adversarial stance than Paul and the author of Revelation. But this more lax stance did not win the day.

31   See, e.g., J. N. Sevenster, *The Roots of Pagan Anti-Semitism in the Ancient World*, Novum Testamentum Supplements 41 (Leiden: Brill, 1975); Louis H. Feldman, "Anti-Semitism in the Ancient World," in *History and Hate: The Dimensions of Anti-Semitism*, ed. D. Berger (Philadelphia: Jewish Publication Society, 1986), 15–42.

32   As noted, e.g., by Nock, *Conversion*, 227–28.

33   L. W. Hurtado, *How on Earth Did Jesus Become a God? Historical Questions about Earliest Devotion to Jesus* (Grand Rapids: Eerdmans, 2005), 56–82 ("To Live and Die for Jesus: Social and Political Consequences of Devotion to Jesus in Earliest Christianity"); and also *Why on Earth Did Anyone Become a Christian in the First Three Centuries?*

34   "Sacrifice keeps the tenuous balance between the human world and the divine realm intact, [and] assures that the dramatic vagaries of

divine dissatisfaction will be held in check. In the Roman context, where sacrifice serves as the first line of defense in the preservation of political stability, the refusal to sacrifice or the perversion of the carefully balanced sacrificial relations produces threatening seismic fissures running underneath the foundations of society." Elizabeth A. Castelli, "Imperial Reimaginings of Christian Origins: Epic in Prudentius' Poem for the Martyr Eulalia," in *Reimagining Christian Origins: A Colloquium Honoring Burton L. Mack*, ed. Elizabeth A. Castelli and Hal Taussig (Valley Forge, Pa.: Trinity International, 1996), 179 (173–84).

35   Shaye J. D. Cohen, "Crossing the Boundary and Becoming a Jew," *Harvard Theological Review* 82 (1989): 13–33; Joshua Ezra Burns, "Conversion and Proselytism," in *The Eerdmans Dictionary of Early Judaism*, ed. John J. Collins and Daniel C. Harlow (Grand Rapids: Eerdmans, 2010), 484–86. In contrast to a somewhat larger number of Gentiles who more informally showed varied levels of interest in, and respect for, Jewish beliefs and practices, full/formal proselyte conversions seem not to have been very frequent in the Roman era.

36   Biblical passages that Paul likely saw himself as fulfilling may include Isaiah 60:1-17; and note that Paul's reference to his "call" by God (Galatians 1:15-16) appears to draw on wording from Isaiah 49:1-6, which portrays a figure called by God "as a light to the nations" (49:6).

37   Note, e.g., Paul's exhortations in 1 Corinthians 7:17-21 that the Corinthian believers should "remain in the condition in which you were called" (7:20), whether circumcised (Jewish) or uncircumcised (pagan), married or unmarried, slave or free.

38   For references to Gentile converts as adopted into Abraham's family, see, e.g., Galatians 3:23-29; Romans 4:1-12. For a cogent discussion of how Paul regarded his Gentile converts in God's redemptive plan, see Matthew V. Novenson, "The Jewish Messiahs, the Pauline Christ, and the Gentile Question," *Journal of Biblical Literature* 128 (2009): 357–73.

39   "Not requiring complete affiliation with Judaism via circumcision, insisting that family and urban cults nonetheless be renounced, the early apostles walked these Christ-fearing pagans into a social and religious no-man's land." Paula Fredriksen, "How Later Contexts

Affect Pauline Content; or, Retrospect Is the Mother of Anachronism," in *Jews and Christians in the First and Second Centuries: How to Write Their History*, ed. Peter J. Tomson and Joshua Schwartz (Leiden: Brill, 2014), 45 (17–51); and see her similar statements in "Christians in the Roman Empire in the First Three Centuries CE," in *A Companion to the Roman Empire*, ed. David S. Potter (London: Blackwell, 2006), 596–97 (587–606). Granted, as Shaye Cohen showed, there were various ways in which Gentiles could relate to Jews and Jewish religion, including abstaining from idolatry without making a full proselyte conversion to Judaism. "Crossing the Boundary." But the point is that those who did this could not plead any ethnic basis for it and so could incur harassment from fellow Gentiles.

40 Adolf von Harnack, *Der Vorwurf des Atheismus in den drei ersten Jahrhunderten*, Texte und Untersuchungen 13/1 (Leipzig: J. C. Heinrichs, 1905). Anders Bjorn Drachman (*Atheism in Pagan Antiquity* [London: Gyldenhal, 1922]) surveys the various expressions of philosophical and religious atheism of the ancient period; and now also Jan N. Bremmer, "Atheism in Antiquity," in *The Cambridge Companion to Atheism*, ed. Michael Martin (Cambridge: Cambridge University Press, 2007), 11–26.

41 *Martyrdom of Polycarp* 9:2; and also 3:2. Whenever the text was put into its present form (which may well have been considerably later than the events it recounts), the charge that Christians were atheists is authentic. The same charge is replied to by Justin Martyr (*1 Apology* 6:1–2; 13:1).

42 Indeed, one scholar has expressed doubts about this, stating, "We may be forced to accept the idea that not all non-Jews who were connected to the Jesus movement were wholeheartedly committed to worship only the God of Israel through Christ. In fact, Paul's discussion of 'idolatry' in 1 Corinthians 8–10, could be taken as an indication that he knew and to some extent accepted that people within the community participated in social events where Grace-Roman cults were performed." Magnus Zetterholm, "Jews, Christians, and Gentiles: Rethinking the Categorization within the Early Jesus Movement," in *Reading Paul in Context: Explorations in Identity Formation*, ed. Kathy Ehrensberger and J. Brian Tucker (London: T&T Clark, 2010), 252 (242–54). I think he misreads the Pauline text.

Paul's comments do seem to reflect a diversity in practices among the Corinthian believers, but I see no indication that Paul accepted his converts participating in what he regarded as "idolatry."

43 Beard, North, and Price, *Religions of Rome*, 311.

44 So also Keith Hopkins, "Christian Number and Its Implications," *Journal of Early Christian Studies* 6 (1998): 187 (185–226). In saying "most" other religious groups, I allow for a similar exclusivity in Judaism of the time. But I know of no other example.

45 The book of Acts posits (entirely plausibly to my mind) that early Jewish believers in Jerusalem frequented the Jerusalem temple at times of daily prayer (Acts 3:1; 22:17) and to make sacrificial offerings too (Acts 21:20-26). But, of course, this reflects their sense of also remaining part of the Jewish people and continuing to worship their ancestral deity according to their traditional practices. There is no indication of new shrines set up specifically for circles of early Christians.

46 See, e.g., Wayne A. Meeks, "Social and Ecclesial Life of the Earliest Christians," in *The Cambridge History of Christianity*, vol. 1, *Origins to Constantine*, ed. Margaret M. Mitchell and Frances M. Young (Cambridge: Cambridge University Press, 2006), 145–73, esp. 160–65; and the wide-ranging survey of various early Christian ritual and worship practices by Andrew B. McGowan, *Ancient Christian Worship: Early Church Practices in Social, Historical, and Theological Perspective* (Grand Rapids: Baker Academic, 2014).

47 So also, e.g., McGowan, *Ancient Christian Worship*, 135 ("almost universal in earliest Christianity").

48 The Greek preposition used is sometimes "in" (Greek: *en*) and sometimes "into" (Greek: *eis*), without a major difference in connotation. For a fuller discussion, see Lars Hartman, *"Into the Name of the Lord Jesus": Baptism in the Early Church* (Edinburgh: T&T Clark, 1997).

49 Hartman, *Into the Name*, 37–50. Everett Ferguson's *Baptism in the Early Church: History, Theology, and Liturgy in the First Five Centuries* (Grand Rapids: Eerdmans, 2009) is now the major discussion of the rite more generally. Robin M. Jensen (*Baptismal Imagery in Early Christianity* [Grand Rapids: Baker Academic, 2012]) highlights visual references to the rite.

50 "In the initiations of the [pagan] mysteries . . . what is protected as 'pure' is the sacred space or the sacred rites themselves. Hence, e.g., washing *precedes* initiation. In Christian initiation [baptism], what is to be kept pure is the *community*. Moreover, that purity is defined in moral as well as theological—that is-monotheistic—terms." Wayne A. Meeks, *The Origins of Christian Morality: The First Two Centuries* (New Haven: Yale University Press, 1993), 33 (emphasis original).

51 Other Old Testament examples of the expression include Genesis 12:8; 21:33; 26:25; 2 Kings 18:24, plus a number of references to calling "upon his [God's] name/him," which likewise designate invoking or appealing to God.

52 See, e.g., Jerome Kodell, *The Eucharist in the New Testament* (Wilmington, Del.: Michael Glazier, 1988).

53 There is a valuable survey of shared meals in various Roman-era groups, in Dennis E. Smith, *From Symposium to Eucharist: The Banquet in the Early Christian World* (Minneapolis: Fortress, 2003), 13–172. But his handling of early Christian evidence is somewhat less adequate. See my review: http://www.bookreviews.org/pdf/ 3112_3417.pdf.

54 A number of invitations to such meals survive from the ancient world and are discussed helpfully in G. H. R. Horsley, *New Documents Illustrating Early Christianity* (North Ryde, Australia: Macquarie University, 1981), 5–9.

55 Paul's references to eating or drinking "in an unworthy manner" (1 Corinthians 11:27) and "without discerning the body" seem to reflect the social divisions and disdainful attitude that he complains about in 11:17-22. The "body" to be discerned, thus, must be the church as the "body" of Christ.

56 McGowan (*Ancient Christian Worship*, 183–215) reviews evidence of Christian practices of the first several centuries.

57 This seems to be reflected in Matthew 6:5-15 and Luke 11:1-4 (although we have two distinguishable forms of the prayer in these texts) and is more explicitly affirmed in the early (second-century?) Christian text known as the *Didache* (8.2–3), where the prayer is prescribed for recitation three times daily.

58 Erik Peterson, "Das Kreuz und das Gebet nach Osten," in *Frühkirche, Judentum und Gnosis: Studien und Untersuchungen* (Rome:

Herder, 1959), 15–35; D. Plooij, "The Attitude of the Outspread Hands ('Orante') in Early Christian Literature and Art," *Expository Times* 23 (1912): 199–203, 265–69. Kneeling was reserved for prayers of contrition.

59 Larry W. Hurtado, *God in New Testament Theology* (Nashville: Abingdon, 2010).

60 See, e.g., David T. Runia, "God and Man in Philo of Alexandria," *Journal of Theological Studies* 39 (1988): 48–75.

61 For a concise citation and discussion of relevant philosophical texts, see Robert M. Grant, *Gods and the One God* (Philadelphia: Westminster, 1986), 75–83; and also the classic analysis in Nock, *Conversion*, 212–53.

62 Other early expressions include John 3:16; Ephesians 2:4-7. Indeed, references to God's love are so frequent in early Christian texts/ discourse that it quickly became a commonplace.

63 Werner Beierwaltes, "The Love of Beauty and the Love of God," in *Classical Mediterranean Spirituality*, ed. A. H. Armstrong (New York: Crossroad, 1986), 293–313.

64 The discussion of attested uses of *agapē* and *agapaō* (in James Hope Moulton and George Milligan, *The Vocabulary of the Greek Testament Illustrated from the Papyri and other Non-literary Sources* [London: Hodder & Stoughton, 1930; repr., Grand Rapids: Eerdmans, 1972], 1–2) remains important. Also useful, esp. for New Testament usage, is Gerhard Schneider, "αγαπη," *Exegetical Dictionary of the New Testament*, ed. Horst Balz and Gerhard Schneider, 3 vols. (Grand Rapids: Eerdmans, 1990–1993), 1:8–12.

65 Campbell Bonner ("Some Phases of Religious Feeling in Later Paganism," *Harvard Theological Review* 30 [1937]: 119–40) discussed "the emotional response to participation in worship" in ancient Greek religion, and the "contemplation or experience of the divine" (120n2), and he urged attention to "love felt towards a god, or conceived to be felt by a god towards his worshippers" (121). He cited Aeschylus' (fifth century BC) reference to Athenians as "beloved [or friends] of the Beloved Maiden" (*parthenou philas philoi* Athena) in *Eumenides* 998–1000. But, despite Bonner's sense of a "genuine and heartfelt" feeling in the passage, we should note that in other works, such as *Agamemnon* and *Libation-Bears*, Aeschylus presents the gods in their more typically amoral character. So, I find

it difficult to judge how much his treatment of them in *Eumenides* reflects a genuine religious development and/or, in any case, a widely shared religious feeling. Bonner (138–39) urged, however, that "the Christian's attitude towards God and towards Christ" can be found also in "the older religion" directed towards Asklepios, Sarapis, Isis, or others, including "the sense of loving communion." Consequently, he posited that "the victory of the Christian church was an intellectual one and that it was a moral one" and (a bit reluctantly) that Christianity "deserved the victory it had won" (139); nevertheless, he felt that in "Hellenic religion" there was revealed "a beauty so soul-stirring" that it generated "a sigh of regret at its passing" (140). Compare, however, Lautaro Roig Lanzillotta ("Christian Apologists and the Greek Gods," in *The Gods of Ancient Greece: Identities and Transformations*, ed. Jan Bremmer and Andrew Erskine [Edinburgh: University of Edinburgh Press, 2010], 442–64), who cites the second-century Christian criticism of pagan notions of the gods. The second-century apologists were somewhat one-sided, but also Bonner's claims may be exaggerated. We should be cautious in taking poetic texts of this or that person of elite status as really indicative of the attitudes of most/many ordinary people.

66   By one count, Old Testament references to God's love for individuals or the people of Israel number fewer than twenty-five. But God's love is "an important aspect" in these writings (e.g., Psalm 47:4; Malachi 1:2; Isaiah 43:4; 48:14; Jeremiah 31:3). Indeed, in the book of Hosea, God's love for Israel is memorably described in terms of a husband's fierce love of his wife (e.g., 3:1) and of a parent for a child (11:1). For discussion, Katharine Doob Sakenfeld, "Love (OT)," in *Anchor Bible Dictionary*, ed. David N. Freedman, 6 vols. (Garden City: Doubleday, 1993), 4:375–81.

67   For a similar judgment, see William Klassen, "Love (NT and Early Jewish)," in Freedman, *Anchor Bible Dictionary*, 4:395 (381–96).

68   For a somewhat similar view, see Jan Bremmer, "The Social and Religious Capital of the Early Christians," *Hephaistos* 24 (2006): 269–78; and Bremmer, *The Rise and Fall of the Afterlife* (London: Routledge, 2002), 103–8 ("Appendix 1: Why Did Jesus' Followers Call Themselves Christians?"). In his extended review of W. V. Harris, ed., *The Spread of Christianity in the First Four Centuries: Essays in Explanation* (Leiden: Brill, 2005), John Barclay judged that

"the clearest and most consistent thesis to emerge from the book is that peculiar features of early Christian ideology [that is, doctrines, beliefs] *were* in fact decisive in ensuring its dramatic impact on the ancient world." See *Journal of Roman Studies* 97 (2007): 372–73, citing 372.

69 "Jewish Christianity" and "Jewish Christians" have become more controversial terms in recent decades, partly because today most Jews regard "Christian" and "Christianity" as incompatible with being a Jew. I use the term simply to designate Jews who openly identified themselves as Jesus-followers. See now the excellent set of studies: Oskar Skarsaune and Reidar Hvalvik, eds., *Jewish Believers in Jesus: The Early Centuries* (Peabody, Mass.: Hendrickson, 2007); and also Tobias Nicklas, *Jews and Christians? Second Century "Christian" Perspectives on the "Parting of the Ways"* (Tübingen: Mohr Siebeck, 2014).

70 Note, e.g., the use of the terms "Christianity" (Greek: *Christianismos*) and "Judaism" (Greek: *Ioudaïsmos*) by Ignatius of Antioch (*To the Magnesians* 10:1–3; *To the Philadelphians* 6:1). Granted, the exact dates of Ignatius' letters remain debated, but I go here with what is still likely the most widely held view.

71 Larry W. Hurtado, "'Ancient Jewish Monotheism' in the Hellenistic and Roman Periods," *Journal of Ancient Judaism* 4 (2013): 379–400. More concisely, see Hurtado, "Monotheism," in Collins and Harlow, *Eerdmans Dictionary*, 961–64. Paula Fredriksen has repeatedly emphasized, however, that Roman-era Jews in diaspora settings often were willing to show certain kinds of *respect* for the gods and those who reverenced them, all in an effort to avoid tensions, so far as possible. But she agrees that Jews typically avoided joining in the actual *worship* of pagan deities. See, e.g., her essay "How Later Contexts Affect Pauline Content," in Tomson and Schwartz, *Jews and Christians*, 17–51, esp. 21–23.

72 There were, however, some versions of early Christianity that did not regard Old Testament writings as scriptures, such as Marcionites and so-called "gnostic" Christians. See now Timothy H. Lim, *The Formation of the Jewish Canon* (New Haven: Yale University Press, 2013); he argues that there was a plurality of ancient Jewish notions of what was "canonical" and that the Pharisaic canon ultimately became the one adopted more widely in Judaism.

73 E.g., Larry W. Hurtado, *One God, One Lord: Early Christian Devotion and Ancient Jewish Monotheism* (Philadelphia: Fortress, 1988; 2nd ed., London: T&T Clark, 1998; 3rd ed. London: Bloomsbury T&T Clark, 2015) and *At the Origins of Christian Worship*, esp. 63–97.

74 "All Israel" as used by Paul here likely designates not every Jew who has ever lived but a final critical mass of Jews, probably a divinely ordained number that comprises the "fullness" (Greek: *plērōma*) or "full number" of redeemed Israel. For a full discussion of Romans 11:25-26 see, e.g., Robert Jewett, *Romans: A Commentary* (Minneapolis: Fortress, 2007), 696–702.

75 So, I do not find persuasive Pamela Eisenbaum's quip that, for Paul, "Jesus saves, but he only saves Gentiles." Cf. Pamela Eisenbaum, *Paul Was Not a Christian* (New York: HarperOne, 2009), 242. This seems to go directly against the whole thrust of Paul's view that there is one God, who has appointed the one Lord (Jesus) as the universal redeemer and the Messiah for all peoples, Jews as well as Gentiles.

76 The earliest firsthand reference to Pharisees is by Paul in Philippians 3:5, where he refers to his own former adherence to Pharisaic observance. The other key ancient sources are other New Testament references in the Gospels and Acts, and in writings of Flavius Josephus, who discusses various Jewish religious parties, with particular attention to the Pharisees. For a brief introduction, see Roland Deines, "Pharisees," in Collins and Harlow, *Eerdmans Dictionary*, 1061–63.

77 Deines, "Pharisees," in Collins and Harlow, *Eerdmans Dictionary*, 1062.

78 Compare the discussion of the categories "sect" and "sectarianism" by Jutta Jokiranta, "Sectarianism," in Collins and Harlow, *Eerdmans Dictionary*, 1209–11.

79 For a recent analysis of theories about the relationship between the Qumran site and the Jewish groups reflected in the scrolls found there, see John J. Collins, "Sectarian Communities in the Dead Sea Scroll," in *The Oxford Handbook of the Dead Sea Scrolls*, ed. Timothy H. Lim and John J. Collins (Oxford: Oxford University Press, 2010), 151–72. Note his judgment that "the sectarian status of this movement [reflected in the Qumran scrolls] is hardly in dispute" (163).

80 Note also 2 Corinthians 3:12–4:6, where Paul characterizes fellow Jews who do not recognize Jesus' glorious status as having

"hardened" minds (3:14), a "veil" lying over their hearts (3:15) that is removed only "in Christ." Those such as Paul who have had this veil over their hearts removed now see "the glory of the Lord [Jesus]" (3:18) and "the light of the gospel of the glory of Christ, who is the image of God" (4:4).

81 This translation more readily reflects the Greek version of Deuteronomy 6:4: *Kyrios ho Theos hēmōn Kyrios heis estin.* But it is also one plausible way to translate the Hebrew original.

82 *Maranatha* in 1 Corinthians 16:22 (and also in *Didache* 10.6) is a transliteration of an Aramaic expression, *māránā' thā* (or *mārán 'athā*), probably meaning "Our Lord, come!" It likely originated as "an ancient acclamation" of Jesus as "Lord" that derived from "some primitive Palestinian liturgical setting," and expressed the hope of Jesus' future return in a regal and judicial capacity. See esp. Joseph A. Fitzmyer, "New Testament Kyrios and Maranatha and Their Aramaic Background," in his collection of essays, *To Advance the Gospel*, 2nd ed. (Grand Rapids: Eerdmans, 1998), 218–35; he judged that *maranatha* "gives evidence of a veneration of Jesus by early Jewish Christians as 'Lord,' as a figure associated with Yahweh of the Old Testament, even as one on the same level with him, without saying explicitly that he is divine" (229).

83 Paul refers casually to "a hymn, a lesson, a revelation, a tongue, or an interpretation" as if they are regular features of the gatherings of his churches (1 Corinthians 14:26), and he refers to singing "with/ in the Spirit" and singing "with the mind," which in the immediate context seem to refer respectively to singing "in a tongue" and in regular language under the impulse of a religious exaltation that he ascribed to God's Spirit. Colossians 3:16 urges that "psalms, hymns and spiritual odes" be sung to God, and Ephesians 5:19 urges the same to be sung "to the Lord" (probably Jesus). Revelation 5:9 pictures God's heavenly court erupting in a "new song" of praise to Jesus ("the Lamb"), which obviously depicts what the author intends as ideal/true worship. See, e.g., Martin Hengel, "The Song about Christ in Earliest Worship," in *Studies in Early Christology* (Edinburgh: T&T Clark, 1995), 227–91.

84 Philippians 2:6-11 has often been cited as (or as adapted from) the wording of an early Christian ode, as has Colossians 1:15-20. E.g., Leonard L. Thompson, "Hymns in Early Christian Worship,"

Anglican Theological Review 55 (1973): 458–72. But there are now also strong critics of this view, such as Benjamin Edsall and Jennifer R. Strawbridge ("The Songs We Used to Sing? Hymn 'Traditions' and Reception in Pauline Letters," *Journal for the Study of the New Testament* 37 [2015]: 290–311), who cite other critics as well. Their main point seems to be that these passages are not referred to as hymns/odes in early Christian writers. This is significant but perhaps not as determinative as they seem to think. In any case, whatever one makes of Philippians 2:6-11 or Colossians 1:15-20, "hymns" and "odes" in praise of Jesus were clearly a part of earliest Christian worship practice, as shown by the references to the practice cited here.

85   Hurtado, *One God, One Lord.*

86   George W. E. Nickelsburg and James VanderKam's *1 Enoch: The Hermeneia Translation* (Minneapolis: Fortress, 2012) is a handy and recent translation. The same authors give detailed commentary in *1 Enoch 2: A Commentary on the Book of 1 Enoch Chapters 37–82* (Minneapolis: Fortress, 2012). On the expression "son of man" and its usage in the Gospels, see my discussion in "Summing Up and Concluding Observations," in *Who is This Son of Man? Latest Scholarship on a Puzzling Expression of the Historical Jesus*, eds. Larry W. Hurtado and Paul Owen (London: T&T Clark, 2011), 159-77.

87   L. W. Hurtado, "Early Jewish Opposition to Jesus-Devotion," *Journal of Theological Studies* 50 (1999): 35–58; reprinted in Hurtado, *How on Earth*, 152–78.

88   "In the end we must acknowledge that Christianity represented something genuinely novel, if not absolutely *sui generis.* The expansion of Christianity was not simply an example of another successful cult within the Graeco-Roman world, but a development that ultimately entailed the fundamental transformation of that world." J. B. Rives, "Christian Expansion and Christian Ideology," in *The Spread of Christianity in the First Four Centuries*, ed. William V. Harris (Leiden: Brill, 2005), 41 (15–41).

3: A Different Identity

1   E.g., Mary Beard, John North, and Simon Price, *Religions of Rome*, vol. 1, *A History* (Cambridge: Cambridge University Press, 1998), 157, 338–40.

2 E.g., the famous quip in Juvenal, *Satires* 3.59, that "Syrian Orontes has poured its sewage into the Tiber," referring to the many peoples of the East who settled in Rome, bringing their foreign customs and religions with them.

3 Beard, North, and Price, *Religions of Rome*, 157–60.

4 Beard, North, and Price, *Religions of Rome*, 158.

5 This is a point made effectively by Simon R. F. Price, *Rituals and Power: The Roman Imperial Cult in Asia Minor* (Cambridge: Cambridge University Press, 1984), with particular reference to the emergence of worship of the Roman emperor.

6 Beard, North, and Price, *Religions of Rome,* 158–60.

7 See, e.g., Beard, North, and Price, *Religions of Rome*, 348–63, on which I draw heavily in these paragraphs. Emperor cult has become again a focus of scholarly discussion, nearly all of it shaped in some way by Price, *Rituals and Power*. Recent works include Ittai Gradel, *Emperor Worship and Roman Religion* (Oxford: Clarendon, 2002); Jeffrey Brodd and Jonathan L. Reed, eds., *Rome and Religion: A Cross-Disciplinary Dialogue on the Imperial Cult* (Atlanta: Society of Biblical Literature, 2011).

8 Beard, North, and Price, *Religions of Rome*, 348.

9 Duncan Fishwick, *The Imperial Cult in the Latin West*, 3 vols. (Leiden: E. J. Brill, 1987–2005).

10 E.g., see Beard, North, and Price, *Religions of Rome*, 353–54.

11 Beard, North, and Price, *Religions of Rome*, 360.

12 Scholars use the term "cult" in a nonpejorative sense to designate a group focused on a particular deity. The older term "mystery religion" is now deemed inappropriate because the various circles devoted to Isis or Mithras, for example, did not form a translocal network. Instead, each local circle operated pretty much on its own. For an excellent and up to date study of these groups, see Jan N. Bremmer, *Initiation into the Mysteries of the Ancient World* (Berlin: De Gruyter, 2014). For a handy selection of primary sources in English translation, see Marvin W. Meyer, ed., *The Ancient Mysteries: A Sourcebook* (San Francisco: Harper & Row, 1987).

13 The early classic study that provoked much reaction was Richard Reitzenstein, *Die hellenistischen Mysterienreligionen nach ihrer Grundgedanken und Wirkungen* (Berlin: Teubner, 1910); English translation of the 1927 German edition, *Hellenistic Mystery Religions*

(Pittsburgh: Pickwick, 1978). Among early critical responses was H. A. A. Kennedy, *St. Paul and the Mystery-Religions* (London: Hodder & Stoughton, 1913). Another early and influential figure was Franz Cumont, particularly in early views of the significance of Mithraism, but his work has come in for very damaging criticism in subsequent decades: e.g., the critical analysis by Ramsay MacMullen, *Paganism in the Roman Empire* (New Haven: Yale University Press, 1981), 122–27; and now esp., Bremmer, *Initiation into the Mysteries.* Furthermore, in the ancient pagan world, a "mystery" (Greek: *mystērion*) did not necessarily connote some exotic and highly secretive ritual performed in darkness and among devotees sworn to secrecy (MacMullen, *Paganism,* 23).

14   See now, Bremmer, *Initiation into the Mysteries,* 110–41.

15   Robert Turcan, *The Cults of the Roman Empire,* trans. Antonia Nevill (Oxford: Blackwell, 1996), 195–247; Manfred Clauss, *The Roman Cult of Mithras,* trans. Richard Gordon (Edinburgh: Edinburgh University Press, 2000); Roger Beck, *The Religion of the Mithras Cult in the Roman Empire: Mysteries of the Unconquered Sun* (Oxford: Oxford University Press, 2006).

16   MacMullen, *Paganism,* 122.

17   Turcan, *Cults of the Roman Empire,* 247.

18   "The attraction of the cult lay rather in a broad range of feelings and experiences: in roasting sacrificial hens and pork ribs . . . with one's friends; descending into the barrel-vaulted dusk of the chapel, into the very presence of the god, for a long meal with much wine; thereafter (it may be imagined) communal chanting of a prayer, fortifying thoughts, perhaps some special verses or paean pronounced by the priest." MacMullen, *Paganism,* 124.

19   Turcan, *Cults of the Roman Empire,* 75–129; Rory B. Egan, "Isis: Goddess of the Oikoumene," in *Goddesses in Religions and Modern Debate,* ed. Larry W. Hurtado (Atlanta: Scholars Press, 1990), 123–42. Tim Hegedus attempted an analysis of the growth of Isis worship, in "The Urban Expansion of the Isis Cult: A Quantitative Approach," *Studies in Religion/Sciences religieuses* 27 (1998): 161–78.

20   Images of Isis and Horus are readily viewable online via a search "Isis and Horus."

21   English translation in Meyer, *Ancient Mysteries,* 172–74.

22   Beard, North, and Price, *Religions of Rome*, 308. See pp. 301–11 on "Homogeneity and Exclusivity" in Roman-era cults.

23   Beard, North, and Price, *Religions of Rome*, 159.

24   John North, "The Development of Religious Pluralism," in *The Jews among Pagans and Christians in the Roman Empire*, ed. Judith Lieu, John North, and Tessa Rajak (New York: Routledge, 1992), 184 (174–93).

25   Wayne Meeks made this same point that the devotion to Isis affirmed by Apuleius was not exclusive. *The Origins of Christian Morality: The First Two Centuries* (New Haven: Yale University Press, 1993), 28.

26   Beard, North, and Price, *Religions of Rome*, 309.

27   Beard, North, and Price, *Religions of Rome*, 310.

28   North, "Development of Religious Pluralism," in Lieu, North, and Rajak, *Jews among Pagans*, 178: "Pagans could and did experiment with foreign cults and certainly might sacrifice to foreign gods when abroad—indeed, it would always have been prudent to do so. They might also belong to, or join, a philosophical sect that held particular views about the gods and their activities. But none of this involved a fundamental decision, affecting the individual's religious loyalty and identity."

29   See, e.g., David G. Horrell, "Idol-Food, Idolatry and Ethics in Paul," in *Idolatry: False Worship in the Bible, Early Judaism and Christianity*, ed. Stephen C. Barton (London: T&T Clark, 2007), 120–40.

30   By contrast, see the author's commendation of the church in Ephesus for rejecting "the works of the Nicolaitans" (2:6), a group also mentioned in 2:15. The Nicolaitans' error is not specified. Steven J. Friesen proposed that they reflect another distinguishable stance "with a different level of social complexity than is the case with Jezebel or Balaam," noting that we cannot tell whether the objectionable feature of the Nicolaitans in the eyes of the author of Revelation was "sexual or culinary or both." *Imperial Cults and the Apocalypse of John: Reading Revelation in the Ruins* (Oxford: Oxford University Press, 2001), 193. See also the discussion of the texts in G. K. Beale, *The Book of Revelation: The New International Greek Testament Commentary* (Grand Rapids: Eerdmans, 1999), 248–51, 260–63.

31   The claim that these prophets encouraged "fornication" may be a metaphor, connoting unfaithfulness to God, or it may refer to the

sort of sexual activities that could sometimes form a part of a "symposium" (drinking banquet), in which slave girls and boys might be brought in to service sexually those invited as guests.

32   As noted also by Beale, *Book of Revelation*, 249.

33   Friesen, *Imperial Cults*, 193.

34   See, e.g., Peder Borgen, " 'Yes,' 'No,' 'How Far?' The Participation of Jews and Christians in Pagan Cults," in *Paul in His Hellenistic Context*, ed. Troels Engberg-Pederson (Minneapolis: Fortress, 1995), 30–59.

35   Philo of Alexandria vividly portrays the major move in religious and ethnic identity for a Gentile convert/proselyte. They have abandoned "their kinfolk by blood, their country, their customs and the temples and images of their gods . . . [and] they have taken a journey to a better home, from idle fables to the clear vision of truth and the worship of the one and truly existing God" (*On the Virtues*, 102). On the various ways that Gentiles could relate to Jewish religion, see Shaye J. D. Cohen, "Crossing the Boundary and Becoming a Jew," *Harvard Theological Review* 82 (1989): 13–33.

36   Among the numerous studies of the Roman-era Jewish diaspora, see John M. G. Barclay, *Jews in the Mediterranean Diaspora: From Alexander to Trajan (323 BCE–117 CE)* (Edinburgh: T&T Clark, 1996); and Eric S. Gruen, *Diaspora: Jews amidst Greeks and Romans* (Cambridge, Mass.: Harvard University Press, 2002).

37   John North, "Pagan Ritual and Monotheism," in *One God: Pagan Monotheism in the Roman Empire*, ed. Stephen Mitchell and Peter Van Nuffelen (Cambridge: Cambridge University Press, 2010), 35 (34–52).

38   Larry W. Hurtado, "The Place of Jesus in Earliest Christian Prayer and Its Import for Early Christian Identity," in *Early Christian Prayer and Identity Formation*, ed. Reidar Hvalvik and Karl Olav Sandnes (Tübingen: Mohr Siebeck, 2014), 35–56.

39   Paul refers to this project in 1 Corinthians 16:1-4; 2 Corinthians 8–9; and Romans 15:22-33. I think it is also referred to in Galatians 2:7-10, but some scholars see this text as referring to some other collection. For a brief introduction to Paul's project, see Scot McKnight, "Collection for the Saints," in *Dictionary of Paul and His Letters*, ed. Gerald F. Hawthorne, Ralph P. Martin, and Daniel G. Reid (Downers Grove, Ill.: InterVarsity, 1993), 143–47.

Among larger scholarly studies, see Ze'ev Safrai and Peter J. Tomson, "Paul's 'Collection for the Saints' (2 Cor 8–9) and Financial Support of Leaders in Early Christianity and Judaism," in *Second Corinthians in the Perspective of Late Second Temple Judaism*, ed. Reimund Bieringer, Emmanuel Nathan, Didier Pollefeyt, and Peter J. Tomson (Leiden: Brill, 2014), 132–220; they judge that Paul's Jerusalem collection "has no parallel in rabbinic literature and is an original development of the global Christian community" (217).

40 See, e.g., D. R. de Lacy, "Gentiles," in Hawthorne, Martin, and Reid, *Dictionary of Paul and His Letters*, 335–39; Gary Gilbert, "Gentiles, Jewish Attitudes Toward," in Collins and Harlow, *Eerdmans Dictionary*, 670–73. Ishay Rosen-Zvi and Adi Ophir ("Paul and the Invention of the Gentiles," *Jewish Quarterly Review* 105 [2015]: 1–41) contend that Paul is the first to refer to non-Jews collectively as an undifferentiated body of "Gentiles," and that he may even have influenced the subsequent use of the term *goy* in rabbinic texts. But I find their argument unpersuasive and faulty on methodological grounds.

41 I note again Paula Fredriksen, "How Later Contexts Affect Pauline Content; or, Retrospect Is the Mother of Anachronism," in *Jews and Christians in the First and Second Centuries: How to Write Their History*, ed. Peter J. Tomson and Joshua Schwartz (Leiden: Brill, 2014), 45 (17–51); she referred to Paul leading his pagan converts into a religious and social "no-man's land."

42 The origins and original connotation of the term "Christian(s)" have often been explored by scholars. For recent discussions, see David G. Horrell, "The Label Χριστιάνος: 1 Peter 4:16 and the Formation of Christian Identity," *Journal of Biblical Literature* 126 (2007): 361–81; and Paul Trebilco, *Self-Designations and Group Identity in the New Testament* (Cambridge: Cambridge University Press, 2012), 272–97. See also Jan Bremmer, "*Christianus sum:* The Early Christian Martyrs and Christ," in *The Rise and Fall of the Afterlife* (New York: Routledge, 2001), 103–8, 175–78; and Philippa Townsend, "Who Were the First Christians? Jews, Gentiles and the *Christianoi*," in *Heresy and Identity in Late Antiquity*, ed. E. Iricinischi and H. M. Zellentin (Tübingen: Mohr Siebeck, 2008), 212–30.

43 Horrell, "The Label Χριστιάνος," 362.

44   On the Jewish messianic notions and hopes to which early Chris-
     tian claims originally referred, see, e.g., Kenneth E. Pomykala,
     "Messianism," in Collins and Harlow, *Eerdmans Dictionary*, 938–42;
     and, more fully, John J. Collins, *The Scepter and the Star: The Mes-
     siahs of the Dead Sea Scrolls and Other Ancient Literature* (New York:
     Doubleday, 1995); and Joseph A. Fitzmyer, *The One Who Is to Come*
     (Grand Rapids: Eerdmans, 2007).

45   "Quakers" is another example of a term originating among out-
     siders to refer to Christian groups who referred to themselves as
     "Friends of Truth" and other preferred expressions. But, at some
     point, they accepted also "Quakers." See further discussion of this
     process, in Trebilco, *Self-Designations*, 9–10.

46   E.g., Ignatius of Antioch (5×), *Martyrdom of Polycarp* (4×), and *Epis-
     tle to Diognetus* (14×), plus uses in non-Christian writers such as
     Tacitus, Suetonius, Josephus, Pliny the Younger, and Trajan.

47   So Horrell ("The Label Χριστιάνος," 367), citing previous scholars
     also, and he reviews various other proposals as well (362–67).

48   *Herōdianoi* are mentioned in Mark 3:6; 12:13; Matthew 22:16.
     Note also the reference to "the partisans of Herod" (Greek: *tous
     ta Herōdou phronountes*) by Josephus (*Jewish Antiquities* 14.450). In
     Mark 8:15, manuscripts differ over whether to read "the leaven of
     Herod" or "the leaven of the Herodians." On the one hand, the lat-
     ter reading is supported in the earliest extant copy of Mark ($\mathfrak{P}^{45}$, the
     third-century Chester Beatty codex of the Gospels and Acts) and a
     number of later manuscripts. On the other hand, the other reading
     is supported by the majority of manuscripts, including those gen-
     erally taken as of superior textual quality (e.g., Codex Sinaiticus,
     Codex Vaticanus). The choice is not decisive for my point.

49   Tacitus and Suetonius say that Nero went after Christians in 64 AD.
     Unless they were using the term anachronistically, reflecting usage
     of it at the time they wrote, their accounts suggest that the term was
     in usage in Nero's time.

50   As noted by Horrell ("The Label Χριστιάνος," 369) in his analysis of
     the use of the term in 1 Peter.

51   See the discussion in Trebilco, *Self-Designations*.

52   For discussion of these categories, see Trebilco, *Self-Designations*, 6–9.

53   In much later Christian usage, the term "saints" was retained
     but applied to certain Christians deemed to have been of special

spiritual status and significance. The original usage, however, was to designate all believers.

54   For further discussion, see L. Coenen, "Church, Synagogue," in *New International Dictionary of New Testament Theology*, ed. Colin Brown, 3 vols. (Grand Rapids: Zondervan, 1975–1978), 1:291–307; J. Roloff, "ἐκκλησία," in *Exegetical Dictionary of the New Testament*, ed. Horst Balz and Gerhard Schneider, 3 vols. (Grand Rapids: Eerdmans, 1990–1993), 1:410–15.

55   This "regular/lawful assembly" contrasts with the riotous assembly (*ekklēsia*) of v. 32.

56   Most recently, see George van Kooten, "Ἐκκλησία τοῦ θεοῦ: The 'Church of God' and the Civic Assemblies (Ἐκκλησίαι) of the Greek Cities in the Roman Empire: A Response to Paul Trebilco and to Richard A. Horsley," *New Testament Studies* 58 (2012): 522–48. I think, however, that van Kooten rests his case far too heavily on the single Pauline reference to Christians as having a "citizenship" (Greek: *politeuma*) in heaven. Van Kooten seems to read all of Paul's uses of *ekklēsia* through this one text, ascribing thereby to Paul a programmatic conceptual contrast between the churches and the political assemblies. The Philippians text obviously makes an implicit contrast between an earthly (Roman) citizenship and a heavenly one. But this one place where Paul makes this contrast is likely conditioned by Philippi as a Roman colony, where matters of citizenship would have been of particular importance. Moreover, Van Kooten seems to me to fail to do justice to the actual statements in which Paul refers to *ekklēsia*, but this is not the occasion to elaborate my own analysis.

57   E.g., Deuteronomy 23:2; 1 Chronicles 28:8; 29:20; Micah 2:5. Scholars typically use "LXX" to refer to the Greek Old Testament.

58   E.g., Psalm 22:22 (LXX 21:22); 26:12 (LXX 25:12); 35:18 (LXX 34:18). Chapter numbers of the Septuagint do not always line up with those of the Hebrew text, which is the usual basis for English translations of the Old Testament.

59   1QM 4.10 (the "War Scroll"). For a handy presentation of texts (the Hebrew with English translation on facing pages), see Florentino Garacía Martínez and Eibert J. C. Tigchelaar, eds., *The Dead Sea Scrolls Study Edition*, 2 vols. (Grand Rapids: Eerdmans, 1997–1998).

60 Paul in particular uses this expression a number of times: the singular form in 1 Corinthians 1:2; 10:32; 11:22; 15:9; 2 Corinthians 1:1; Galatians 1:13; and the plural "assemblies/churches of God" in 1 Corinthians 11:16, 22; 1 Thessalonians 2:14; 2 Thessalonians 1:4.

61 There are several writings ascribed to Paul but certainly, or likely, as the case may be, composed in his name posthumously. These include extracanonical texts, such as "3 Corinthians," and also several included in the New Testament, such as 1 Timothy, 2 Timothy, Titus, Ephesians, and (though opinion on these is a bit more divided) 2 Thessalonians and Colossians.

62 See, e.g., Exodus 19:6.

63 Michelle Murray has argued that the troublemakers in Galatia may have been Gentile Christians who had become convinced that full Torah observance was necessary. *Playing a Jewish Game: Gentile Christian Judaizing in the First and Second Centuries CE* (Waterloo, Ontario: Wilfrid Laurier University Press, 2003). The identity of those whom Paul opposes in Galatians, however, is not decisive for the point I am making here.

64 Among a number of studies, see, e.g., Jeffrey S. Siker, *Disinheriting the Jews: Abraham in Early Christian Controversy* (Louisville: John Knox, 1991); and Stephen G. Wilson, *Related Strangers: Jews and Christians 70–170 C.E.* (Minneapolis: Fortress, 1995).

65 Denise Kimber Buell (*Why This New Race? Ethnic Reasoning in Early Christianity* [New York: Columbia University Press, 2002]) provocatively probed the use of this kind of terminology and the associated claims in early Christian texts. I have both appreciation for some of her discussion and qualms about some other parts, including her use of "race" (with the modern connotations of the term) to characterize early Christian group identity, but I cannot go into the matter further here. I note somewhat similar reservations in an important review of the book: http://bmcr.brynmawr .edu/2006/2006-02-31.html (accessed 7 January 2016).

66 I have treated the matter fully elsewhere: Larry W. Hurtado, *Lord Jesus Christ: Devotion to Jesus in Earliest Christianity* (Grand Rapids: Eerdmans, 2003).

67 J. D. G. Dunn, *Beginning from Jerusalem: Christianity in the Making*, vol. 2 (Grand Rapids: Eerdmans, 2009), 214.

68 North ("Development of Religious Pluralism," in Lieu, North, and Rajak, *Jews among Pagans*, 191) referred to Christianity forcing others "to react to a situation not of their own making" and judged that "in the end the transformation affected every area of life."

69 North, "Development of Religious Pluralism," in Lieu, North, and Rajak, *Jews among Pagans*, 189.

70 This distinction was, of course, quickly erased by Constantine's appropriation of Christianity, and in European Christendom as well, and it reemerged in some early post-Reformation movements but more saliently in the eighteenth century. For a wider-ranging discussion of how early Christianity anticipated modern "secular" notions, see Edwin Judge, "The Religion of the Secularists," *Journal of Religious History* 38 (2014): 307–19.

71 Keith Hopkins, *A World Full of Gods: Pagans, Jews, and Christians in the Roman Empire* (London: Weidenfeld & Nicolson, 1999), 113. And this judgment from a scholar whose general disdain for early Christianity all too often otherwise distorted his portrayal.

72 Tertullian, *To Scapula*, 2; the translation is adapted from Alexander Roberts and James Donaldson, eds., *The Ante-Nicene Fathers*, vol. 3 (Peabody, Mass.: Hendrickson, 1994), 105.

73 Granted, there are precedents, especially in some Jewish texts. The stories in the early chapters of the biblical book of Daniel, for example, insist that Jews can be good servants of the pagan ruler if he does not require them to worship the pagan gods. Likewise, Jews were allowed the special arrangement of offering sacrifice *to their own God* and *on behalf of the emperor*, and they were excused from worshipping the pagan deities. But, to reiterate the point, this was a special *ethnic* arrangement and was not seen as precedent setting for any other people.

4: A "Bookish" Religion

1 The key work is Harry Y. Gamble, *Books and Readers in the Early Church* (New Haven: Yale University Press, 1995); although I find his handling of the Christian preference for the codex (49–66) flawed. Compare my discussion of the matter in *The Earliest Christian Artifacts: Manuscripts and Christian Origins* (Grand Rapids: Eerdmans, 2006), 43–93 (cited hereafter as *Artifacts*). On early Christian books, see also Michael J. Kruger, "Manuscripts, Scribes,

and Book Production within Early Christianity," in *Christian Origins and Greco-Roman Culture: Social and Literary Contexts for the New Testament*, ed. Stanley E. Porter and Andrew Pitts (Leiden: Brill, 2012), 15–40; Larry W. Hurtado and Chris Keith, "Writing and Book Production in the Hellenistic and Roman Periods," in *The New Cambridge History of the Bible: The Bible, From the Beginnings to 600*, ed. James Carleton Paget and Joachim Schaper (Cambridge: Cambridge University Press, 2013), 63–80; and H. Gregory Snyder, *Teachers and Texts in the Ancient World: Philosophers, Jews and Christians* (New York: Routledge, 2000), esp. 189–227.

2   Kim Haines-Eitzen has criticized "scholarly imaginings of a scholarly and *bookish* Alexandrian Christianity" (emphasis original), contending that our earliest manuscripts of New Testament writings do not exhibit the marks that characterize those produced in scriptoria but instead look more like copies of texts produced more informally and in a "non-scholarly" tradition. "Imagining the Alexandrian Library and a 'Bookish' Christianity," in *Reading New Testament Papyri: Lire les papyrus du Nouveau Testament dans leur context*, ed. Claire Clivaz and Jean Zumstein (Leuven: Peeters, 2011), 218 (206–18). I take her point. But, as indicated above, I use the term "bookish" more loosely here simply to point to the importance and prominence of texts in early Christian groups. On the place of texts in Roman-era Jewish circles, see, e.g., Snyder, *Teachers and Texts*, 122–89.

3   Gamble, *Books and Readers*, 141; Snyder, *Teachers and Texts*, 10; Margaret M. Mitchell, "The Emergence of the Written Record," in *The Cambridge History of Christianity*, vol. 1, *Origins to Constantine*, ed. Margaret M. Mitchell and Frances M. Young (Cambridge: Cambridge University Press, 2006), 178 (177–94); Guy G. Stroumsa, "Early Christianity—A Religion of the Book?" in *Homer, the Bible, and Beyond: Literary and Religious Canons in the Ancient World*, ed. Margalit Finkelberg and Guy Stroumsa (Leiden: Brill, 2003), 153 (153–73).

4   In an earlier statement (*First Apology* 66.3), Justin explicitly identifies the "memoirs" of the apostles as the Gospels. Note that he knows of the use of multiple Gospels, although he does not name the ones used. On Justin, see the recent multiauthor volume edited by Sara Parvis and Paul Foster, eds., *Justin Martyr and His Worlds*

(Minneapolis: Fortress, 2007), which includes Oskar Skarsaune, "Justin and His Bible," 53–76 (on the texts Justin regarded as scriptures), and C. E. Hill, "Was John's Gospel among Justin's *Apostolic Memoirs?*" 88–94 (who argues for a positive answer). For general discussion about the reading of texts in ancient worship, see Gerard Rouwhorst, "The Bible in Liturgy," in *The New Cambridge History of the Bible*, vol. 1, *From the Beginnings to 600*, ed. James Carleton Paget and Joachim Schaper (Cambridge: Cambridge University Press, 2013), 822–42.

5   On these and other "pseudonymous" writings in the New Testament, see, e.g., Bart D. Ehrman, *The New Testament: A Historical Introduction to the Early Christian Writings* (Oxford: Oxford University Press, 1997), 320–40; Delbert Burkett, *An Introduction to the New Testament and the Origins of Christianity* (Cambridge: Cambridge University Press, 2002), 436–45. I do find Ehrman's reference to "forgery" a bit misleading, however. Forgery today is most often done for financial gain, whereas authors of ancient "pseudonymous" works sought mainly to have their contents read and given some respect.

6   Consequently, I find dubious McGowan's recent claim that the regular reading of scripture texts in early Christian assemblies, which he refers to as "the 'scripturization' of Christian worship," "seems to be a second- or third-generation phenomenon." Andrew B. McGowan, *Ancient Christian Worship: Early Church Practices in Social, Historical, and Theological Perspective* (Grand Rapids: Baker Academic, 2014), esp. 83, 110.

7   I count some fifty-two statements referring to "scripture" and "scriptures" in New Testament writings, twelve of them in Paul's undisputed letters. In the latest (28th) edition of the Nestle-Aland edition of the Greek New Testament, *Novum Testamentum Graece* (Stuttgart: Deutsche Bibelgesellschaft, 2012), there are forty-two double-column pages of quotations and allusions to Old Testament and extracanonical Jewish writings (pp. 836–78), thirty-three pages of references to writings in the Hebrew Bible alone (pp. 836–69). See, e.g., Bradley H. McLean, *Citations and Allusions to Jewish Scripture in Early Christian and Jewish Writings through 180 C.E.* (Lewiston: Edwin Mellen, 1992); G. L. Archer and G. C. Chirichigno, *Old Testament Quotations in the New Testament: A Complete Survey* (Chicago: Moody, 1983).

8   Early Christian writers sometimes acknowledged that there were uneducated and illiterate Christians, as noted by Origen (*Against Celsus* 1.27) and Justin Martyr (*First Apology* 60.11). But Justin also asserts a diversity of Christians of his time, including "philosophers and scholars" as well as "artisans and people entirely uneducated" (*Second Apology* 10.8). On the social makeup of second-century Roman Christianity, see Peter Lampe, *From Paul to Valentinus: Christians at Rome in the First Two Centuries*, trans. Michael Steinhauser (Minneapolis: Fortress, 2003).

9   As Gamble observed, "We must assume, then, that the large majority of Christians in the early centuries of the church were illiterate, not because they were unique but because they were in this respect typical" (*Books and Readers*, 6).

10 I have discussed these matters in earlier publications: Larry W. Hurtado, "What Do the Earliest Christian Manuscripts Tell Us about Their Readers?" in *The World of Jesus and the Early Church: Identity and Interpretation in Early Communities of Faith*, ed. Craig A. Evans (Peabody, Mass.: Hendrickson, 2011), 179–92; and "Manuscripts and the Sociology of Early Christian Reading," in *The Early Text of the New Testament*, ed. Charles E. Hill and Michael J. Kruger (Oxford: Oxford University Press, 2012), 49–62.

11 The earliest extant lectionary manuscripts date from the fourth century AD and later. See Carroll Osburn, "The Greek Lectionaries of the New Testament," in *The Text of the New Testament in Contemporary Research: Essays on the* Status Quaestionis, 2nd ed., ed. Bart D. Ehrman and Michael W. Holmes (Leiden: Brill, 2013), 93–113. There may have been systems of planned reading of scriptures in ancient synagogues, but I know of no evidence of pre-Christian lectionary *manuscripts*. Stephen Reed ("Physical Features of Excerpted Torah Texts," in *Jewish and Christian Scripture as Artifact and Canon*, ed. Craig A. Evans and H. Daniel Zacharias [London: T&T Clark, 2009], 82–104) discusses *tefillin, mezuzot*, and manuscripts comprised of excerpts of the Pentateuch. But these are not really lectionaries.

12 Rouwhorst ("Bible in Liturgy," in Paget and Schaper, *New Cambridge History*, 833–35) describes three reading schemes followed in Christian circles in different regions in Late Antiquity.

13   Charles Perrot, "The Reading of the Bible in the Ancient Synagogue," in *Mikra: Text, Translation, Reading and Interpretation of the Hebrew Bible in Ancient Judaism and Early Christianity*, ed. Martin Jan Mulder (Philadelphia: Fortress, 1988), 137–60; Lawrence H. Schiffman, "The Early History of Public Reading of the Torah," in *Jews, Christians, and Polytheists in the Ancient Synagogue: Cultural Interaction during the Greco-Roman Period*, ed. S. Fine (London: Routledge, 1999), 44–56; Stephen K. Catto, *Reconstructing the First-Century Synagogue: A Critical Analysis of Current Research*, Library of New Testament Studies 363 (London: T&T Clark, 2007), 116–25.

14   For a stout defense of a first-century date for the inscription, and for full references to other scholarly publications on the item, see John S. Kloppenborg Verbin, "Dating Theodotos (CIJ 1404)," *Journal of Jewish Studies* 51 (2000): 243–80; and also Anders Runesson, Donald D. Binder, and Birger Olsson, *The Ancient Synagogue from Its Origins to 200 C.E.: A Source Book*, Ancient Judaism and Early Christianity 72 (Leiden: Brill, 2008), 52–54.

15   Donald Drew Binder, *Into the Temple Courts: The Place of the Synagogues in the Second Temple Period*, Society of Biblical Literature Dissertation Series 169 (Atlanta: Society of Biblical Literature, 1999), 399.

16   Referring to what they called the "sacral graphocentrism" of early Judaism and Christianity, the editors of a multiauthor volume on literacy in the ancient world judged that the ancient Jewish and Christian attitudes to their sacred texts "contrast markedly with the extensive but very different uses of writing in Greek and Roman religion," in which "texts never occupied the same position as the Jewish or Christian scriptures." Alan K. Bowman and Greg Woolf, eds., *Literacy and Power in the Ancient World* (Cambridge: Cambridge University Press, 1994), 13.

17   Edwin A. Judge has contended that in this and other features early Christianity resembled philosophical groups of that day. "The Early Christians as a Scholastic Community," *Journal of Religious History* 1 (1961): 4–15, 125–37; republished in E. A. Judge, *The First Christians in the Roman World* (Tübingen: Mohr Siebeck, 2008), 526–52.

18 Snyder, *Teachers and Texts*, 1. Snyder's excellent discussion probes similarities and differences in the ways that texts were used in various philosophical groups of the Roman period.

19 On the emergence of a body of texts treated as scriptures in ancient Jewish tradition, see now Timothy H. Lim, *The Formation of the Jewish Canon* (New Haven: Yale University Press, 2013).

20 Note what seem to be references to several Christian circles in Rome in Romans 16:5, 10, 11, 14, 15. But houses were not the only venue for the gatherings of early Christians, as contended recently by David L. Balch, "Rich Pompeiian Houses, Shops for Rent, and the Huge Apartment Building in Herculaneum as Typical Spaces for Pauline House Churches," *Journal for the Study of the New Testament* 27 (2004): 27–46; and Edward Adams, *The Earliest Christian Meeting Places: Almost Exclusively Houses?* (London: T&T Clark, 2013).

21 In Paul's day, "Galatia" could refer either to a traditional territory by that name in central Anatolia or to the Roman province of Galatia to the south. Scholars differ over which Paul meant, but the issue is not important here. See, e.g., Hans Dieter Betz, *Galatians* (Philadelphia: Fortress, 1979), 3–5. Note also the reference to "the churches of Galatia" in 1 Corinthians 16:1. Galatian Christians are also mentioned in 2 Timothy 4:10 and 1 Peter 1:1.

22 E. Randolph Richards (*Paul and First-Century Letter Writing* [Downers Grove, Ill.: InterVarsity, 2004]) judged that "it is scarcely plausible" that Paul dispatched multiple copies, as this would have been prohibitively expensive, and he proposed that Paul sent the Galatians letter by a carrier, who "followed the Roman highway, stopping at each town in succession" (187n7).

23 The seven cities, Ephesus, Smyrna, Pergamum, Thyatira, Sardis, Philadelphia, and Laodicea, were all connected by roads. See Colin J. Hemer, *The Letters to the Seven Churches of Asia in Their Local Setting* (Sheffield: JSOT Press, 1986).

24 As Gamble (*Books and Readers*, 95) observed, Paul's letters were occasioned by particular circumstances but were hardly casual communication.

25 Cf. Robert W. Funk, "The Apostolic *Parousia*: Form and Significance," in *Christian History and Interpretation: Studies Presented to John Knox*, ed. W. R. Farmer, C. F. D. Moule, and R. R. Niebuhr (Cambridge: Cambridge University Press, 1967), 249–68; and the

critique by Margaret M. Mitchell, "New Testament Envoys in the Context of Greco-Roman Diplomatic and Epistolary Conventions: The Example of Timothy and Titus," *Journal of Biblical Literature* 111 (1992): 641–62; Mitchell contends that Paul deliberately chose letters (and/or emissaries) over a personal visit in at least some cases because he regarded them as more effective.

26 The variant reading in many later manuscripts, "to all the saints," is surely secondary and likely reflects the practice of Paul's letters being read more widely as scripture.

27 See Gamble's discussion of the matter, in *Books and Readers*, 99–101. He proposes that the initial collection may have been "based on copies retained by Paul and preserved after his death by his associates" (100).

28 In his classic study (*The Text of the Epistles: A Disquisition upon the Corpus Paulinum; The Schweich Lectures, 1946* [London: Oxford University Press for the British Academy, 1953], 279), Günther Zuntz proposed that an archetypal collection of Pauline epistles was made by ca. 100 AD.

29 As Skarsaune notes ("Justin and His Bible," in Parvis and Foster, *Justin Martyr*, 71–72), Justin may also have been influenced by his Christian predecessor, Papias, who referred to the Gospel of Mark as a collection of what he remembered of Peter's teaching about Jesus (reported by Eusebius, *Ecclesiastical History* 3.39.15–16).

30 Skarsaune, "Justin and His Bible," in Parvis and Foster, *Justin Martyr*, esp. 64–74. Noting "almost an established dogma of scholarship" that Justin did not use the Gospel of John, Skarsaune points to "echoes of John" in Justin ("case studies" in *First Apology* 35.5–8 and 52.10–12) and cites (184n64) as "an effective deconstruction and refutation of this consensus." See Charles E. Hill, *The Johannine Corpus in the Early Church* (Oxford: Oxford University Press, 2004), esp. 11–59.

31 Most recently, see Joseph Verheyden, "Justin's Text of the Gospels: Another Look at the Citations in *1 Apol. 15.1–8*," in *The Early Text of the New Testament*, ed. Charles E. Hill and Michael J. Kruger (Oxford: Oxford University Press, 2012), 314–15 (313–35); and, earlier, Charles E. Hill, *Who Chose the Gospels: Probing the Great Gospel Conspiracy* (Oxford: Oxford University Press, 2010), 132–43; Skarsaune, "Justin and His Bible," in Parvis and Foster,

Justin Martyr, esp. 64–68; and Graham Stanton, "Jesus Traditions and Gospels in Justin Martyr and Irenaeus," in *The Biblical Canons. Bibliotheca Ephemeridum Theologicarum Lovaniensium CLXIII*, ed. J.-M. Auwers and H. J. de Jonge (Leuven: Leuven University Press, 2003), 353–70, esp. 360–66.

32   For an argument for an early fourfold Gospel collection, see, e.g., Graham N. Stanton, "The Fourfold Gospel," *New Testament Studies* 43 (1997): 317–46. Skarsaune ("Justin and His Bible," in Parvis and Foster, *Justin Martyr*, 187n95) also points to "certain or probable echoes of 1 Corinthians, Philippians, and Colossians . . . and possible allusions to 1 and 2 Thessalonians, 1 Timothy, and Titus."

33   On Marcion, cf. Paul Foster, "Marcion: His Life, Works, Beliefs, and Impact," *Expository Times* 121 (2010): 269–80; Sebastian Moll, "Marcion: A New Perspective on His Life, Theology, and Impact," *Expository Times* 121 (2010): 281–86; and Heikki Räisänen, "Marcion," in *A Companion to Second-Century Christian "Heretics,"* ed. Antti Marjanen and Petri Luomanen (Leiden: Brill, 2005), 100–124.

34   As noted, e.g., by Skarsaune, "Justin and His Bible," in Parvis and Foster, *Justin Martyr*, 73.

35   Marcion (and those who followed his teachings), however, also rejected the "Old Testament" writings.

36   The influential study is William V. Harris, *Ancient Literacy* (London: Harvard University Press, 1989). But cf. the views in Mary Beard et al., *Literacy in the Roman World*, Journal of Roman Archaeology Supplement Series 3 (Ann Arbor: University of Michigan, 1991).

37   Gamble (*Books and Readers*, 8–9) noted that the likely limited extent of literacy in the Roman-era "had little adverse effect on the ability of Christians generally to gain a close acquaintance with Christian literature."

38   Larry W. Hurtado, "Oral Fixation and New Testament Studies? 'Orality,' 'Performance' and Reading Texts in Early Christianity," *New Testament Studies* 60 (2014): 321–40.

39   See Lincoln H. Blumell, *Lettered Christians: Christians, Letters, and Late Antique Oxyrhynchus* (Leiden: Brill, 2012); although his evidence comes from mainly the third through seventh centuries AD and thereafter. As for "apocryphal" writings, such as the *Gospel of Thomas*, they often seem to have been intended for circulation among loose networks of like-minded individual Christians rather

than used as scripture by formal circles of believers such as the phantom "Thomas community." On the topic, see Larry W. Hurtado, "Who Read Early Christian Apocrypha?" in the *Oxford Handbook of Early Christian Apocrypha*, ed. Christopher Tuckett and Andrew Gregory (Oxford: Oxford University Press, 2015), 153–66.

40 Larry W. Hurtado, "A Fresh Analysis of P.Oxyrhynchus 1228 ($\mathfrak{P}^{22}$) as Artefact," in *Studies on the Text of the New Testament and Early Christianity: Essays in Honor of Michael W. Holmes on the Occasion of His 65th Birthday*, ed. Daniel M. Gurtner, Juan Hernández Jr., and Paul Foster (Leiden: Brill, 2015), 153–66.

41 On this papyrus and the other early copies of the *Gospel of Thomas* in Greek, see Larry W. Hurtado, "The Greek Fragments of the *Gospel of Thomas* as Artefacts: Papyrological Observations on Papyrus Oxyrhynchus 1, Papyrus Oxyrhynchus 654 and Papyrus Oxyrhynchus 655," in *Das Thomasevangelium: Entstehung—Rezeption—Theologie*, ed. Jörg Frey, Enno Edzard Popkes, and Jens Schröter (Berlin: De Gruyter, 2008), 19–32.

42 For a similar judgment, see, e.g., Kruger, "Manuscripts," in Porter and Pitts, *Christian Origins*, 16.

43 Claudio Moreschini and Enrico Norelli, *Early Christian Greek and Latin Literature: A Literary History*, vol. 1, *From Paul to the Age of Constantine*, trans. Matthew J. O'Connell (Peabody, Mass.: Hendrickson, 2005).

44 See, e.g., the discussion of works attributed to Hippolytus of Rome, in Moreschini and Norelli, *Early Christian Greek and Latin Literature*, 232–47.

45 Robin Lane Fox (*Pagans and Christians* [New York: Alfred A. Knopf, 1987], 270) noted that the early Christian literary output was "conspicuous" in size.

46 E.g., Anna Collar (*Religious Networks in the Roman Empire* [Cambridge: Cambridge University Press, 2013]) analyzed inscriptional evidence for the spread of several religious groups, including Jupiter Dolichenus and the "Most High God," for neither of which is there any evidence of the production of texts.

47 The seven letters accepted as genuinely Paul's by virtually all scholars are (in their traditional ordering in the New Testament) Romans, 1 Corinthians, 2 Corinthians, Galatians, Philippians, 1 Thessalonians, and Philemon. There is less of a consensus on the

others. The "Pastoral Epistles" (1 Timothy, 2 Timothy, and Titus) are most widely judged pseudonymous, the remaining epistles (Ephesians, Colossians, 2 Thessalonians) also often (but somewhat less widely) so judged.

48 Martin R. P. McGuire, "Letters and Letter Carriers in Christian Antiquity," *Classical World* 53 (1960): 148–53, 184–85, 199–200.

49 These figures taken from David E. Aune, *The New Testament in its Literary Environment* (Philadelphia: Westminster, 1987), 205. Cf. the similar figures given by Richards, *Paul and First-Century Letter Writing*, 163.

50 Richards, *Paul and First-Century Letter Writing*, 164.

51 Aune, *Literary Environment*, 167.

52 So also Gamble, *Books and Readers*, 95. There are now numerous studies in which Paul's letters are analyzed in the light of ancient rhetorical practice: e.g., Anders Eriksson, *Traditions as Rhetorical Proof: Pauline Argumentation in 1 Corinthians* (Stockholm: Almqvist & Wiksell, 1998). But there are also critics of this who judge that Paul's acquaintance with rhetorical techniques was limited: e.g., R. Dean Anderson Jr., *Ancient Rhetorical Theory and Paul* (Kampen: Kok Pharos, 1996); Philip H. Kern, *Rhetoric and Galatians: Assessing an Approach to Paul's Epistles* (Cambridge: Cambridge University Press, 2007). It is not necessary here to engage the issue of how sophisticated an acquaintance with rhetoric Paul had. It is sufficient simply to note that his letters are obviously serious vehicles for teaching on subjects that Roman-era philosophy engaged, such as right behavior.

53 Aune, *Literary Environment*, 167–70. See also the categories of letters described by Stanley K. Stowers, *Letter Writing in Greco-Roman Antiquity* (Philadelphia: Westminster, 1986).

54 See esp. Richard A. Burridge, *What Are the Gospels? A Comparison with Graeco-Roman Biography* (Cambridge: Cambridge University Press, 1992; 2nd ed., Grand Rapids: Eerdmans, 2004); and similarly Aune, *Literary Environment*, 17–76; and my discussion in *Lord Jesus Christ: Devotion to Jesus in Earliest Christianity* (Grand Rapids: Eerdmans, 2003), 270–82.

55 See the specific comparison of the Gospel of Mark with Roman-era biographical works, by David E. Aune, *Jesus, Gospel Tradition*

and Paul in the Context of Jewish and Greco-Roman Antiquity (Tübingen: Mohr Siebeck, 2013), 50–51.

56 This has been noted by several scholars: Philip S. Alexander, "Rabbinic Biography and the Biography of Jesus: A Survey of the Evidence," in *Synoptic Studies*, ed. C. M. Tuckett (Sheffield: JSOT Press, 1984), 19–50, esp. 40–41; also Jacob Neusner, *Why No Gospels in Talmudic Judaism?* (Atlanta: Scholars Press, 1988); Richard A. Burridge, "Gospel Genre, Christological Controversy and the Absence of Rabbinic Biography: Some Implications of the Biographical Hypothesis," in *Christology, Controversy and Community: New Testament Essays in Honour of David R. Catchpole*, ed. David G. Horrell and Christopher M. Tuckett (Leiden: Brill, 2000), 137–56; and my discussion in *Lord Jesus Christ*, 274–77.

57 To be sure, Flavius Josephus wrote a substantial autobiography, *The Life of Josephus*, but that is not really the same thing.

58 David E. Aune (*Literary Environment*, 27–36) gives a survey of examples and key features.

59 Simon Swain, "Defending Hellenism: Philostratus, *In Honour of Apollonius*," in *Apologetics in the Second Century: Pagans, Jews, and Christians*, ed. Mark Edwards, Martin Goodman, Simon Price, and Christopher Rowland (Oxford: Oxford University Press, 1999), 157–96.

60 It has been widely thought among New Testament scholars that the Gospel of John may have gone through at least one prior edition or that it may have reached its present form through a compositional process of several stages. Cf. e.g., Raymond E. Brown, *The Community of the Beloved Disciple: The Life, Loves, and Hates of an Individual Church in New Testament Times* (New York: Paulist, 1979); and Martin Hengel, *The Johannine Question* (London: SCM Press, 1989), 83–108. In John 21:20-25, the "beloved disciple" is posited as the author or chief source for the Gospel, but in those same verses his death is mentioned and in v. 24 an unspecified "we" affirm his validity as witness to Jesus' ministry. So, at the very least, in its present form the Gospel of John seems to be a posthumous text.

61 Edouard Massaux, *The Influence of the Gospel of St. Matthew on Christian Literature before St. Irenaeus*, part 1, *The First Ecclesiastical Writers*, ed. A. J. Bellinzoni, trans. N. J. Belval and S. Hecht (Macon, Ga.: Mercer University Press, 1990).

62 Noted by Gamble, *Books and Readers*, 104.

63 Scholarly estimates of the date of Revelation have tended to the reign either of Nero (54–68 AD) or of Domitian (81–96 AD), most now favoring the latter. For an extensive discussion of this and other introductory questions about Revelation, see David E. Aune, *Revelation 1–5*, Word Biblical Commentary 52 (Dallas: Word Books, 1997), xvii–ccxi (lvi–lxx on the date); he proposes a two-stage composition, the present form completed toward the end of the first century AD (lxxiv). See Aune, *Literary Environment*, 226–40, on "apocalypticism," "apocalyptic eschatology," and "apocalypses."

64 George W. Nickelsburg, *1 Enoch 1: A Commentary on the Book of 1 Enoch, Chapters 1–36; 81–108* (Minneapolis: Fortress, 2001), 21–26. Jewish "apocalyptic" writings also include *The Book of Jubilees* and various others that are introduced and translated in *The Old Testament Pseudepigrapha*, vol. 1, *Apocalyptic Literature and Testaments*, ed. James H. Charlesworth (Garden City, N.Y.: Doubleday, 1983).

65 Aune, *Revelation 1–5*, lxxii–lxxv.

66 It appears that the use of a "grace benediction" as a concluding formula for letters began with the apostle Paul: e.g., 1 Thessalonians 5:28; Philippians 4:23; Galatians 6:18; Philemon 25; Romans 16:20; 1 Corinthians 16:23; and the more elaborate form in 2 Corinthians 13:14. That Revelation uses the basic formula suggests that the author may have adopted it from an acquaintance with Pauline letters. On this and other features of early Christian letters, see Aune, *Literary Environment*, 183–225.

67 Aune (*Literary Environment*, 240) suggested that John's exile on the island of Patmos, apparently as a penalty for his Christian profession (Revelation 1:9), may signal that he was "upper-class," noting, "otherwise the penalty might have been death."

68 The other major exception is the enigmatic second-century AD work known as the *Shepherd of Hermas*. "Hermas" is apparently the author's real name, and it seems to have been sent to the recipients identified in it (*Vision* 2.4.3). But, as we have it, the work appears to be a composite, either of one author writing at different stages or of the work of two or three different authors writing at different times. See, e.g., Michael W. Holmes, ed., *The Apostolic Fathers:*

Greek Texts and English Translations, 3rd ed. (Grand Rapids: Baker Academic, 2007), 442–47.

69   Aune, *Literary Environment*, 241. But, later, in his commentary, Aune urged, "the literary unity and coherence of Revelation have been exaggerated, though they certainly exist in some levels of composition" (*Revelation 1–5*, cviii). He proposed a two-stage composition process, or two "editions" of Revelation (cxx–cxxxiv). It is neither necessary nor relevant to engage this question here, but compare, e.g., Richard Bauckham, *The Climax of Prophecy: Studies on the Book of Revelation* (Edinburgh: T&T Clark, 1993), 1–37 ("Structure and Composition").

70   Notwithstanding various proposals that Revelation is composite and/or the end product of some multistage editorial process. For a brief overview of the form of Revelation, see Aune, *Literary Environment*, 240–43; and the review of various detailed proposals about its structure in G. K. Beale, *The Book of Revelation* (Grand Rapids: Eerdmans, 1999), 108–16.

71   Gamble, *Books and Readers*, 104.

72   Also, as Gamble observed (*Books and Readers*, 108), as well as Revelation, the second-century text *Shepherd of Hermas* "exemplifies the bookish aspect of apocalyptic literature." This body of revelations and visions, too, was from the first intended to be communicated as a *text* (e.g., Hermas, *Vision* 3.3).

73   See esp. 24–31, 36–46, 47–58, drawing on his earlier work: *The Secretary in the Letters of Paul* (Tübingen: J. C. B. Mohr [Paul Siebeck]), 1991); and also Gordon J. Bahr, "Paul and Letter Writing in the First Century," *Catholic Biblical Quarterly* 28 (1966): 465–77.

74   Richards also emphasizes the role of secretaries in ancient composition practices, arguing that Paul's letters reflect his use of such assistants, who may even have served as coauthors in some cases (*Paul and First-Century Letter Writing*, esp. 59–93).

75   On the legal issues and options, see Adela Yarbro Collins, *Crisis and Catharsis: The Power of the Apocalypse* (Philadelphia: Westminster, 1984), 102–4. Patmos is about sixty kilometers off the western coast of Turkey and was part of the Roman province of Asia (Minor), but today it is part of Greece.

76   We will look more closely at the copying and circulation of early Christian texts in the next section of this chapter.

77 Edgar J. Goodspeed, ed., *Die älteste Apologeten: Texte mit kurzen Ein-leitungen* (Göttingen: Vandenhoeck & Ruprecht, 1914; repr., 1984).

78 It may be that the early third-century scholar Origen is the ear-liest Christian author to be freed to devote himself to scholarship with support from a wealthy patron. Ambrose, who as described by Eusebius (*Ecclesiastical History*, 6.23), provided Origen "with what was necessary," including seven shorthand writers (for dictation), copyists, and "girls skilled in penmanship" (for making the final, fair copies). On Origen's remarkable literary and scholarly produc-tions, see now Anthony Grafton and Megan Williams, *Christianity and the Transformation of the Book: Origen, Eusebius, and the Library of Caesarea* (Cambridge, Mass.: Belknap, 2006); and on Origen him-self, see Henri Crouzel, *Origen: The Life and Thought of the First Great Theologian* (San Francisco: Harper & Row, 1989).

79 Richards, *Paul and First-Century Letter Writing*, 164–65. Richards rightly noted that we need to allow for attendant tasks of preparing papyrus for copying, resharpening pens, and the limited number of daylight hours. If, however, copyists worked by lamplight, and were exceptionally motivated, they might have worked more than five hours a day.

80 Richards, *Paul and First-Century Letter Writing*, 165. He gives a table of estimates for each letter of the traditional Pauline corpus.

81 As illustrations, in Oxyrhynchus there were copies of *Shepherd of Hermas* (composed in Rome), Irenaeus' *Against Heresies* (composed in Gaul), and writings by Melito of Sardis, all of them dated within only a decade or two after they were composed. See my discussion in *Artifacts*, 27.

82 Gamble, *Books and Readers*, 111.

83 For introduction, Greek text, and English translation of *1 Clement*, Polycarp's *Letter to the Philippians*, and *Shepherd of Hermas* (as well as a number of other early texts), see Holmes, *Apostolic Fathers*.

84 So, Gamble, *Books and Readers*, 108. See his lengthy discussion of the publication and circulation of early Christian texts (82–143).

85 Gamble, *Books and Readers*, 109.

86 Eldon J. Epp, "The Significance of the Papyri for Determining the Nature of the New Testament Text in the Second Century: A Dynamic View of Textual Transmission," in *Gospel Traditions in*

the Second Century: Origins, Recensions, Text, and Transmission, ed. William L. Petersen (Notre Dame, Ind.: University of Notre Dame Press, 1989), 81 (71–103).

87   S. R. Llewelyn, *New Documents Illustrating Early Christianity,* vol. 7 (North Ryde, Australia: Macquarie University Ancient History Documentary Research Centre, 1994), 57 (1–57).

88   Gamble, *Books and Readers,* 112.

89   As noted by Gamble, *Books and Readers,* 112 (and 289n93). Origen (*Against Celsus* 4.52) cites Celsus as having attacked Aristo's work. On it, see Johannes Quasten, *Patrology,* vol. 1, *The Beginnings of Patristic Literature* (Westminster, Md.: Christian Classics, 1986 [original publication 1950]), 195–96.

90   Philo of Alexandria's *Embassy to Gaius* might serve as a kind of precedent. But the sheer number of Christian *apologia* texts is unprecedented.

91   Larry W. Hurtado, "The Earliest Evidence of an Emerging Christian Material and Visual Culture: The Codex, the *Nomina Sacra* and the Staurogram," in *Text and Artifact in the Religions of Mediterranean Antiquity: Essays in Honour of Peter Richardson,* ed. Stephen G. Wilson and Michel Desjardins (Waterloo, Ontario: Wilfrid Laurier University Press, 2000), 271–88.

92   For full discussion and references to other scholarly work, see Hurtado, *Artifacts,* 43–93.

93   E. G. Turner, *The Typology of the Early Codex* (Philadelphia: University of Pennsylvania Press, 1977; repr., Eugene, Ore.: Wipf & Stock, 2014), 73–88, includes examples of pagan literary texts in codex form.

94   See the discussion of the Ulpian text (*Digesta* 32.52) and also comments of the jurist Paulus, by C. H. Roberts and T. C. Skeat, *The Birth of the Codex* (London: Oxford University Press, 1983), 30–32; noted also by Stephen Emmel, "The Christian Book in Egypt: Innovation and the Coptic Tradition," in *The Bible as Book: The Manuscript Tradition,* ed. John Sharpe and Kimberly van Kampen (London: British Library, 1998), 35–36 (35–43).

95   See, e.g., William A. Johnson, "The Ancient Book," in *The Oxford Handbook of Papyrology,* ed. Roger S. Bagnall (New York: Oxford University Press, 2009), 256–81.

96   These figures are derived from the Leuven Database of Ancient Books, http://www.trismegistos.org/ldab/ (accessed 11 January 2016). I drew attention to similar figures earlier in Hurtado, *Artifacts*, esp. 44–49.

97   My figures are derived from the Leuven Database of Ancient Books. I have excluded from these figures items listed as either "sheet" or "fragment" (i.e., items that were single sheets of writing material or that were not classified by editors as either bookroll or codex).

98   About 79 percent of all third-century manuscripts of pagan literary texts in the Leuven Database are bookrolls, whereas 75 percent of third-century Christian manuscripts are codices.

99   See discussion of individual manuscripts, some of which are difficult to classify as to whether they are from Christian provenance, in Hurtado, *Artifacts*, 53–59.

100 I exclude the four New Testament "opisthographs"—i.e., reused rolls—with New Testament texts copied onto the reverse side of a roll originally used for some other text. These copies were likely made for someone's personal reading/study. For details, see Hurtado, *Artifacts*, 57n49. In a forthcoming article, however, Geoffrey Smith proposes that the "Willoughby Fragment" (parts of John 1:49–2:1 written along the papyrus fibers) comes from a bookroll copy of John. "The Willoughby Fragment: A New Fragment of John 1:49–2:1 and an Unidentified Christian Text." *Journal of Biblical Literature* (forthcoming). I thank Smith for allowing me to read his article at prepublication stage.

101 Emmel's claim ("Christian Book in Egypt," in Sharpe and van Kampen, *Bible as Book*, 37) that in the early centuries "Christian books in roll format are scarcely known" is, thus, an exaggeration. It is true only for copies of texts treated as scriptures by early Christians, but not for all Christian texts.

102 Johnson ("Ancient Book," in Bagnall, *Oxford Handbook of Papyrology*, 267) refers to putative practical reasons for preferring the codex as "red-herrings." I have discussed these matters more fully in *Artifacts*, 61–80.

103 Hurtado, *Artifacts*, 63–67. Likewise unconvincing is the proposal that Christians preferred the codex because they came from lower socioeconomic levels of Roman-era society and so were more

accustomed to subelite texts written in codex format (*Artifacts*, 68–69).

104 Irven M. Resnick ("The Codex in Early Jewish and Christian Communities," *Journal of Religious History* 17 [1992]: 1–17) contended that the codex functioned in particular to distinguish Christian copies of biblical (Old Testament) texts from Jewish copies.

105 I discuss the production of codices, in *Artifacts*, 83–89.

106 As writing material, papyrus had one side with vertical fibers and one with horizontal fibers. It was easier to copy on the latter surface.

107 Emmel, "Christian Book in Egypt," in Sharpe and van Kampen, *Bible as Book*, 37.

108 I draw here on my fuller discussion in *Artifacts*, 95–134.

109 In addition to the Greek words for "Jesus," "Christ," "Lord," and "God," the Greek words for the following also came to be treated as *nomina sacra*: "son" (as in "son of God"), "spirit" (as in "Holy Spirit"), "David," "cross," "mother" (esp. referring to Mary), "father" (esp. referring to God), "Israel," "savior," "man" (esp. in referring to Jesus, as in "son of man"), "Jerusalem," and "heaven."

110 Larry W. Hurtado, "The Origin of the *Nomina Sacra*: A Proposal," *Journal of Biblical Literature* 117 (1998): 655–73; *Artifacts*, esp. 111–20.

111 The Hebrew alphabet is a set of consonants. So, God's name was written as the four letters in question: *yod, hē, vav, hē*, which can be transliterated as *YHWH*. The name is commonly thought to have been vocalized as "Yahweh" or "Yahveh."

112 Discussion and references in *Artifacts*, 101–4.

113 Robert Kraft ("The 'Textual Mechanics' of Early Jewish LXX/ OG Papyri and Fragments," in *The Bible as Book: The Transmission of the Greek Text*, ed. Scot McKendrick and Orlaith O'Sullivan [London: British Library, 2003], 51–72) proposed that the *nomina sacra* practice was taken over from Jewish scribal practice. But there is no evidence of Jewish copyists using the practice prior to the date of early Christian manuscripts.

114 But Frank Shaw (*The Earliest Non-mystical Jewish Use of IAO* [Leuven: Peeters, 2014]) shows that the avoidance of pronouncing *YHWH* was not completely observed.

115 See, e.g., Robin Margaret Jensen, *Understanding Early Christian Art* (New York: Routledge, 2000), 9 (and 183–84n2): "Christian art

as such cannot be dated any earlier than the end of the second or beginning of the third century."

116 Hurtado, "Earliest Evidence," in Wilson and Desjardins, *Text and Artifact.*

117 See also Kruger, "Manuscripts," in Porter and Pitts, *Christian Origins,* 17.

5: A New Way to Live

1   See the similar exhortation in A. D. Nock, *Conversion: The Old and the New in Religion from Alexander the Great to Augustine of Hippo* (Oxford: Oxford University Press, 1933), 218.

2   William V. Harris ("Child-Exposure in the Roman Empire," *Journal of Roman Studies* 84 [1994]: 1–22) gives a full discussion of the practice.

3   P. Oxyrhynchus 4.744. Greek text and English translation (from which I quote here) in A. S. Hunt and C. C. Edgar, *Select Papyri I: Private Affairs* (Cambridge, Mass.: Harvard University Press, 1932), 294–95.

4   Harris ("Child-Exposure," 3) presumed that discarding their infants "often caused parents deep regret." We do not know this, but it seems a reasonable surmise that mothers especially may have had qualms, perhaps more so than fathers.

5   Harris, "Child-Exposure," 2.

6   There have been news stories of couples today using prenatal scanning to determine the sex of the unborn child, with a view to aborting a female in preference for having a male baby. And poverty does not seem to be a factor.

7   Harris, "Child-Exposure," 11, 15.

8   Harris, "Child-Exposure," 18, and more fully 18–19.

9   William V. Harris, "Demography, Geography and the Sources of Roman Slaves," *Journal of Roman Studies* 89 (1999): 74 (62–75).

10 Hermas, *Vision* 1.1. For further discussion of the passage, see Carolyn Osiek, *Shepherd of Hermas: A Commentary* (Minneapolis: Fortress, 1999), 42.

11 As one study of prostitution in the Roman era noted, "the basic premise that prostitutes broadly become such through enslavement (or, at least, that the great majority of prostitutes are slaves) is certainly borne out in numerous sources." Rebecca Fleming, "*Quae*

Corpore Quaestum Facit: The Sexual Economy of Female Prostitution in the Roman Empire," *Journal of Roman Studies* 89 (1999): 41 (38–61).

12 In addition to Justin, see, e.g., Tertullian, *Apology* 9.17–18; *Epistle to Diognetus* 5.6; *Didache* 2.2; 5.2; *Epistle of Barnabas* 19.2; 20.2; Clement of Alexandria, *Christ the Educator* 3.3.21.5. For still further Christian texts, see Harris, "Child-Exposure," 17n148.

13 Carolyn Osiek, "The Self-Defining Praxis of the Developing *Ecclesia*," in *The Cambridge History of Christianity*, vol. 1, *Origins to Constantine*, ed. Margaret M. Mitchell and Frances M. Young (Cambridge: Cambridge University Press, 2006), 281 (274–92).

14 Daniel Schwartz, "Did the Jews Practice Infant Exposure and Infanticide in Antiquity?" *Studia Philonica* 16 (2004): 61–95. It is likely that some Jews engaged in the practice, but it was not religiously acceptable among self-identifying Jews collectively.

15 Philo presents his stance as based on Exodus 21:22-25, which addresses a situation in which a man may injure a pregnant woman, causing her to miscarry or deliver prematurely. The text does not, however, obviously address the matter of infant exposure! He worked with the Greek text (the "Septuagint"), which differs from the Hebrew in making the distinction between a miscarriage of a fetus not fully formed (a fine to be imposed on the man) and a premature delivery and death of a fully formed fetus (in which case, the man pays with his life). There is now a recent translation of the Greek "Old Testament": Albert Pietersma and Benjamin G. Wright, eds., *A New English Translation of the Septuagint* (Oxford: Oxford University Press, 2007).

16 As noted by Osiek, "Self-Defining Praxis," in Mitchell and Young, *Cambridge History of Christianity*, 281; citing Tacitus (*Histories* 5.5), and Diodorus Siculus (40.3).

17 Musonius Rufus, fragment 15. He left no writing of his own, and his teachings have been collected from various later sources. A standard introduction, with Greek text and English translation, is Cora E. Lutz, "Musonius Rufus: 'The Roman Socrates,'" *Yale Classical Studies* 10 (1947): 3–147. A more readily available English translation now is by Cynthia King, *Musonius Rufus: Lectures and Sayings* (Createspace, 2011). The last saying cited has obvious resonance with the saying ascribed to Jesus in Matthew 6:25-26, exhorting

against anxiety about what to eat or drink and pointing to God's provision for the birds of the air who "neither sow nor reap nor gather into barns."

18   Tertullian refers to laws that forbid the killing of newborn infants (*To the Heathen* 1.15), and then claims, "no laws are evaded with more impunity . . . with the deliberate knowledge of the public, and the suffrages of this entire age." But Harris ("Child-Exposure," 16) judged that he must have been referring to the law against murder, not to any specific ordinance against infant exposure.

19   Harris, "Child-Exposure," 17.

20   Among accessible treatments of the topic, see Fik Meijer, *The Gladiators: History's Most Deadly Sport*, trans. Liz Waters (London: Souvenir, 2004); and Roger Dunkle, *Gladiators: Violence and Spectacle in Ancient Rome* (London: Pearson Education, 2008). For a more wide-ranging review of the various sorts of events that comprised "spectacles" in the Roman era, see David S. Potter, "Spectacle," in *A Companion to the Roman Empire*, ed. David S. Potter (London: Blackwell, 2006), 385–408.

21   We should not imagine our time to be immune to the lure of such things. Perhaps, in our time, in Western societies, the closest that we get to a similar kind of sport is the "cage-fighter" contest, typically two men who punch bare-knuckled, kick, choke, and otherwise seek to defeat each other, crowds cheering on the violence.

22   Perhaps today there is a similar distancing that allows the enjoyment of the violence in the various vampire and zombie movies (those killed not really/fully human) and in computer games in which various monsters or aliens are killed off by the players.

23   *Deeds of the Divine Augustus*, 22; translation cited from P. A. Brunt and J. M. Moore, *Res Gestae Divi Augusti: With an Introduction and Commentary* (Oxford: Oxford University Press, 1969). The text was in the form of an inscription likely erected after Augustus' death in 14 AD. Meijer (*Gladiators*, 33–38) describes the role of various early emperors in gladiatorial shows.

24   For more extended discussion, see "A Day at the Colosseum," in Meijer, *Gladiators* (135–75), on which I draw here.

25   Corpus Inscriptionum Latinarum 4.3884. Cited in Meijer, *Gladiators*, 135.

26   The notorious movie *Satyricon*, by Fellini, is an illustration of the Hollywood stereotype.

27   My citations are from Michael W. Holmes, ed., *The Apostolic Fathers: Greek Texts and English Translations*, 3rd ed. (Grand Rapids: Baker Academic, 2007), 686–719. For other recent introductory discussions, see Clayton N. Jefford et al., *Reading the Apostolic Fathers: An Introduction* (Peabody, Mass.: Hendrickson, 1996), 159–69; and Paul Foster, ed., *The Writings of the Apostolic Fathers* (London: T&T Clark, 2007), 147–56.

28   "Wives" translates the preferred Greek variant, *koitēn* ("marriage bed"), which is an emendation of the word *koinēn*, reported (in transcriptions) as the reading in the one manuscript in which *Diognetus* was preserved (which was destroyed in 1870 in a fire during the Franco-German War). *Koinēn* ("common, shared") is likely a copyist error and yields a sentence that does not make sense.

29   The reference to Jesus as God's "child" translates a Greek word, *pais*, that featured in very early Christian circles but largely dropped from usage later (in favor of the term "Son"; Greek: *hyios*). *Pais* appears as an honorific term applied to Jesus in Acts 3:13, 26; 4:27, 30, and in a few other early texts. This usage likely derived from its honorific application in the Greek Old Testament writings to Israel (e.g., Isaiah 41:8; 42:1) and to David (e.g., Psalm 18:1; taken up also in Luke 1:69; Acts 4:25). Its application to David gave it a royal-messianic connotation, and this is its probable nuance when applied to Jesus in early Christian texts.

30   Holmes, *Apostolic Fathers*, 688, mentions some proposals about who this Diognetus may have been.

31   Nock (*Conversion*, 192) judged that there is little indication that the second-century literary defenses of Christianity were read by anyone other than Christians, people "on the way to be such," or serious students (and critics) of Christianity such as Celsus.

32   I cite, as an ally, Nock (*Conversion*, 193), who noted that an educated pagan visiting a Christian gathering might get the impression that it had resemblances to a philosophical school, and would "have difficulty in recognizing it as cultus in any ordinary sense," but would likely conclude that "this was of the nature of superstition, that is ungentlemanly popular religion."

33   Scholars debate the appropriate application of the term "ethics," some reserving it for systems and theories of good and bad behavior, and others using the term more loosely to designate any kind of teaching about conduct. I tend here toward the latter use of the word.

34   Of course, Paul's Thessalonian converts were themselves "Gentiles" (Greek: *ethnē*; "nations/peoples"), a Jewish term designating non-Jews. But here Paul distinguishes between his converts and (other?) non-Christian Gentiles. This may be an early stage in the later use of the term "Gentiles" in early Christian texts with the sense of non-Christians, with the connotation of another later term, "pagans."

35   Kyle Harper, "*Porneia*: The Making of a Christian Sexual Norm," *Journal of Biblical Literature* 131 (2012): 378 (363–83); and his briefer discussion in his book *From Shame to Sin: The Christian Transformation of Sexual Morality in Late Antiquity* (Cambridge, Mass.: Harvard University Press, 2013), 86–93. Jennifer A. Glancy took issue with a point in Harper's article, contending that in ancient Jewish texts *porneia* did not include sex with one's own household slaves and also that the absence of an explicit prohibition against sexual use of household slaves in Paul's references to *porneia* likely means that he, too, implicitly accepted this practice. "The Sexual Use of Slaves: A Response to Kyle Harper on Jewish and Christian *Porneia*," *Journal of Biblical Literature* 134 (2015): 215–29. She develops this argument more fully in her book *Slavery in Early Christianity* (New York: Oxford University Press, 2002). I think, however, that her argument about Paul fails to take account of the wider evidence that he and other early Jesus-believers confined legitimate sex to marriage. But there is neither space nor necessity to engage the matter further here. See also Margaret Y. MacDonald, "Slavery, Sexuality and House Churches: A Reassessment of Colossians 3.18–4.1 in Light of New Research on the Roman Family," *New Testament Studies* 53 (2007): 94–113; and Carolyn Osiek, "Female Slaves, *Porneia*, and the Limits of Obedience," in *Early Christian Families in Context: An Interdisciplinary Dialogue*, ed. David L. Balch and Carolyn Osiek (Grand Rapids: Eerdmans, 2003), 255–74.

36   There was a different Greek word for "adultery": *moicheia*. But, as this passage in 1 Thessalonians shows, in early Christian usage the

term *porneia* could cover this and all other forms of sexual activity deemed sinful.

37 On the passage and term *skeuos* as used here, see, e.g., Ernest Best, *A Commentary on the First and Second Epistles to the Thessalonians* (New York: Harper & Row, 1972), 160–66. The suggestion of Glancy (*Slavery in Early Christianity*, 60) that the term designates a man's slave and so Paul here implicitly approves Christians making sexual use of their slaves seems to me far-fetched. For one thing, it goes against the whole thrust of Paul's strictures against a variety of sexual practices that he refers to as "*porneia(s)*" ("fornication[s]").

38 Demosthenes, *Against Neaera*, 3.122.

39 So also Amy Richlin, "Sexuality in the Roman Empire," in *A Companion to the Roman Empire*, ed. David S. Potter (London: Blackwell, 2006), 350 (327–53).

40 The instruction may also be directed against the sort of crudely put sexual demands on a wife reflected, for example, in one of Martial's epigrams (11.104), complaining that the wife will not allow anal sex and will not masturbate him, and demanding that she act more in the role of a prostitute for him, clearly reflecting the view that sexual pleasure is for men, women simply there to provide it.

41 On 1 Thessalonians 4:1-8 and Paul's instructions about sexual behavior in 1 Corinthians 7, see Larry O. Yarbrough, *Not Like the Gentiles: Marriage Rules in the Letters of Paul* (Atlanta: Scholars Press, 1985); Yarbrough argues that Paul's exhortations about sex in 1 Thessalonians here were not prompted by any particular problem (86–87). But Robert Jewett contended precisely the opposite, in *The Thessalonian Correspondence: Pauline Rhetoric and Millenarian Piety* (Philadelphia: Fortress, 1986), 105–6.

42 The word *parousia* here seems to liken Jesus' return to the arrival of a ruler—e.g., to a city to demonstrate his rule.

43 Leviticus 18:6-18 specifies a list of near kin with whom a man is forbidden to have sex, including (v. 8) "your father's wife." A similar prohibition appears in Leviticus 20:11 and in Deuteronomy 22:30. Paul refers to this situation as something not even known among pagans, but the famous tragedy of Euripides, *Hippolytus*, is based on the love of Phaedra for her stepson Hippolytus (thanks to Jan Bremmer for this reference).

44 Paul does not really explain why he condemns the relationship, as if he felt it unnecessary to do so. Perhaps it was simply that he saw it as one of the relationships forbidden in Leviticus 18, a text that for him was part of God's law and remained valid for the behavior of his Gentile converts.

45 But Raymond F. Collins (*First Corinthians* [Collegeville, Minn.: Liturgical, 1999], 240) contended that there is no reason to think that men in the Corinthian church were having sex with prostitutes. I think, however, that Collins did not fully appreciate the diversity of opportunities for extramarital sex presented in Roman-era urban life, which included not only prostitutes (based in brothels) but also courtesans and slave girls brought in for male pleasure at dining events, etc.

46 See, e.g., the discussion of views by Anthony C. Thiselton, *The First Epistle to the Corinthians* (Grand Rapids: Eerdmans, 2000), 462–63.

47 More recently, some scholars have contended that the latter slogan also included the following statement: "but/and God will destroy both the one and the other." E.g., Thiselton, *First Epistle to the Corinthians*, 462–63. This is not, however, crucial to my discussion here.

48 The oft-cited study is Dale B. Martin, *The Corinthian Body* (New Haven: Yale University Press, 1995).

49 In his survey of uses of the word in ancient Greek texts over a number of centuries, Harper ("*Porneia*," 369) found it in only four classical authors. By contrast, it is used hundreds of times in ancient Jewish and Christian texts.

50 In 1 Corinthians 15:42-49, Paul distinguishes between the characteristics of the present/mortal body and the resurrection body in a series of contrasts: perishable/imperishable, dishonor/glory, weakness/power, physical/spiritual. "Spiritual," however, seems to designate the source and nature of the animating power of the resurrected body: it will be empowered by God's spirit. And he directly states that resurrected believers will "bear the image of the man of heaven" (the risen Jesus; v. 49).

51 One of the better attempts to show how all of 1 Corinthians 7:1-40 forms a coherent discussion of a connected series of issues relating

to sex and marriage is Gordon D. Fee, *The First Epistle to the Corinthians* (Grand Rapids: Eerdmans, 1987), 267–357.

52 The two attitudes might go hand in hand. It was a widespread notion that sex with prostitutes or slaves was an important (even necessary) means of preventing males from committing adultery. So, if (as a number of commentators surmise) some in the Corinthian church developed the notion that married believers should not have conjugal sex (perhaps because they saw it as unspiritual of them), they might, nevertheless, have allowed sex with prostitutes as an indifferent kind of sexual activity.

53 It is interesting that the second part of the statement, which I have put in italics, is omitted in some manuscripts (in the Gregory-Aland list, F and G, and a few others). The repetition of the Greek verb may have resulted in some copyists accidentally omitting the phrase; or the omission may have been deliberate, reflecting perhaps a more patriarchal view of marriage.

54 In Paul's wording here, each spouse "has authority" (Greek: *exousiazei*) over the other's "body." As Collins (*First Corinthians*, 259) judged, Paul's point is that neither spouse has "complete self-determination," but each is responsible to the other.

55 "Lest Satan tempt you (to sexual sin) because of your lack of self-control" (v. 5). "Lack of self-control" translates the Greek term *akrasia*, used in the New Testament writings only here and in Matthew 23:25; it can also be rendered "self-indulgence." Note that in the Matthew text it is linked with another vice term, "*harpagē*," meaning "plundering," or "robbery," or (as in the NRSV) "greed."

56 I repeat that I do not find Glancy's argument persuasive (*Slavery in Early Christianity*) that the absence of an explicit condemnation of sexual abuse of slaves in the writings of Paul (and other early Christian texts) means that it was tacitly accepted by him and in early Christian circles. I am not alone in this stance, as illustrated, for example, in John Nordling's review of the book in *Journal of the American Academy of Religion* 73 (2005): 1212–15.

57 As noted by Harper, "*Porneia*," 379.

58 For examples of *monandros*, see Liddell, Scott, Jones, Lexicon 1143; and for studies, see Jean-Baptiste Frey, "La signification des termes μονανδρος et *univira*: Coup d'oeil sur la famille Romaine aux premier siècles de notre ère," *Recherches de Science Religieuse* 20 (1930):

48–60; and Marjorie Lightman and William Zeisel, "*Univira*: An Example of Continuity and Change in Roman Society," *Church History* 46 (1977): 19–32.

59 In 1 Timothy 5:9, likewise, the author does not use the term *monandros* in laying down requirements for widows but instead uses the phrase *henos andros gynē* ("wife of one husband"). Does this perhaps reflect the author's desire to distinguish the requirement verbally from the way the topos was often expressed in the wider culture?

60 Bernhard Kötting, "'Univria' in Inschriften," in *Ecclesia Peregrinans, Das Gottesvolk unterwegs: Gesammelte Aufsätze* (Muenster: Aschendorff, 1988), 345–55; see esp. 353, where he notes that the new standard expressed in the text in 1 Timothy is to expect the same of husbands as of wives.

61 Amy Richlin ("Reading Boy-Love and Child-Love in the Greco-Roman World," in *Sex in Antiquity: Exploring Gender and Sexuality in the Ancient World*, ed. Mark Masterson, Nancy Sorkin Rabinowitz, and James Robson [London: Routledge, 2015], 352–73) surveys the changing attitudes toward pederasty in scholarship across the past two centuries, earlier scholarship often depicting an "aestheticized pederasty" (368).

62 Excerpts and discussion in Richlin, "Sexuality in the Roman Empire," in Potter, *Companion to the Roman Empire*, 334–38.

63 These terms all derive from a combination of the Greek words *pais* ("child/boy") and *eraō* ("to love sexually/passionately").

64 John W. Martens, "'Do Not Sexually Abuse Children': The Language of Early Christian Sexual Ethics," in *Children in Late Ancient Christianity*, ed. Cornelia B. Horn and Robert R. Phenix (Tübingen: Mohr Siebeck, 2009), 227–54. In an inscription (that I discuss shortly) giving requirements for members of a local pagan cult group from Philadelphia, Lydia, one of the prohibited activities is "anything fatal to children" (*ti paidophthonon*), a term also used in some earlier classical texts and probably referring to child exposure. Still closer to the Christian terminology, another line of the inscription prohibits seduction and/or sexual relations (*mē phtherein*) with another man's wife or with boys or virgin girls, probably, however, referring to freeborn children.

65 Martens, "Do Not Sexually Abuse Children," in Horn and Phenix, *Children in Late Ancient Christianity*, 252.

66   I cite translations in Holmes, *Apostolic Fathers*. In the edition by Bart Ehrman, *The Apostolic Fathers* (Cambridge, Mass.: Harvard University Press, 2003), the verb *paidophthoreō* is translated as "pederasty," which does not capture as well the strongly negative tone of the verb as established by Martens.

67   Martens, "Do Not Sexually Abuse Children," in Horn and Phenix, *Children in Late Ancient Christianity*, 244.

68   For citations of these other early Christian writers, see Martens, "Do Not Sexually Abuse Children," in Horn and Phenix, *Children in Late Ancient Christianity*, 247, and 244–47.

69   Clement of Alexandria, *Stromata* 2.23.140.1; as cited in Richlin, "Sexuality in the Roman Empire," in Potter, *Companion to the Roman Empire*, 345; and further discussion in Peter Brown, *The Body and Society: Men, Women, and Sexual Renunciation in Early Christianity* (New York: Columbian University Press, 1988), 132–35; and now Harper, *From Shame to Sin*, 107–33.

70   Citing the text in Lutz, "Musonius Rufus," at 12.10–14, 30–34.

71   Lutz, "Musonius Rufus," 15.25–30.

72   Cf. Anders Klostergaard Petersen, "Finding a Basis for Interpreting New Testament Ethos from a Greco-Roman Philosophical Perspective," in *Early Christian Ethics in Interaction with Jewish and Greco-Roman Contexts*, ed. Jan Willem van Henten and Joseph Verheyden (Boston: Brill, 2013), 53–81. He describes his own stance as arguing that "the early Christian and Graeco-Roman ethics reflect different, but comparable manifestations of a *Zeitgeist* common to particular segments and wider parts of the Mediterranean area during the Hellenistic period" (58). He draws attention to what he calls "therapeutic philosophy" (that is, the philosophical aim of "curing" the soul of individuals, promoting in them a robust ethical effort). But he seems to fail to appreciate adequately the remarkable difference between formulating certain values for teaching a small number of pupils and the sort of aggressive effort at wider group formation and group identity reflected in many early Christian texts.

73   Harper, *From Shame to Sin*, 11. In pp. 70–78, he discusses what he calls "The Gloomy Ones: The Philosophers and Sexuality," focusing on Musonius and his successors (Dio Chrysostom and Epictetus), and judged: "His strictures on the use of slaves and prostitutes

may have been no more effective than his (far less celebrated) disapproval of shoes, but they are in the same spirit and equally account for the spread of his legend" (73).

74 Harper, *From Shame to Sin*, 7.

75 Richard Walzer, *Galen on Jews and Christians* (London: Oxford University Press, 1949), 15.

76 The inscription has been referred to by various scholars for a century or so. See, in particular, the detailed analysis by Stephen Barton and G. H. R. Horsley ("A Hellenistic Cult Group and the New Testament Churches," *Jahrbuch für Antike und Christentum* 24 [1981]: 7–41), which includes the Greek text and their translation (8–10); and for a critique of some previous uses of the inscription, see Stanley K. Stowers, "A Cult from Philadelphia: Oikos Religion or Cultic Association?" in *The Early Church in Its Context: Essays in Honor of Everett Ferguson*, ed. Abraham J. Malherbe et al. (Leiden: Brill, 1998), 287–301. Earlier references to the inscription include Nock, *Conversion*, 216–17. The inscription also appears in the recent collection edited by Philip A. Harland, *Greco-Roman Associations: Texts, Translations, and Commentary*, vol. 2, *North Coast of the Black Sea, Asia Minor* (New York: De Gruyter, 2014), #141, available online: http://philipharland.com/greco-roman-associations/divine-instructions-for-the-household-association-of-dionysios/.

77 Cogently shown by Stowers, "A Cult from Philadelphia," in Malherbe et al., *Early Church in its Context*.

78 Note, e.g., Michael B. Thompson, "The Holy Internet: Communication between Churches in the First Christian Generation," in *The Gospels for All Christians: Rethinking the Gospel Audiences*, ed. Richard Bauckham (Grand Rapids: Eerdmans, 1998), 49–70.

79 See, e.g., Roger W. Gehring, *House Church and Mission: The Importance of Household Structures in Early Christianity* (Peabody, Mass.: Hendrickson, 2004). However, Edward Adams (*The Earliest Christian Meeting Places: Almost Exclusively Houses?* [London: T&T Clark, 2013]) points to evidence of a variety of physical settings of earliest Christian worship, but he grants that houses of Christians were a common, perhaps the most common, venue.

80 E.g., on the social levels of Pauline Christians, see Wayne A. Meeks, *The First Urban Christians: The Social World of the Apostle Paul* (New Haven: Yale University Press, 1983), 51–73. For a more recent

study, see Alexander Weiss, *Soziale Elite und Christentum: Studien zu ordo-Angehörigen unter den frühen Christen* (Boston: De Gruyter, 2015); Weiss contends that higher-status individuals joined the Christian movement earlier, and somewhat more frequently, than has been noticed in the past.

81   Also, note that Musonius urged that daughters and wives should study philosophy specifically so that they could be better wives and daughters. He hardly advocated any radical reordering of society.

82   There are similar texts in other early Christian writings, such as *1 Clement* 21.6–9; *Didache* 4.9–11; Ignatius, *Letter to Polycarp* 4.1–5.2; Polycarp, *Letter to Philippians* 4.1–6.1; but these are much shorter and do not always address all the groups addressed in the New Testament passages.

83   In addition to discussion of these texts by Gehring (*House Church and Mission*, 229–87, with ample citation of previous scholarship), other recent studies include James P. Hering, *The Colossian and Ephesian Haustafeln in Theological Context: An Analysis of Their Origins, Relationship, and Message* (New York: Peter Lang, 2007); and now the important study by Margaret Y. MacDonald, *The Power of Children: The Construction of Christian Families in the Greco-Roman World* (Waco, Tex.: Baylor University Press, 2014), esp. 1–32. The Colossians text has received particular attention, in part because it is widely thought that Ephesians drew upon Colossians: e.g., Angela Standhartinger, "The Origin and Intention of the Household Code in the Letter to the Colossians," *Journal for the Study of the New Testament* 79 (2000): 117–30. For a concise introduction, see P. H. Towner, "Households and Household Codes," in *Dictionary of Paul and His Letters*, ed. G. F. Hawthorne, R. P. Martin, and D. G. Reid (Downers Grove, Ill.: InterVarsity, 1993), 417–19.

84   Aristotle, *Politics* 1.12–13; Plutarch, *Advice on Marriage* 16, 31–32; Xenophon, *Oeconomicus* 3.1–15; 9.14–15. For discussion of these and other such texts, see MacDonald, *Power of Children*, 9–18.

85   As noted by MacDonald, *Power of Children*, 5.

86   MacDonald, *Power of Children*, 7; MacDonald cites also Marlis Gielen, *Tradition und Theologie neutestamentlicher Haustafelethik: Ein Beitrag zur Frage einer christlichen Auseinandersetzung mit gesellschaftlichen Normen* (Frankfurt am Main: Anton Hain, 1990), 37–38, 69–71, 102, 118, 145.

87   See, e.g., K. R. Bradley, *Slaves and Masters in the Roman Empire: A Study in Social Control* (Oxford: Oxford University Press, 1987).
88   The freedman-philosopher, Epictetus, is a prominent example.

Conclusion

1   Agrippa's execution of James is cited in Acts 12:1-2. Nero's pogrom is referred to by Tacitus (*Annals* 15.44.2–5) and Suetonius (*Nero* 16.2). Revelation 2:13 refers to the killing of a Pergamum Christian named Antipas, and Pliny's oft-cited letter to Trajan (*Epistles* 10.96) describes his handling of those denounced as Christians.

2   Candida Moss (*The Myth of Persecution: How Early Christians Invented a Story of Martyrdom* [San Francisco: HarperOne, 2013]) alleges that Christianity exaggerated the number of martyrs, but I think that her complaint is a bit exaggerated and seems shaped overmuch in reaction to what she sees as inappropriate claims of martyrdom by some right-wing versions of American Christianity today. Her earlier book is a much better discussion: *Ancient Christian Martyrdom: Diverse Practices, Theologies, and Traditions* (New Haven: Yale University Press, 2012).

3   See my discussion in *Why on Earth Did Anyone Become a Christian in the First Three Centuries* (Milwaukee: Marquette University Press, 2016).

4   I cite again the classic study by A. D. Nock (*Conversion: The Old and the New in Religion from Alexander the Great to Augustine of Hippo* [Oxford: Oxford University Press, 1933]), who demonstrated this point.

Appendix

1   Edwin Hatch, *The Influence of Greek Ideas and Usages upon the Christian Church: The Hibbert Lectures 1888* (London: Williams & Norgate, 1907), 353, 23. Other early and influential pioneers were Otto Pfleiderer, *Das Urchristenthum: Seine Schriften und Lehren in geschichtlichem Zusammenhang* (Berlin: Georg Reimer, 1887); and Hermann Gunkel, *Zum religionsgeschichtlichen Verständnis des Neuen Testaments*, Forschungen zur Religion und Literatur des Alten und Neuen Testaments 1 (Göttingen: Vandenhoeck & Ruprecht, 1903).

2   Note Hatch's belief that he was contributing "a new chapter to Christian apologetics" that would "confirm the divinity of Christianity by showing it to be in harmony with all else that we believe to be divine" (*Influence*, 24).

3   Key figures of the initial circle included Hermann Gunkel, William Wrede, Ernst Troeltsch, Wilhelm Heitmüller, Paul Wernle, and, esp. influential, Wilhelm Bousset. For fuller discussion, see, e.g., Werner Kümmel, *The New Testament: The History of the Investigation of Its Problems*, trans. G. McLean Gilmour and Howard C. Kee (Nashville: Abingdon, 1970), 206–308. Other major works are in German: the influential account and critique of the *Schule* by Carsten Colpe, *Die religionsgeschichtliche Schule: Darstellung und Kritik ihres Bildes vom gnostischen Erlösermythus* (Göttingen: Vandenhoeck & Ruprecht, 1961); and note also Karsten Lehmkühler, *Kultus und Theologie: Dogmatik und Exegese in der religionsgeschichtliche Schule* (Göttingen: Vandenhoeck & Ruprecht, 1996).

4   E.g., Lehmkühler, *Kultus und Theologie*.

5   Suzanne L. Marchand, *German Orientalism in the Age of Empire: Religion, Race, and Scholarship* (Cambridge: Cambridge University Press, 2009), esp. 252–91.

6   On Reitzenstein, see now Jan Bremmer, "Richard Reitzstein's Die Hellenistischen Mysterienreligionen," in *Between Crazy Mythologists and Stupid Theologians: Early Christianity and the Pagan Mystery Cults in the Work of Franz Cumont and in the History of Scholarship*, edited by A. Lannoy and D. Praet (Stuttgart: Steiner, forthcoming).

7   Richard Reitzenstein, *Die hellenistischen Mysterienreligionen nach ihrer Grundgedanken und Wirkungen* (Berlin: Teubner, 1910; 2nd ed., 1920, 3rd ed., 1927, which is the basis for the English translation of 1978). Nowadays, scholars prefer to refer to these as "mystery cults"—i.e., groups with distinguishing deities and practices that formed part of the variety of the Roman-era religious environment, but not full-scale "religions" in their own right.

8   See, e.g., Günter Wagner, *Pauline Baptism and the Pagan Mysteries: The Problem of the Pauline Doctrine of Baptism in Romans 6:1-11, in the Light of Its Religio-historical "Parallels"* (Edinburgh: Oliver & Boyd, 1967); A. J. M. Wedderburn, *Baptism and Resurrection: Studies in Pauline Theology Against Its Graeco-Roman Background*, Wissenschaftliche

Untersuchungen zum Neuen Testament 44 (Tübingen: Mohr Siebeck, 1987).

9   See esp. Fritz Graf, "Mysteries, Baptism, and the History of Religious Studies: Some Tentative Remarks," in *Dans le laboratoire de l'historien des religions: Mélanges offerts à Philippe Borgeaud*, ed. Francesca Prescendi and Youri Volokhine (Geneva: Labor et Fides, 2011), 94–95 (91–103); which partially overlaps with his "Baptism and Graeco-Roman Mystery Cults," in the massive multiauthor work on ritual use of water in antiquity, *Ablution, Initiation, and Baptism: Late Antiquity, Early Judaism, and Early Christianity*, ed. David Hellholm et al., 3 vols. (New York: De Gruyter, 2011), 1:101–18.

10 See now the major work by Everett Ferguson, *Baptism in the Early Church: History, Theology, and Liturgy in the First Five Centuries* (Grand Rapids: Eerdmans, 2009), e.g., 25–37 (on washings in pagan religion), 60–82 (Jewish washings and baptisms).

11 A second edition appeared in 1921 and was reprinted several times thereafter. An English translation was published in 1970 (Abingdon Press). For further details, especially how Bousset's book fared in scholarly circles, see my introduction to the recent reprint edition of the English translation: Wilhelm Bousset, *Kyrios Christos: A History of the Belief in Christ from the Beginnings of Christianity to Irenaeus* (Waco, Tex.: Baylor University Press, 2013), v–xx. The following citations are to this edition.

12 Bousset, *Kyrios Christos*, 119–52.

13 Bousset, *Kyrios Christos*, 153. The date of Jesus' crucifixion is placed by various scholars between 27 and 33 AD, most opting for 30–33 AD, and so Paul's "conversion" is typically dated by them ca. 32–35 AD. See, e.g., L. C. A. Alexander, "Chronology of Paul," in *Dictionary of Paul and His Letters*, ed. G. F. Hawthorne and R. P. Martin (Downers Grove, Ill.: InterVarsity, 1993), 115–23, esp. 116.

14 Larry W. Hurtado, "New Testament Christology: A Critique of Bousset's Influence," *Theological Studies* 40 (1979): 306–17; idem, *Lord Jesus Christ: Devotion to Jesus in Earliest Christianity* (Grand Rapids: Eerdmans, 2003), 11–18; and idem, "Wilhelm Bousset's *Kyrios Christos*: An Appreciative and Critical Assessment," *Early Christianity* 6 (2015): 1–13.

15 See, e.g., Edmondo Lupieri, *The Mandaeans: The Last Gnostics* (Grand Rapids: Eerdmans, 2002).

16 H. A. A. Kennedy, *St. Paul and the Mystery-Religions* (London: Hodder & Stoughton, 1913).

17 Geerhardus Vos, "The Kyrios Christos Controversy," *Princeton Theological Review* 15 (1917): 21–89. The responses were mainly from German-speaking scholars, and Vos noted that the heated debate continued all through the conflict of World War I.

18 J. Gresham Machen, *The Origin of Paul's Religion* (London: Hodder & Stoughton, 1921; repr., Grand Rapids: Eerdmans, 1965); A. E. J. Rawlinson, *The New Testament Doctrine of the Christ* (London: Longmans, Green, 1926).

Index of Ancient Sources

Index of Subjects and Modern Authors